ALL OF MY LIFE WITH YOU

ALL OF MY LIFE WITH YOU

A Memoir

Janis Rice Grogan

To Jo + Rick,
Thanks for many years
of love and support,
Janis R. Grogan

POSTERITY PRESS

ISBN 978-1-889274-52-2

Book design by Denise Arnot
Typeset in Requiem

The *Night Prayer* quoted in the epilogue is
reprinted, with permission, from *A New Zealand
Prayer Book—He Karakia Mihinare o Aotearao.*

POSTERITY PRESS

POSTERITY PRESS, INC.
P.O. Box 71002
Chevy Chase, MD 20813

Printed in the United States of America

to my children

Patrick, Lisa and Suzanne

for your love, encouragement and trust

CONTENTS

Prologue

PROLOGUE

THIS IS A LOVE STORY. Covering nineteen moves, living on five continents, as my husband Gene and I roamed our fascinating world, we strived to make a place that felt like home for ourselves and our children. We could not have imagined the life we lived.

However, I doubt that I would be writing this book without an event that occurred almost fifty years ago. We search continually for meaning but a decision or experience that occurs but once can change the trajectory of one's life. As Robert Frost wrote in his poem *The Road Not Taken*:

> *I shall be telling this with a sigh*
> *Somewhere ages and ages hence:*
> *Two roads diverged in a wood, and*
> *I took the one less traveled by,*
> *And that has made all the difference.*

In 1967 I began a spiritual journey that has lasted a lifetime. I accepted my mother's invitation to attend a Christian retreat in Oklahoma that was a popular place of renewal for her prayer group. I knew Sara Porter, her closest friend, would be there. I looked forward to a week of sleeping late, playing tennis and relaxing without meals to prepare or children and husband to care for. I was shocked to discover near the week's end that my self-satisfied attitude toward my practice of Christianity had vanished, leaving me uncomfortable and envious of the other attendees. These Christians, from various denominations, races and cultures, seemed joyful, confident, loving and tolerant.

Desperate to be like them, in a small group composed of people who were strangers to me, I requested prayer, cringing when our leader, a little Pentecostal preacher, invited me to sit in a chair in the middle of the circle. He put his hands on my shoulders and asked me, "Well, sister, what do you want prayer for?" "I have no idea," was my reply. Undeterred, he began to pray aloud. I never heard a word as I was riveted by a vision that appeared before my closed eyes.

I watched the green globe of earth turning on its axis glowing in the dark sky. Suddenly, a box inserted in an upper corner of this peaceful scene drew my attention to our kind neighbors, Señor and Señora Garay, feeding chickens in their backyard. The Garays had been essential to our survival during a nightmare year in Patagonia in 1963. I heard this message from God: "Don't you understand that I have been caring for you for your entire life?" The spell was broken when the preacher said, "Amen." The rest of the day I prowled the campground wondering what had happened. Was it a hallucination? Was God actually communicating with me? Finally, approaching Sara, a deeply spiritual woman, I asked to speak with her privately. She promised to come to my room. Alone in the dark I asked God, if He existed, to make Himself known to me. And He did. I can't explain how, but I knew that it was real. I was not alone in that room. When Sara arrived she found me laughing and crying at the same time.

My curiosity about God began in 1946 when I was nine. The subject of religion was always treacherous territory during my childhood. Mother had become a Christian at a Methodist tent revival in 1935, which completely changed her personality and behavior, converting her from a drinking, smoking, dancing, card-playing Roaring Twenties flapper into a devout believer who gave up all of those vices. She was no longer the woman my father had married. He considered religion "the opiate of the masses," using ridicule as his weapon of choice. My sister, thirteen years my senior, sided with him while Mama took me to church. One Sunday, I went forward during an altar call that followed a terrifying sermon in which the minster had described hell in graphic detail. Rapidly reviewing my past nine years, convinced of my utter sinfulness, I went forward as the congregation sang many verses of the hymn "Just as I Am" and was baptized. I soon fled to the Presbyterian Church of my friend, where the message was less frightening. For the rest of my childhood, I faithfully attended church services and was active in the youth group.

Being a Christian seemed to be a simple set of moral rules to follow, while church was a safe atmosphere for social interaction. These assumptions stayed with me during my adolescence, young adulthood and through the early years of my marriage. Suddenly, during that retreat in Oklahoma, I knew that God was no longer the stern judge of my childhood but a loving father, eager to lead me personally into a life of joy and transform me into the person He had created me to be. I saw clearly that a lot of work needed to be done but hopefully embraced the future.

I was on the road "less traveled . . . And that has made all the difference."

One

OUR JOURNEY BEGINS

Norman and Bartlesville
June 1956 / May 1958

MY SORORITY SISTER swept through the front door followed by a young man, all ears and bony frame, carrying a load of her clothes. Looking up from my books, I said, "Hi, I'm Jan." He replied that his name was Gene and asked if he could invite his mother inside for a drink of cool water before she drove on home. In walked my future mother-in-law.

In June 1956, my Kappa Alpha Theta sisters Margot Moore and Sally Caldwell and I were renting a small house while attending summer school at the University of Oklahoma. In the process of severing a romantic relationship with a young man who was already an alcoholic at the age of twenty-two, I was taking medication to alleviate the hives covering my body. They were undoubtedly caused by stress added to my afternoons in the organic chemistry lab, where the temperature averaged 110 degrees. Sally and Margot were planning a backyard barbecue for their boyfriends and wanted me to invite someone. Sally suggested Gene Grogan, whom she knew through mutual friends. I demurred, but to my surprise he called early that week and invited me out for a coke with his Delta Upsilon fraternity brother Bob West and his fiancée, Judy Crumpler. Sally again suggested inviting Gene to the barbecue.

He wanted to see me every evening after that, and within the month, told me that he loved me. My response—that he didn't know me—only made him more adamant. The conquest was too easy. I could have lost interest, except for Sally's warning: "Please don't hurt him." Tall, slim, dressed in T-shirts and army fatigues, he wasn't much to look at, except for his penetrating blue eyes and ready smile. I thought he was lying when he told me he was twenty-three. His quiet self-confidence was baffling. Where did that come from and what did he see in me? Eighteen years old, I had just completed my sophomore year and looked a mess, covered with ugly welts and spaced out on tranquilizers. In my romantic dream, the ideal man would write me sonnets and bring flowers. Instead he patiently slathered calamine lotion on my hive-covered back and took me to play putt-putt golf. Because of my poor health I withdrew from the chemistry class, but remained in Norman to pay my part of the house rent.

When summer school ended, I returned home to Lawton, Oklahoma. Gene went to the university's geology camp in Colorado for the month of August. I normally went out in the evenings but this August, turning down all invitations, I retired to my room after dinner to write to Gene. My behavior must have appeared unusually antisocial to my parents. He wrote me every evening as well, letters full of the day's activities, very little romance.

Gene had returned to college after three years in the army. Starting in 1950 on a journalism scholarship, he had no desire to be a journalist but needed financial assistance. Then, with the Korean War raging, the reinstated GI Bill guaranteed a free university education for returning veterans. Gene enlisted in February 1951 and was accepted into the Corps of Engineers Officer Candidate School at Fort Belvoir, Virginia, in 1952. He graduated on June 24 as the youngest Second Lieutenant in his class. Later he credited his experience in OCS for the leadership skills he needed to become a successful manager. In December of 1952 he flew to South Korea, where at night he spent the first six months on the front line supervising the building of machine gun bunkers for the Greek infantry. When his men set off explosives to blast holes in the granite, they had to dive for cover as the North Koreans and Chinese responded by shelling their location. He never talked much about that period of his life but continued to have nightmares for a few months after our marriage.

On our first date that autumn, he took me to Glen's Hik'ry Inn, a famous steak house in Oklahoma City. Although he really couldn't afford it, he recognized that he was dating a spoiled eighteen-year-old with no concept of financial restraints. When the appetizers arrived, he produced a small box containing a pair of tumbled amethyst earrings. When the next course arrived he produced another box, this time a necklace and earring set with gold flecks embedded in Lucite. With dessert, another box appeared. This time, I was shocked to see a sterling silver DU pendant, which would signify we were going steady. My first big lesson in knowing Gene Grogan: He was a strategic planner. Having accepted the first two gifts, it would have been churlish to reject the third. To be fair, he later pointed out that by writing him each night I had indicated serious interest.

Shortly after school resumed, my mother made an unusual trip to Norman to meet Gene. We went out to eat, and while I was in the powder room she told him that I was not a strong person. Her comment surprised me, when Gene told me about their conversation later, as she was normally a quiet, unobtrusive woman. We went to Lawton one weekend for Gene to meet my father. He seemed friendlier than usual at meeting a prospective suitor; at least he was not scowling. My first visit to Gene's home was quite different. His mother gave me a big hug at the front door and his grandmother followed suit, a startling show of affection to a girl from a home where we rarely touched one another.

As Gene and I shared our childhood experiences, the differences were evident at once. My parents, Wilbur and Lucile, were not demonstrative toward each other or their children, my sister Beverly and me. My father's red hair was matched by his temper. A self-taught polymath, he didn't suffer fools gladly, and used his razor-sharp wit to both entertain and intimidate. His abilities as the advertising manager of the local newspaper were valued to the extent that he shared in the profits with the publisher. He was respected for his high ethical standards, his artistic skill at crafting advertisements and his ability to attract business; however, he instilled fear in me from an early age. My mother was a gentle, kind woman with a deep faith in God. I knew that she loved me unconditionally. Her model of Christian love and charity toward every person she met impressed me deeply. But as a child I did not feel safe. She and I were like two mice in a house with two cats.

By contrast, Gene's large extended family, whose members lived in close proximity to each other, was admired by everyone in town as compatible, outgoing and generous. Gene's father died suddenly in 1938 when he was six; his mother, grandparents, aunts, uncles and cousins surrounded him with the love and support that imbued him with confidence and optimism. His uncles, all university graduates and pillars of their community, served as role models for him.

In November Gene and I got pinned, joining his fraternity pin and my sorority pin, which signified a step of commitment prior to engagement. His fraternity brothers came to the Theta house on a prearranged date to serenade me and my Theta sisters. He proposed at another dinner at Glen's in December 1956. Although everything seemed to be moving too fast for me, Gene had a deadline in mind— his graduation in August.

The next weekend we drove to Lawton on a mission. Excusing myself early, I went upstairs to bed. Gene told my father that he would like to talk to him and was invited into his office located right beneath my bedroom. Our house was heated by steam radiators on the ground floor with louvered vents between the floors. Wrapping myself in a blanket on the floor by the vent, I listened to Gene ask for my hand in marriage. He started with his birth, slowly progressing through his life to date. He told about his father's death, his employment as a janitor at the bank, delivering groceries for his grandfather's grocery store, selling magazine subscriptions door to door, working on an oil rig and construction during the summers, and his army career. The only clue that there was another person in the room was the occasional squeak of my father's chair and the smell of smoke from his ever-present cigarette. When Gene finally finished, I expected to hear Daddy's objections to his lack of finances and my young age. He did mention my youth but his next words were a shock. He said, "Gene, Jan doesn't know the value of a dollar." I was furious. Of course he was right, but whose fault was that? Had he ever tried to teach me frugality or refuse me anything material? He bought me a new car for my sixteenth birthday and gave me charge authorization at major shops in town. Little did I know that his statement would shackle me to doing our family finances for the rest of my life!

In January 1957, Gene made an appointment with Miss Emma Jordan, the proprietor of the jeweler Harry Winston in Oklahoma City. I felt worried and excited, fearing that he didn't have the money to buy me an engagement ring but was determined to do so. Miss Jordan ushered us into a private viewing room where she began to display beautiful engagement rings—unbeknownst to me, within the price range that she and Gene had agreed upon. We chose one especially pleasing to Gene because it was shaped like a football, the favorite sport he had played in high school. From there we walked to a nearby cinema. During the film, Gene excused himself; I thought he had gone to the men's room. After dinner that evening, he astonished me by producing the ring and slipping it on my finger.

The summer became a magical time for us, not that it began happily. After a year of always feeling things were progressing at breakneck speed, the reality of making a lifetime commitment came crashing down on me. I confessed to Gene my apprehension. A mistake in the choice of a mate, in my mind, would mean a life of misery; divorce was a word that was only whispered in polite society.

In fact, I was convinced if I divorced that I would not be welcomed at home. Until now, our romance seemed like a fairy tale but what did "happily ever after" really mean? I had no role models for that.

As I thought about Gene, his frequent playful recitation of the Boy Scout Law came to mind. This Eagle Scout loved to reel off the attributes: trustworthy, loyal, helpful, friendly, courteous, kind, obedient, cheerful, thrifty, brave, clean and reverent. He was also intelligent, exuberant and sensitive. After a few miserable days of uncertainty, I realized that I would be devastated if he left me and that I really loved him. His terse response, when I told him so, struck me like a bucket of ice water. He said, "Jan, I won't go through that again." At last, I realized that he was a mature man to whom I could trust my life.

While Gene worked to complete his course in geological engineering, I was enrolled in two courses in Far Eastern history taught by a charming, fascinating professor who had spent his childhood in China with his Presbyterian missionary parents. He offered us premarital counseling, a new concept to us, which we gratefully accepted.

Each morning, Gene collected me at my rooming house; we ate breakfast, lunch and dinner together at the student union. Geological engineering was a five-year program, but because the GI Bill expired after four years his mother provided some funds for the fifth year by purchasing Gene's share of the car they had bought together when he returned from Korea. His three part-time jobs barely covered books, tuition and lodging for the summer session, so we ate vegetarian meals. At his graduation in August, our parents met for the first time. Gene said that my dad showed up just to be sure that he graduated. His mother gave him one hundred dollars, which fed and housed him for two weeks until he received his first paycheck. Graduation day was the perfect finish to our idyllic summer but also a day of sorrow. A week later, Gene started work for Cities Service Oil Company in their engineering training program. I planned to spend the next semester at the university taking the organic chemistry course that I had dropped the previous summer. A Bachelor of Science in medical technology also required a nine-month laboratory internship. The thought of a long separation distressed us both.

The weekend following graduation, Gene traveled with me back to Norman. While he carried my bags to the room, I sat on the bed and cried. We started talking of alternatives and settled on a plan for me to return home, spend three months planning a wedding, and he would pay for me to attend summer school the next year. We retraced our path to Lawton. The glare on my father's face when he opened the front door was the beginning of an acrimonious discussion. However, when we told my parents our plan, they reluctantly assented. Mother believed I would never finish my degree and said so. She asked me, privately, if I was sure of my choice of a husband. My response—"Absolutely!"—satisfied her. That my father liked and respected Gene was obvious from the friendship they had developed. He gave me one thousand dollars for the wedding and never asked another word about it. Mama became more engaged, helped me shop for my wedding dress and trousseau, but left the other details to me. Family friends had parties and opened their homes to accommodate Gene's family and our attendants. The three months I spent at home were a peaceful, happy time for my parents and me.

Our wedding on Saturday, December 7, 1957, was the first formal ceremony in the beautiful new Presbyterian Church. Four hundred guests attended. The simplicity of the A-frame design was enhanced by the altar filled with flocked Christmas trees decorated with turquoise balls, flowers and glowing candlelight. We each had five attendants, including our sisters. The reception was held in the church hall because his family did not approve of alcoholic drink. Around eleven o'clock on that bitterly cold, blustery night, my father joyfully carried my bag out to the car while everyone waved us on our way.

Cities Service had given Gene one week off work to get married. He had rented a garage apartment in Bartlesville, Oklahoma, located across the street from the Price Tower, designed by Frank Lloyd Wright. Our aerie over the garage was so old and fragile that a strong wind shook it sufficiently to roll our bed on wheels across the bare bedroom floor. However it was convenient to downtown, the Cities Service office, the library, supermarket and other amenities. As I was totally unskilled in domestic arts, Gene spent the week teaching me to cook breakfast, run the vacuum cleaner and use our landlady's washer. On several weekends, we drove to Garber for his mother to teach me how to iron his heavily starched shirts.

Cooking was a challenge but Gene said all my chemistry courses would surely help. The menu of fried eggs, bacon and toast became scrambled eggs when I broke the yolks. Seeing the blackened bacon and toast, Gene refused to toss them so we had dry scrambled eggs, charcoaled bacon and scraped toast submerged in jelly. Mama's gift of a Betty Crocker cookbook became my textbook each day after Gene left for work. When I read a recipe that I understood—with ingredients we could afford—I forged ahead. More than once, Gene came home to a flood of tears because of culinary disasters. His grandmother patiently taught me to make the egg noodles served in a broth with chicken, an essential family recipe. His mother had warned him never to complain about my cooking or compare me with her. Bless her!

Gene's starting salary was a generous $440 a month, but with no savings or health insurance, we needed a cushion in case of emergencies. He produced a budget for us to save a hundred dollars per month, which we adhered to until our first child was born two years later. No lights on our tiny Christmas tree, one movie a month, lots of chicken and hamburger, no alcohol...but we were happy, living like most of the other young couples we knew. We ate at friends' homes, listened to music, played bridge, went to the library and took long walks.

My first attempt at entertaining provided fodder for teasing for years. The guests were Gene's cousin June Alexander and her husband, Lloyd, and Bob and Judy West. On Valentine's Day 1958, after creating a dining table out of two card tables pushed together and covered with a white sheet tablecloth, red construction paper place cards, and red candles in our silver candlesticks to set the stage, I wrote down the exact time to the minute when each part of the meal—a roast and vegetables—should be started. Regrettably, I missed seeing "per pound" following the thirty minutes cooking time for the roast. With no aroma coming from the kitchen, June finally asked if she could take a peek in the oven, after which she softly suggested making other plans. I dashed to the supermarket and bought six steaks. Although we ate beans for the rest of the month, it was a good lesson in being a relaxed hostess no matter what happened. Going from a family who rarely had guests to one where anyone dropping by was invited to stay for dinner was a big transition. Having an open-door policy to friend and stranger alike became the Grogan norm.

Two

THE KINDNESS *of* STRANGERS

Wichita Falls, Electra and Owensboro
June 1958 / February 1963

IN MAY 1958 Gene was assigned for a month to the Cities Service research laboratory in Tulsa. We lived in a furnished garage apartment again, this one on the back lot of a welding business. Although we had no neighbors it was close enough for Gene to walk to work. Passing the Frito-Lay factory on the way home at noon gave him a healthy appetite for lunch. We bought him a handsome dark-brown silk suit at a store that sold fire-sale goods; only one dry cleaning removed the smell of smoke. Polyester suits were the height of fashion for engineers so Gene stood out when he made his first presentation to management. From then on, no matter the strain on our budget, he always had at least one handsome suit and a good pair of shoes.

Gene's first permanent assignment took us to North Texas. In June we packed a U-Haul trailer with all our possessions and drove south to Wichita Falls, where we moved into our first unfurnished apartment. The next day I departed for summer school at the University of Oklahoma for six long and lonely weeks living in a campus dorm. With no distractions, I had plenty of time to study. The reward was an A in the dreaded organic chemistry.

Al Comstock, the Cities district superintendent, was well known for his ability to break in young engineers. We soon learned that meant working seven days a week including holidays. Al didn't believe in spoiling engineers by spending good money for hotel rooms, so they slept in their company cars at oil drilling sites, often in stifling heat with the windows shut against mosquitoes. The complex where we lived was full of young Cities couples with whom we forged friendships and commiserated about our hard lives under Comstock.

I applied for a job in the laboratory at Wichita General Hospital, hoping to complete a nine-month internship, the only remaining obstacle to my degree. I started in the bacteriology section with two other young trainees under the mysophobic chief bacteriologist, who shaved his entire body including his head. Although the lab work was repetitious and boring, when the pathologist in charge of the lab learned of my fascination with autopsies he began to invite me to watch. As we sat at our card table over dinner one evening, I eagerly began to describe my day, especially the bright red fingernails of the corpse who had prepared herself carefully before taking her own life. When I began describing the screeching circular saw cutting an arc into the woman's skull, Gene turned an interesting shade of gray and pushed back from the table. Thus ended sharing my work stories at dinnertime.

Our friendship with newlyweds Bill and Sue Montgomery was soon tested. Bill and Gene shared an office at work. With Gene frequently away from home "sitting on a well," I suffered from a debilitating fear of being alone. Although we were the center apartment of a triplex unit whose walls were paper thin, I was afraid to get into bed and close my eyes. Every tiny sound I interpreted as someone trying to break in. Each night my vow to overcome my terror vanished by nine o'clock and I was calling Sue to request the use of their guest room. They patiently took me in night after night for months. We became life-long friends.

Since my parents lived only sixty miles away, they occasionally drove down on Sunday afternoons. Our furniture, except for a bed and night-stands, consisted of two card tables and four folding chairs. On the second visit, my father presented us with an old overstuffed armchair, which he occupied on subsequent visits. The meager sum I made was put into a special account with which we purchased a sofa, armchair, slate-topped side table and a lamp. At last visitors actually stayed a while.

In early 1959 Gene was asked to move thirty miles west to Electra, Texas, to work in a Cities production office located in an oil field on the W. T. Waggoner ranch. Since the pathologist had failed to get the accreditation required for me to receive credit for my months of work, I quit my job.

Named for the feisty daughter of W. T. Waggoner, Electra was located on the edge of a ranch homesteaded in 1852 by Daniel Waggoner and expanded by his son W. T. to cover half a million acres. When early settlers drilled wells for water, they were contaminated with oil that seeped in, a great disappointment for Electra residents. However, by 1911 a wildcat well was drilled for the petroleum that was rapidly replacing whale oil as the fuel of choice. It was a gusher and the oil boom was on. The town population swelled to six thousand. In 1959, it was still a viable town with ranching and oil production the main sources of income. The bars and churches vied for first place as centers of social life. We were warmly welcomed into the First Presbyterian Church community, where Gene was elected an elder at the tender age of twenty-eight.

We rented a tiny run-down box of a house on the wrong side of the railroad tracks. From my kitchen window, I could see several old men staggering around near their cardboard shacks. I was terribly afraid of them until I began to volunteer at our church's thrift shop and discovered that the church women knew them all by name and outfitted them with warm clothes each winter.

Gene bought a small black-and-white TV hoping the noise would make me less fearful when alone. It helped a little but the flimsy locked front door frequently blew open in a strong wind, which terrified me. A wash house across the street was equipped with old-fashioned open tub washers with electric wringers. Women in Electra were judged by how early their wash was on the clothesline on Monday mornings. It was a contest I never entered. However, when I did go outside to hang out clothes, I had company. A large black snake lived under the back stoop and liked to sun himself under the clothesline, but courteously raced for his hole when I appeared. He earned my respect by keeping the rodent population down. I seemed to have unexpected bravery for real threats but suffered debilitating fear of imagined ones.

Gene's new boss was a bear of a man with a speech impediment and an eighth-grade education. When he was just thirteen, Ace Broderson had run away from the brutal uncle who raised him; he was self-sufficient from that time forward. He always answered the phone with, "Dis here Ace." He had strongly resisted having a university-educated engineer in his office but Gene soon won him over with his respectful approach and eagerness to learn. Ace and his wife, Carrie, had six grown children and many grandchildren. They adopted us as their own, inviting us to fish fries featuring catfish Ace had caught, coleslaw and hush puppies made by Carrie, and plenty of beer. Gene called him the most honest person he had ever known. For years, Gene received calls from Ace, who said, "Gene, Electra, it not move." Over the years we were able to visit them a few times.

A couple with another oil company moved in across the street. Diane and I, both avid readers, quickly became fast friends. Every morning at ten she came over for coffee for precisely one hour to discuss literature. Her knowledge greatly expanded my reading. She gave me a treasured copy of *The Prophet* by Khalil Gibran. Her intellectual and creative pursuits contrasted starkly with her husband Clayton's main interests in beer and sports. My obvious happiness with Gene spawned her nickname for him, "the perfect husband." I wasn't surprised when this marriage ended. Diane raised their two daughters while she continued to write, became an Episcopal deacon, and found her soul mate in Vickie. Diane Marquart Moore is a prolific author of poetry and prose, deeply connected to her Louisiana roots.

Not long after our arrival in Electra, I got pregnant. On December 3, 1959, our son, Patrick Deane, was born at Wichita General Hospital, where I had worked. My mother had told me not to expect her as she was afraid of newborn infants. We mistakenly thought it would be an imposition on Gene's mother to ask her to spend her annual vacation helping us, so we asked Gene's sister, Betty

Hurst, who graciously left her husband, Bill, and seven-year-old daughter, Janet, to spend a week with us. How little we understood about grandmothers.

What Gene and I knew about infants consisted of a thorough reading of Dr. Spock's seminal book, Baby and Child Care. We discounted his psychological advice but carefully followed the rest. My old fears were replaced by new ones. Baby noises masked the creaks of the old house that I had invariably assumed were being made by an intruder. New fears took the form of dreams that I had forgotten the baby somewhere. Fortunately, he was healthy and performed Spock's developmental steps right on time. His pediatrician was encouraging and pleased that I was a pioneer in the resurgence of breastfeeding, unlike my obstetrician, who was aghast. Gene took an active role in parenting. He became an expert in soothing a colicky baby and changed diapers through the night—when he wasn't sitting on a well.

We made our first big purchase, trading our Oldsmobile two-door coupe for a Chevrolet station wagon, paying it off in monthly installments. As we entered a new decade, we were in debt for the first time but optimistic and confident. Gene was thriving in his job and we had a beautiful baby boy.

When Patrick was eight months old we were posted back to the district office in Wichita Falls. We were in our small rental house only four days when tragedy struck.

I was scrubbing the kitchen cabinets before unpacking the dishes; Patrick was playing on the floor behind me. It was Sunday and Gene was at work on the Waggoner Ranch. Our range was not connected to the gas line yet so I had filled an electric pot with water because Patrick was still drinking boiled water. Hearing a thump and scream, I turned to see that he had grabbed the cord and pulled the pot off. Sweeping him into my arms, I removed the soaked knit top. To my horror, chunks of his flesh came off with it. Swaddling the shrieking baby in a clean sheet, I dialed 0 for an operator, then the company office, and ran with him to the window looking for the rescue squad. The few minutes it took for them to arrive seemed like an eternity.

One paramedic took Patrick into the back of the ambulance and began to care for him while the other drove and tried to soothe a frantic mother. With siren blaring, we raced through the city to the hospital. When he suddenly stopped screaming, I thought he was dead. He had fainted; a few seconds later, the piercing screams resumed. In the emergency room, the staff, who remembered me, took pity on us and administered morphine before his doctor arrived. I wasn't allowed in the examining room but could still hear him wailing. Shortly after Gene got there, Patrick's pediatrician gave us the good news that the boiling water had sterilized and burned less than 50 percent of his body so he was not in immediate danger of death. The bad news was that he could have no more morphine because it would mask his progress, which had to be monitored closely. The two dangers were infection and pneumonia. Patrick was smeared with ointment and placed into a baby bed tented in sterile linen, heated with light bulbs. A cot was put in the room for us to sleep on; we slept in two- to five-minute increments like Patrick did.

When he jolted awake, we stuck a bottle of water into his mouth. In the middle of the first night he suddenly went rigid and his eyes rolled back in his head. Calling for help, we were shocked to discover that there was only one registered nurse in this huge hospital at 2:00 a.m. and she wasn't on the pediatric wing; there was no physician. She called his doctor, who said Patrick was too hot and told her to unscrew one of the light bulbs. Gene was constantly with us the first forty-eight hours but then resumed work. I never again felt confident that there was anyone at night to help if another incident occurred.

It was reassuring to see a healing film rapidly covering the baby's burns. By the fourth day, Patrick was pulling up, holding on to the rails, and begging to be held. The naked baby made everyone who entered the room a target for a wetting. Our pastor in his suit was the first victim. During this ordeal, the feared Al Comstock and his lovely wife visited us. They were so kind and thoughtful. I discovered that he wasn't such an ogre after all.

One week after the accident, Patrick was dismissed completely healed except for one small spot. When we arrived home he took an uninterrupted three-hour nap. Exhausted from lack of sleep, I drove to the market for groceries. Backing out, I hit a concrete block and caved in the back of the station wagon. When Gene took Patrick with him to get quotes from body shops, he patiently explained the red scars on the baby's arms and the cause of the car accident. The day he collected the repaired car, there was no bill. The owner of the shop said he thought we had had enough anguish. When we think of the kindness of strangers we remember that man.

The career of a petroleum engineer was similar to that of a military man or diplomat; one could expect to be moved every two to three years. The rationale was to give the engineer varied experience in the oil business and management the opportunity to evaluate him. During Gene's first assignment in North Texas he learned the method of secondary recovery using a technique called water-flooding. As the quantity of oil began to decline in older fields, a well in the center of a formation would be chosen for recovery while wells around the periphery of the formation were injected with water that pushed more oil toward the center well. Gene's new expertise qualified him for the next move.

In March of 1961 we were transferred to Owensboro, Kentucky. We arrived ahead of the moving truck and quickly found a beautiful brick house for rent on a corner lot in a good neighborhood. The price of $125 per month was really more than we could afford but we were thrilled with the luxury of three small bedrooms, a carpeted living-dining room, and kitchen-den combination. It even had air-conditioning units in the living room and bedrooms.

Owensboro, the third largest city in Kentucky, was located west of Louisville on the Ohio River, equipped with locks that controlled boats and barges passing through. The population of thirty thousand was over 90 percent white, a very Southern city famous for its barbecue and bourbon. Three businesses provided most of the employment: General Electric, Texas Gas Transmission and a distillery. In those years, the small African American population was almost invisible, working at menial jobs, living in a segregated neighborhood and having absolutely no voice in civic affairs.

Restaurants and cinemas were segregated. As I look back I wonder how they or we could have tolerated such an arrangement but we accepted that was just the way things were. When the civil rights movement led by Dr. Martin Luther King Jr. began to make national headlines, Gene and I felt their liberation and equality were long overdue but we didn't take an active role in the movement.

One morning shortly after our arrival, Patrick awakened with a slight fever and some strange spots. At noon, the mail arrived with the diagnosis. Our friends in Bartlesville with whom we had spent a day on our way to Owensboro wrote to say apologetically that their children had developed chicken pox shortly after we departed. The neighbor next door gave me the name of a pediatrician. He prescribed over the phone for the entire duration of Patrick's illness, and treated a subsequent ear infection by phone too. We never received a bill; however, when I tried to sign the baby up as a patient, I was informed that his practice was full. We were referred to a young, single, newly arrived pediatrician with the aristocratic-sounding name of Duvall Bushong. He declared Patrick to be in perfect health but suggested that he needed a brother or sister. We took his advice.

The First Presbyterian Church was an unusual combination of the southern and northern branches of the Presbyterian Church, the result of a schism dating from the Civil War. This church split its funds according to the declared preferences of its members, 70 percent southern and 30 percent northern. They also ordered teaching materials from the two branches in the same percentages. There was a Wednesday night potluck supper that we attended as well as an adult Sunday Bible study class. At church, we met John and Nancy Blewer, whose son, John Jr., was two weeks younger than Patrick. The boys played beautifully together so Nancy and I had play dates once or twice weekly. We alternated having dinner and bridge together in our homes, trying out new recipes on each other. Our friendship was further cemented when we discovered that we were both expecting with delivery dates a week apart. Gene's boss, L.D. Todd, and his wife, Rubye, who had two young daughters, became friends as well.

Gene was again often away from home traveling as far as West Virginia, and I keenly felt his absence. It seemed to me that his work took precedence over the family. He felt that doing his work to the best of his ability was the way to take care of the family. Our difference of opinion as to his primary duty caused me to resent him and the company that didn't appear to consider the needs of families.

We were also struggling financially. Every Thanksgiving, about forty relatives met at Grandma Southwick's in Garber. We wanted to go but Gene said the drive to Oklahoma would be impossible without new tires. In May I started scrimping and saving, pinching pennies from our food budget. However, we still had only half the money needed for the four tires when November arrived. We compromised and bought two new tires for the front and started for Oklahoma. Just beyond Paducah, Kentucky, in southern Missouri we got into a blinding snow storm. We stopped for dinner at a tiny café with lots of cars around it including several highway patrol cars, always the sign of good food at reasonable prices. We were seated, but before we were given menus the waitress arrived with a big bowl of mashed potatoes, chicken and noodles for Patrick—the waitress declaring that babies don't like to wait for their food. That kind of thoughtfulness was rare even in the 1950s. He tucked in and we followed eagerly with the same meal.

Thanksgiving at Grandma's was a huge production, with Aunt Hazel next door baking the forty-pound turkey overnight. She also prepared the dressing, mashed potatoes and gravy. Aunt Violet, next door on the other side, Aunt Jane from Bartlesville, and Helen Hurst, mother of Gene's brother-in-law, Bill, from Chandler, Oklahoma, all provided their same contributions each year. Gene's mother, Thelma, made all the pies, getting up early on Thanksgiving morning to bake them fresh. The younger women were in charge of setting the tables, putting out the food and washing dishes afterward. The men watched football games on TV and kept a loose eye on the children. We all ate until we couldn't force down another bite. When the dishes were done it was time to set out the leftovers for more eating, followed by more washing and drying. All the women were exhausted by the end of the day but the joyful reunion filled us with happy memories until the next year.

On March 18, 1962, Lisa Lynn arrived a few days after Nancy delivered baby Susan. As planned, Grandmother Thelma arrived to assist for the first ten days. She and I both cried when she left, especially since Patrick was running a fever that preceded a case of the red measles. Fortunately, my immunity provided Lisa protection.

Gene traveled to the mountains of West Virginia to look at property that Cities might be interested in leasing. He ventured into the "hollers" with some trepidation as the inhabitants were none too friendly to strangers. They were always on the lookout for "revenuers" because making moonshine was their prime source of income. After many generations in those backwoods, the people still spoke with the distinct British accent of their forebears. He met a self-taught lawyer whose cabin walls were lined with law books. Gene's work proved fruitful when, a few years later, Cities developed a large waterflood operation in West Virginia.

In January 1963 Gene received a call from corporate headquarters in New York City. They were looking for an engineer with waterflood experience to take over an operation in southern Argentina. He flew to New York and, after discussing it with me, accepted the job. Thus began the most exciting, challenging and terrifying year of my life.

Three

ANNUS HORRIBILIS

Comodoro Rivadavia
February 1963 / February 1964

"SHE MAY SURVIVE because she has a thin layer of fat," the doctor told our interpreter. Fortunately, I spoke no Spanish then.

A week after our arrival in the coastal city of Comodoro Rivadavia in southern Argentina, one-year-old Lisa developed a fever and diarrhea. Unbeknownst to us, bacterial dysentery was killing babies in Buenos Aires. The doctor began a series of penicillin shots administered with old syringes and needles that she sharpened herself. Sometimes, it took her three jabs before she could penetrate Lisa's tender skin. She directed us to keep her hydrated with rice water and the juice extracted from raw beef. This trial was only one of many.

Comodoro had sounded exciting and romantic, but had we known what living there would be like, Gene never would have accepted the job. He had signed a two-year contract with no interim home leave. Cities Service was taking over operations from a partner oil company and he was told to evaluate the economic viability of the oil field.

Saying good-bye to our parents was painful. Indelible memories linger of our mothers tearfully standing at their front doors watching us depart. Gene's uncle Hugh, an amateur photographer, solemnly took formal photographs as though they would never see us again. While we were in Lawton, a family friend gave us her copy of *The Voyage of the Beagle* by Charles Darwin. In 1835 Darwin anchored in Comodoro's Bay of St. George, where he began his epochal journey into Patagonia. We discovered how little had changed during the intervening 125 years. A vast pampas, home to unique species of animals and birds and ideal for raising sheep, Patagonia was a naturalist's wonderland. For young adults, eager to explore the world, it would have been paradise. For Gene and me, with young children to protect, it turned out to be a dangerous place full of perilous pitfalls and obstacles. Life got no easier when I became pregnant shortly after our arrival.

At home we had plunged into preparations: physical examinations, shots, passport photos, visas, purchasing supplies, and storing our worldly goods including the car. We were allowed to take only the bare essentials plus the baby bed and highchair. We were told there was a good house, fully furnished, ready for us. L.D. Todd, Gene's Owensboro boss, asked, "A good house by U.S. standards or a good house for Comodoro?" To our dismay it was neither.

On our way, we checked into the Biltmore Hotel in New York City. Gene awakened the next morning with chills and a fever that quickly escalated to 104 degrees. I requested a doctor from the hotel staff and called the Cities Service office to report that Gene was ill. The doctor diagnosed influenza. When a representative from the office arrived, Gene was so delirious that the man just shook his head and called the airline to postpone our flight. Gene refused to delay our trip more than one day; he worried about what the hotel was costing Cities Service, well known for its parsimony. In fact, before Gene went to New York to interview for the job, the domestic company increased his monthly salary by one hundred dollars because they were embarrassed by its meagerness. He was told that the increase would be rescinded if he rejected the transfer. Looking back, I wonder why we did not ask more questions or even decline the assignment. The promise of adventure and Gene's opportunity to be a manager must have been more compelling than reason. The following morning, the Cities representative returned. With the baby on my hip, Patrick holding on to my coat, and the Cities man and I supporting Gene between us, we slowly made our way out of the hotel and into a taxi. The Cities man happily waved us good-bye. At JFK Airport, we learned that our flight was delayed. I spent five hours pushing Lisa in her stroller through the terminal while Patrick tagged along and Gene sat slumped in a chair. The nightmare was beginning.

With unexpected extravagance, the company had booked us in first class for the eighteen-hour flight, with two refueling stops. At Port of Spain, Trinidad, the low, thatched, un-air-conditioned terminal building had passed-out drunks littering the floor. At Rio, in the middle of the night, we picked our way through rubble remaining from a recent attempted coup. The children slept; we did not. Lisa refused to go in the claustrophobic bassinet attached to the plane's bulkhead so we stretched both children across our seats and sat on the edges. We arrived in Buenos Aires about five o'clock in the morning.

Since we were five hours later than expected, the driver and our interpreter had spent those hours eating, smoking and drinking. The stench of sweat, tobacco, garlic and wine in the car during the ninety-minute drive was overpowering. We were dropped at the Hotel California, which, we soon discovered, was infested with roaches. Months later, at the luxurious Claridge's Hotel on a rest-and-recuperation trip, we asked why we had been put in the Hotel California and were told that Argentines believed all Americans required a hotel with a twenty-four-hour bar.

By late afternoon of the first day, Gene again had a fever. Unable to speak Spanish, I found a maid and showed her my husband in bed looking quite ill. About two hours later, there was a knock at our door. In the hall stood a seven-foot-tall gentleman dressed completely in white from his hat to his spats. The doctor opened Gene's mouth and said, "Oh, dear boy, you have quinsy!" Seeing our look of consternation, he explained that Gene had an abscessed tonsil and would need to remain in Buenos Aires to be treated at the British hospital. For a week, Gene left by taxi each morning and returned later in the day. I never knew how to contact him or when I would see him again. The children and I chased roaches and ordered room service.

One evening when Gene was feeling better, our Irish Argentine interpreter, Paddy Logan, invited us to his home for an asado (barbecue). It was a beautiful evening and we sat in the garden dining on parts of animals we didn't recognize. Gene was glad to be able to avoid most of it because of his sore throat. Finally Paddy offered pudding, and I gratefully thought dessert had arrived—my first experience with the savory dish known as blood pudding. The food was strange but the hospitality was comforting and greatly appreciated.

When Gene recovered, we boarded a French Caravelle for our first flight on a jet, and flew the thousand miles south to our new home. We landed on a typical day in Patagonia, which meant that a raging wind was blowing. To get from the airplane into the terminal, the passengers formed a human chain that snaked across the tarmac.

We were met by Glen Hamilton, who would be Gene's production foreman, and his wife. During the ride into town, Helen described in graphic detail what a hellhole Comodoro Rivadavia was. It was a testament to my numbed state that I didn't burst into tears or hysterical laughter. It didn't take long to discover that Helen solved her problems by rarely leaving her apartment, soothing herself with her small dog and a large bottle of gin. Glen, an old hand in the oil business, was a charmer. He had lived in South America for over twenty-five years, was fluent in Spanish, and would prove to be an essential employee. Glen took us directly to the Hotel Comodoro, where we settled into two tiny connecting bedrooms. The German housekeeper was the only staff person who spoke English.

The next morning, Glen arrived to take us to see the "good house," located on a high hill overlooking the Atlantic. On one side was the best house in town, purpose-built for the French firm Schlumberger's manager. It was surrounded by a high security wall. On the other side lived an Argentine couple, the Garays, both in their sixties and retired from the railroad, who became valued friends and mentors.

The house, painted a dismal green, stood behind a low pipe fence and the yard's few scraggly bushes. The interior was worse. The furnishings consisted of a double bed, a single bed, a sofa, a floor lamp, a kitchen table and four chairs. The floors were bare. There was one small space heater in the hall. Surprisingly, there were three American appliances—a gas range, a dryer and an electric clothes washer. The dryer and oven were inoperable because they required more gas pressure to turn on than was available. The washer worked when we had electricity. We learned to check the space heater often because the low flame occasionally went out, letting gas seep into the house. Hot water was provided by an instant heater over the kitchen sink, which shot out flames each time it was turned on. There was no hot water in the bathroom. The house was filthy and infested with bedbugs. Cleaning, painting and de-bugging had to begin immediately because, according to company policy, we were allotted a maximum of six weeks in the hotel.

Gene's office was located in a village eleven miles from town, and without phone service, we had no contact once he left for work. One advantage of this village was a dairy where Gene could buy milk. Milk in the shops was heavily watered and unsafe. The dairy's milk was raw but our predecessor had left a small pasteurizer. Gene's company car was a Russian-designed Argentinian brand, Siam Di Tella, and I had a small Renault. Both were old and battered. After I had driven the Renault for several months, Gene discovered that of the four bolts holding the driver's seat, three were missing.

The next evening, John Bruton, Cities man in Argentina, Paddy Logan and Al Straub arrived from Buenos Aires. Feeling some trepidation, I hired the hotel housekeeper to babysit the children during the dinner party. We were surprised to see Al, Gene's boss from New York. He took me into a side room to assure me that if there was anything I did not like about our situation he would change it. Obviously, he was feeling guilty for not checking out the place before sending us there. I told him that everything was just fine. What else was I going to say when Gene was getting his first chance to show what he could do managing an operation? But because of his concern, Al always occupied a special place in my heart.

Two days after he departed, Lisa fell ill. Once she had recovered, and while our house was being prepared, I began to venture out in the car with the children. We had seen Americans in the hotel dining room but not one approached us. We eventually introduced ourselves. Most were tough oil-field roughnecks, some with families. The women looked as shell-shocked as I felt. At night we studied a workbook, *Spanish Made Simple,* which we had purchased before leaving the States. At the end of six weeks, we moved into the house. The children were happy to see their toys and to have room to play. Lisa had just learned to walk.

Comodoro had a population of one hundred thousand but it appeared smaller because of its density. There were four trees in the entire city. The wind always blew from the land toward the sea and a few times a year it could reach 150 miles an hour. Most houses, like ours, were constructed of concrete with shutters that could be lowered between the double-paned windows. The earth of bentonite clay (decomposed volcanic ash) was able to absorb large quantities of water and expand dramatically. Normal rainfall was ten inches, but in 1963 over forty inches fell, turning the unpaved roads into quagmires. Many days my little Renault was stuck in the driveway. When the weather dried out, dust storms coated everything in the house as well as outside with a deep layer of ash. Wet washcloths over our noses and mouths made it possible to breathe without fits of coughing. Because the bay was shallow, a long jetty was built where the sea was deep enough for the oil tankers to load. Oil spills made the beach a black, gooey mess. I was beginning to think that Helen's hellhole description was apt. Each day felt like a struggle for survival. The thought that we might be there for two years was almost unbearable. Resentment toward the company was growing stronger in me each day.

We quickly tired of our daily fare of beef tenderloin. Glen had imported a case of chickens, plucked but not gutted. He had them in his freezer and split the case with us. Fried chicken was a great treat. Produce, trucked from Buenos Aires over terrible roads, consisted of root vegetables, occasionally rotting oranges, and little else. A café in a fishing village north of Comodoro produced delicious fish soup, though we seldom ventured up there because of the atrocious road. We bought staples like flour and sugar at a small grocery store. Señora Garay was aghast when she saw canned fruit in my kitchen and shook her head no, but I thought she was just old-fashioned. When the cans swelled, I quit buying canned goods. We took an empty bottle to the grocery where we filled it with excellent cheap red wine from a cask. Bread was delivered around town in the back of a dump truck, so I bought chunks of yeast from the wholesale bakery and made my own instead. The Garays had hens and sold us eggs. The water supply, which came on twice a day, was stored in a tank on the roof and required boiling to be safe. Shopping at the central market, with Lisa on one hip and firmly holding Patrick's hand, was awkward, but the merchants were happy to help me get my purchases into the car. The cars were parallel parked bumper to bumper without setting the brakes, even on the steep hills. Idlers lolling on the streets nominated themselves as experts and directed my efforts to push the cars ahead of me enough to make a space to exit.

Comodoro was a hardship post for young doctors who worked there for a few years to pay off their government education loans. There were no specialists. There was no hospital; one had been started during Juan Perón's presidency, to honor his mother who was from Comodoro, but it was never completed. The hospital's massive shell was an ugly carbuncle on the beach. There were no autoclaves, no x-ray machines and no incubators because Argentina levied a 300 percent tariff on imported medical equipment. Only large hospitals in Buenos Aires could afford them. For minor surgery, illness or delivery, the doctors had rooms connected to their offices, but confinement was limited due to the high probability of infection. We flew to Buenos Aires to consult an obstetrician when I became ill with bronchitis. He ordered six weeks of bed rest. Feeling vulnerable and depressed, I tearfully complied. When Gene and I got food poisoning, the local doctor gave us a small vial of extremely bitter liquid; he warned us to put only one drop on our tongues—that two might kill us. It must have been poison, but it worked. Fortunately, the children stayed healthy. We were less than five hundred miles from the tip of the continent; the winter was very cold so the children wore their snowsuits inside the house.

A typical day consisted of washing a large pile of cloth diapers and clothes—in the washer if it was working, by hand otherwise—and hanging them outside to dry in the stiff wind. Cooking required some ingenuity. Devising a stovetop oven by putting a rack inside a large Dutch oven, I was able to bake. I allowed the children into the fenced backyard where there was a sandbox, but kept a close eye from the kitchen. The highlight of the day was Gene's arrival for lunch. On the hill opposite us, separated by an inlet of the ocean, were starving Chilean peasants living in cardboard shacks. They had come to work in the oil fields ten years earlier; but the jobs ended, leaving them stranded and desperate. At night, they prowled our neighborhood stealing anything left outside. Thankfully, they did not try to break into houses. All the same, I anxiously listened for Gene's car to pull into the drive, as it was dark by the time he came home for dinner. Waiting for his return was the most difficult.

While I was hiding my fear, trying to be a good wife and mother, Gene was dealing with difficulties of his own. The manager of the field, which was owned by a Swiss oil company, was a Nazi sympathizer who did not conceal his hatred for Americans. Glen told Gene that this man had organized his employees into military units during World War II, marching them with rifles in preparation for the day when Germany would "liberate" Argentina. He spoke English but refused to speak it with Gene or to provide him the archival information he needed to judge the field's potential. Only Gene's respectful persistence made the man grudgingly relent. Attempting to recover the thick, sticky oil using waterflooding was unsuccessful. Another oil company tried using steam rather than water, also unsuccessfully. In my weekly letters home I did not share my fears or just how bad our circumstances were because I didn't want to alarm the family, but I needed a friend. Then I met Katie Sanderlin.

Katie's husband, Mickey, worked for an American oil service company; she was the principal of the tiny school established by Halliburton Company for the English-speaking community. Gene rarely traveled but when he had to be away, Katie spent the night with the children and me because I was terrified by reports that a ring of slavers was working in the city. Our plan was that I would barricade myself and the children in their windowless bedroom while Katie ran for help. These were not idle fears. One American friend had to fight for her lovely young daughter at the central market. She had one of her daughter's arms and the slaver had the other. No one intervened to help. The fact that blond, blue-eyed Patrick and Lisa were especially desirable only added to my fear.

Children frequently came to the house begging for food. I watched them eat outside our back door knowing larger children or adults were lurking around the corner to snatch the food from them. I taught Patrick a game of taking Lisa into their bedroom to play hide and seek anytime the doorbell rang so they couldn't be seen.

Other friends were David Wilkie, the manager of Amoco, and his wife, Emma, who had four young children near the ages of Patrick and Lisa. We met an Argentine couple while dining at the Hotel Comodoro.

Carlos Ibarguren spoke a little English, but with determination and our little Spanish, we became friends with him and his wife, Mary. Carlos owned huge sheep ranches all over Patagonia. Neighbors Señor and Señora Garay were wonderful to us. She came into my kitchen every morning and taught me Spanish by just talking to me until I started to understand. When we needed help or advice, they were eager to be of assistance. They also babysat the children. My two attempts at having a maid were unsuccessful; both were country girls who had never seen running water and would have needed months of training. I did not trust them to care for the children.

A tiny Southern Baptist mission church with an American missionary held a weekly service in English. Six couples attended. Because the missionary traveled a wide area, we normally conducted the service ourselves, assigning each person a part for the coming week: sermon, prayers, hymns, scripture reading and announcements. One Sunday Gene preached, taking as his text the Beatitudes from Matthew 5. To his astonishment, the person assigned the scripture read that very passage beforehand. Even in deepest, darkest Patagonia, Gene declared, God was with us. I remained skeptical.

On weekends, we ventured onto the coast road with its axle-breaking potholes. We walked on the pebble beaches, sometimes with a picnic, on the lookout for whales and penguins. Or we would watch the gauchos ride their horses into the city for two-day drinking binges. These fierce-looking men evoked tales of the Wild West. Their bravado was on full display as they galloped into town. There was one nightclub, the Penguin, popular with Americans and with Argentines and their mistresses. Our house was too sparsely appointed for entertaining. Most of our friends lived either in mobile homes or apartments, so we met in restaurants—more cheerful than home but with the same few food choices. The Argentine national drink, yerba mate, supposedly supplied the nutrients lacking in the poor diet. Although it was an extravagance, twice we flew to Buenos Aires to sleep in comfort and fill up on fruits and vegetables. The children loved the extensive playground in the beautiful and lush Luna Park near our hotel.

On November 22 at 7:00 p.m., a telegram was delivered to our house. Written in Spanish by an Argentine friend, it said, "For the terrible tragedy that is inundating the world in mourning, please accept my sincere condolences." Without a shortwave radio, we had no idea what had happened. Gene thought there might have been a nuclear explosion somewhere. A new Argentinian president had been elected in October on the platform of canceling the foreign oil contracts. He had fulfilled his promise. I thought we were being warned by our friend to flee the country. My mind filled with frightful scenes of our family in a small boat on the storm-tossed Atlantic. Because Gene was in bed with a fever, I went next door with flashlight in hand to inquire of our French neighbor. He shared the shocking news of President Kennedy's assassination and offered his sympathy. Sad as it was, I felt relief to know we weren't in immediate danger.

The next day, we were flooded with tearful Argentine friends arriving at our door laden with gifts. One brought a whole goat ready for the grill. I dumped it in the bathtub and ran next door to tell the Garays about it. Señor Garay's eyes lit up and he began to sharpen his gaucho knife. That night we had an asado together. Kennedy was the first American president in many years who had taken an interest in our South American neighbors. That, plus the fact that he was Catholic, made him beloved.

Shortly before Christmas, the children and I flew back home. Airlines would not allow a pregnant woman to fly within six weeks of her due date. From the window of the plane, I could see Gene's heaving shoulders as he wept on the observation deck. We believed that he would be following us soon, as he had reported to Cities Service that the oil concession was not financially viable. All the same, it was a wrenching separation.

When we arrived in Oklahoma City, I knelt down at the bottom of the airplane's steps and kissed the ground.

I vowed never to leave the United States again.

Four

ON THE ROAD AGAIN

Lafayett, Odessa, Tulsa and New York
March 1964 / August 1972

OH, THE JOY of being back in the U. S. of A! We spent Christmas
in snowy Garber, Oklahoma, with Gene's mother, Thelma, and her
mother, Grandma Jennie Southwick. Gene drove south from Comodoro
to an oil service company camp where he spent Christmas with American
friends, getting sunburned while horseback riding. In January, we settled
with my parents in Lawton to await the arrival of the baby. By February
Gene, back in the States, had received his new assignment to Lafayette,
Louisiana. There he would learn deep-well drilling, both offshore in the
Gulf of Mexico and onshore in the Atchafalaya Swamp. He collected
our station wagon from storage and had our belongings trucked to
Lafayette, where he rented a small frame house. Although he had accrued
enough vacation time to be with us through the baby's birth, Cities told
him that he was needed urgently in Louisiana. After a short visit with
us, he reported for work.

On March 5, 1964, Suzanne was born in Southwestern
Hospital—the same hospital where I had been born. A crusty old
nurse called Barnes, who worked in the nursery, had also attended

my birth. She brusquely dumped Suzanne into Gene's arms when he surprised me by arriving the following night, his boss having decided he wasn't so essential after all. Although thrilled by his appearance, I was upset with the company—and with Gene—that he was not there for her birth. When Suzanne developed a blood condition that threatened her life and might have required her blood to be exchanged, he had already gone back to Louisiana. He did carefully prepare for our arrival—with everything unpacked and in place, even washing the good crystal—before returning to drive us to Lafayette. Grandmother Thelma traveled down with us and was a tremendous help.

Louisiana was the perfect state for reentry into the United States, with a culture unique to America. It had been settled by Cajuns, who still spoke archaic French as descendants of the Acadians who had come to Louisiana from the maritime provinces of Canada. In the verdant coastal region, they became successful farmers and fishermen. Lafayette was named for the Marquis de Lafayette, the French aristocrat who fought with the founding fathers in our Revolution. In the 1940s petroleum and natural gas discoveries transformed Lafayette into two sometimes clashing cultures: the fun-loving Cajuns and the brash, hard-driving oilmen. Gradually, the Cajuns taught the oilmen to slow down and enjoy the food, music, gaming and dancing.

We were warmly welcomed by our gregarious Cajun neighbors, and soon became members at Grace Presbyterian Church, where Suzanne was baptized. We developed our social life at this new church filled with young couples, and with neighbors and other Cities employees as well. I became active on the Women's Board but did not recognize any spiritual dimension to my church attendance. Perhaps I wasn't looking for it. When one of our members attempted suicide, I was one of several women our minister asked to call on her and help, as he seemed unable to do so. Her sad story of spousal abuse was shocking and left me feeling totally unable to do anything more than listen to her and take food to her house. How could being a Christian make a difference in her life and mine? There was something missing but I could not figure out what it was. It would be several years before I began to understand the power of prayer and trust in God to guide us through life's trials.

We soon learned that there was indeed an acute shortage of production engineers. Gene was almost constantly sitting on an oil rig either in the Gulf or in the swamp. He would arrive home from the Gulf one evening and be told to report to the swamp the next day. In addition to the heavy work schedule, Cities employees' salaries were much lower than other oil companies were paying. Gene and other workers were being offered lucrative contracts, which forced Cities to finally respond with raises in an attempt to retain their good employees. Gene's loyalty to Cities Service was not unusual. During this period, a person's character and abilities were questioned if one frequently went from one firm to another. Additionally, the matching funds that companies added to employee savings plans were not retained by an employee who left a firm.

In spite of the working conditions, living in Lafayette was considered a good posting. All entertainment revolved around food. Cajun cuisine was irresistible, rich and spicy. Shrimp boils and oyster-shucking parties were great family affairs. Wives with absent husbands were always included in the festivities. Our children also took part in most social occasions and had many playmates in the neighborhood.

Hurricane Hilda came roaring through in October 1964. Gene boarded up our windows and sat beside the radio. The ninety-miles-an-hour wind ripped the shingles off the back half of the roof. When the shaking house awakened me from a deep sleep, I found Gene dashing around with pots and pans to catch the rain pouring in. The electric power failed and we sweltered in the house for several days, always on the lookout for venomous snakes that had sought higher ground.

Early in 1965 we purchased our first house, a rambling four-bedroom ranch with a deep-pitched roof set in a native pine forest, the yard filled with beautiful camellias, azaleas and ferns. The unfenced homes of our neighborhood created a giant playground where the children frolicked together under their mothers' watchful eyes. Our friends Frank and Louise Mytinger and their three children, whom we first met in Wichita Falls, lived a few houses from us. Their two youngest were great playmates for Patrick and Lisa. Plucky one-year-old Suzanne tried her best to join in as well.

Gene's schedule did not improve. I hired an adult babysitter to stay with the children one day a week while I did my shopping, went to the hairdresser and took a piano lesson, a diversion that I greatly enjoyed. One evening a week, I played bridge. In September 1965, Hurricane Betsy, like Hilda billed as a storm that only occurred every fifty years, devastated the Louisiana Gulf Coast. We were again without power or water because our well had an electric pump. This time we had learned to be prepared and had filled a new garbage can with water, and fortunately the tall tree that fell in our backyard landed parallel to the house.

At the end of summer 1966, Gene was promoted to district engineer and we moved from lush Louisiana to dry, barren Odessa, Texas, leaving our empty house for sale. At last Gene would finally have more normal working hours. He had always been a loving and attentive father, playing with the children and tucking them into bed each night when he was at home—but he was so often away! Knowing that he would now be able to spend more time with us eased the pain of having to part once more from friends and familiar places.

Named by immigrant men who worked on the railroad, Odessa, Texas, began as a watering stop and cattle shipping point on the Texas and Pacific Railway in 1855. Midland, the other city in the Permian Basin, was known as the region's cultural center while Odessa was called a redneck, blue-collar town. Shortly after we arrived in August of 1966, we bought season tickets for a series of musical performances at Odessa College, one of the few cultural venues in the city. We attended a performance by the jazz musician Peter Nero. Appearing late before a packed house, he sat down at the piano and began to chat to the audience, explaining his delay. He had arrived via Trans-Texas Airways, which he characterized as "Tinkertoy Airways." After a rather long pause, no doubt waiting for laughter, he plowed ahead with, "You know I've always wanted to play Odessa." Gene and I laughed out loud; we were the only ones in the large auditorium who did.

Odessans did joke that they were in the heart of good fishing territory—four hundred miles in any direction—but they didn't joke about much. What they took seriously was high school football. The Permian Panthers' fans, depicted in the film Friday Night Lights, could get ugly on the rare occasion when the team lost a game. The Odessa Meteor Crater, just outside of town, was billed as a tourist attraction. Encounters with rattlesnakes were an additional unexpected treat. Sandstorms in West Texas could blast the paint off the front of a car and bring the visibility down to zero. We had heard that West Texans were uneducated and crude people who literally didn't have two nickels to rub together until oil was struck on their land. The women would be slopping the hogs one minute before throwing a mink coat over their jeans and muddy boots for a trip to town the next. We did not find that to be true. We became active participants in the First Presbyterian Church. The people we met at church were unpretentious, mink coats notwithstanding; they immediately invited us into their homes and hearts. Gene served as an elder; I was invited to join the Women's Board. We were soon asked to teach an adult Sunday School class.

Although we had arrived in town with no money to buy a house, our friends Bill and Sue Montgomery, who were being transferred to Tulsa, sold us their house on a handshake; they were willing to wait for payment until ours sold in Lafayette. A small, well-built brick house near a good elementary school, our new home had a nicely landscaped front yard, but the backyard was a grassless "sticker patch." The lot next door, a dismal sight out my kitchen window, was a designated oil lease, which meant that an oil rig could appear any day and begin drilling in this residential subdivision. However, for the neighborhood children it was a happy hunting ground for collecting horny toads. Most of the children's mothers had jobs, leaving the neighborhood feeling deserted during school hours. Still, we were almost in paradise because Gene had regular hours and loved his new job. Patrick thrived in first grade. The next autumn Lisa was happy in the Lutheran kindergarten. She became a TV star on the popular children's show Romper Room. Suzanne, three, was just happy.

In April 1967, my mother offered me a week's vacation to attend Camps Farthest Out, a Christian retreat at Lake Murray Lodge in Ardmore, Oklahoma. She must have recognized that I was more of a hopeful Christian than a believing one. It was there that I had the experience, described earlier, that changed my life.

Joy, the pure and simple delight in being alive, replaced the fear that had plagued me since childhood. The resentment that had grown in me over the past ten years—that the company controlled our lives and that Gene went along with it—also disappeared. Little things like taking out the garbage rather than nagging him to do it caught his attention. The pressure on Gene to be the sole source of my happiness and security lifted. Trusting that God loved our children even more than we loved them changed me into a calmer mother. I was hungry to learn more about what it meant to be a follower of Jesus when an opportunity to do just that fell into my lap. It was one of the events that I began to believe was the hand of God personally directing my life.

I was asked to brief the women who led Bible studies in their circles (groups that met monthly to study and pray together), but I realized I knew very little about the Bible. The woman I was replacing was a recognized biblical scholar. The topic for the year was the Holy Spirit, and I doubt that I was a great success as a teacher, but my passion for learning about the Holy Spirit's work in our lives carried me through.

Following my mother's wise counsel, I did not talk about my experience at the camp retreat, but Gene, observing the change in me, decided to attend in April 1968. Although we didn't realize it at the time, we had just become part of a charismatic movement that was rapidly spreading across the country. Alas, it had not reached First Presbyterian. A friend took me to the most spiritual place in Odessa, an Al-Anon meeting, a support group similar to Alcoholics Anonymous for friends and families of alcoholics. There I met people who were not interested in superficialities but were looking to God for concrete solutions to their problems and finding help.

In September 1968, Patrick entered third grade and Lisa started first. Patrick's teacher was a delightful, feisty woman who loved teaching. The children loved her back. Barely five feet tall, she told them that if any exceeded her height during the year they could be the teacher for a day. Patrick almost made it. Had we stayed for the entire year, he undoubtedly would have, so he was disappointed when Gene got the word that we were being transferred to Tulsa. The children were sad to be leaving their neighborhood friends. Gene and I realized that our frequent moves, although good for his career, could be detrimental to our children. But this was the life he had chosen as an engineer. We gave them extra attention, were patient with rages and tears, and prayed a lot.

Contrary to our children's reactions, I was thrilled to be going back to Tulsa, located in northeastern Oklahoma's Green Country. Gene's new job in Cities' domestic headquarters would have him working for the treasurer, Burl Watson. It was not a promotion but he recognized it as an opportunity to learn the financial part of the business, and felt it was a step upward in his career.

Answering a knock on the door as our moving van was being unloaded, I encountered an attractive teenager who solemnly handed me a card and disappeared. It read: "My name is Donna Randall. I am fifteen years old. I do baby-sitting. I charge one dollar an hour." Donna became our regular sitter, adored by the children. Over the years we maintained our friendship with her, following this brilliant young woman's career path in academia, and in 2007 joyfully attended her induction as president of Albion College in Michigan. Patrick and Lisa attended Carnegie Elementary by crossing a pedestrian bridge over Little Joe Creek a few steps from our house. Gene caught a public bus to the Cities Service office downtown. We were pleased to be back nearer our parents and already had many friends in Tulsa. The neighborhood was full of school-age children.

We joined Kirk of the Hills Presbyterian Church, a lively congregation nearby. Gene and I immersed ourselves in church activities and were recruited once more to lead a Bible study class for young adults. Suzanne, lonely without her siblings, begged us to enroll her in their nursery school so she could be a big girl like her brother and sister. We did.

A couple we met at church invited us to join a nondenominational Bible study/prayer group. Meeting in homes, this charismatic gathering of about sixty people was the highlight of our week. All the "gifts of the Holy Spirit" were practiced, especially speaking in tongues and prophesying. Gene and I received the gift of speaking in tongues and took part in praying aloud this way during our time in Tulsa. However, we did not find that it was a benefit to other people and eventually discontinued doing it.

A Presbyterian professor led us in Bible study. He emphasized Paul's admonition from I Corinthians 13 that love is the greatest gift. Paul urged Jesus's followers in the letter to the Galatians 5:16-22 to develop the fruits of the Holy Spirit—"love, joy, peace, patience, kindness, goodness, faithfulness, gentleness and self-control." One cannot have too much of those qualities. We made our closest friends in this group. It became a magnet for people with physical and emotional problems. As we grew in our faith, we began to learn to put it into action in the wider community. The men mentored newly paroled felons on Saturday mornings. Gene loved this ministry. Sadly, in later years fundamentalism robbed the charismatic movement of much of its power by incorporating a rigid set of dogmas that a person must believe to be considered a true Christian. However, Gene and I were always grateful for the two years we were in Tulsa where we formed lifelong friendships with this compassionate group of people.

Tulsa, settled between 1829 and 1836 by a band of Creek Indians, became known during the twentieth century as the Oil Capital of the World. Built on the wealth generated from petroleum, it was the cultural center of the state, with two world-renowned art museums as well as opera and ballet companies. Located on a bluff above the Arkansas River, the city frequently flooded. On the evening of May 9, 1970, as we entertained a group of Cities friends, rain began pouring down. What became known as the 1970 Mother's Day Flood inundated large parts of Tulsa, including our neighborhood, as Little Joe Creek breached its banks. The water came within one foot of entering our house. Our real estate agent assured us that if we didn't try to sell for a year, the memory of the flood would not impact its value. However, Gene was already secretly in discussions about transferring to the corporate office in New York City. We lost a large part of our equity in that house. We had to borrow our children's savings to help with the purchase of a new home in central New Jersey, on Shongum Mountain north of Morristown.

When we returned to Tulsa from our house-buying trip, my mother, who had been staying with the children in our absence, suggested we go out for a walk and chat. She and I were always close but in the years since my Christian awakening our relationship was sheer bliss for us both. She told me that she was experiencing an unusual feeling in her abdomen so I suggested she consult her doctor even though she had passed a routine physical six months earlier. The diagnosis was a tumor that the doctor told us was almost always benign but should be removed. In July, I joined my father and sister at the hospital for the surgery. The results were crushing; Mama was told she had only four months to live.

The children went to Lawton with me while I helped my parents during her recovery. Gene reported for work in New York. In late August we left for New Jersey in spite of Daddy's pleas to enroll the children in the local elementary school. He felt helpless to care for my mother and seemed terrified at the prospect of living without her. For the first time in twenty years he told her that he loved her. I felt I was being torn in half.

Much as I loved my parents, I had no doubt that Gene and our children were my primary responsibility. I also believed that my father needed time alone with my mother to make amends for his past behavior. Gene had received permission for us to fly on the company planes that flew daily between New York and Tulsa in case we needed to get home quickly. Once again we uprooted the family after less than two years in one place.

This was a difficult move for all of us. Gene had a two-hour commute to the office in New York: by car to the Morris Plains, New Jersey, train station; from there on the Erie-Lackawanna Railway to Hoboken; under the Hudson River on the Port Authority of New York and New Jersey train; and ending with a six-block walk. He was exhausted each day by the time he reversed this journey to arrive home around 7:00 o'clock. Patrick was teased at school for his Oklahoma accent and not challenged in his studies. Lisa missed her friends in Tulsa; she cried at bedtime for six weeks. We joined the Presbyterian Church on the Green in Morristown, New Jersey. The minister was a dramatic thespian but not a pastor. We met only one couple who became friends. Gene and I taught fifth- and sixth-grade Sunday School but were not involved otherwise. Agonized by the separation from my dying mother, I longed for spiritual fellowship.

"June Gulbrandsen is our only subscriber in your zip code," the woman at *New Wine* magazine told me. A publication aimed at the charismatic community, I was hoping to find through it a prayer group similar to the one we had left in Tulsa. Although Gene was sure that this person would be "a little old Pentecostal woman," I called her number. June was friendly and unfazed by a stranger's voice. She and her husband, Bill, in their thirties, had three young children. She invited me to join her women's Bible study. Thus we became a part of the Christian Norwegian American community in New Jersey. These evangelical women knew how to pray and their love and support were essential to me and my family. Although not charismatic in practicing the gifts of the Spirit, they were deeply committed Christians who graciously befriended us.

In November, my mother was in the hospital when we arrived in Lawton for the Thanksgiving holiday. We were told she had a slight infection. She was weak but not in pain. My sister, Beverly, and I took her for a walk in the hospital corridor. However, the following Monday evening, after we had returned to New Jersey, Beverly called me with the news that Mama was not expected to live through the night. Our next-door neighbor agreed to care for the children so Gene could follow me to Oklahoma. I caught a Cities plane the next morning. During the flight, I planned her funeral service according to her wishes. She died on December 1, 1970, an hour before I arrived in Tulsa—four months after her surgery, just as the doctor had predicted. She was seventy years old.

The First Methodist Church was filled to capacity for her funeral. The pastor read her favorite scripture, the entire eighth chapter of Romans, and we sang uplifting hymns. It truly was a celebration of her life. She was buried in Highland Cemetery not far from her parents, David Crockett Hamilton and Mary Sue Agee Hamilton.

Gene returned home while I spent a few more days with Daddy. Early the next morning, we met in the kitchen. Getting out Mama's favorite skillet, the eggs and butter, I handed him the eggs to crack. By the time I left a few days later he was successfully making breakfast. I urged him to eat out at least one meal daily. Minnie, the elderly housekeeper, cleaned and did the laundry. Beverly frequently checked in on him. Nonetheless, when I returned the next summer I discovered that the fresh produce I had left in the refrigerator was still there, covered in green mold. I asked around and found that a group of his old friends ate together every evening at a local cafeteria. I insisted that he join them, which he did, enjoying the lively political discussions as much as the food.

Back east, we were adapting to our environment. We had bought a house in a new development where several Cities families had settled, near the village of Mount Freedom. Our friends the Mytingers lived about twenty miles away. The children made friends in the neighborhood and enjoyed exploring the surrounding woods, and sledding and ice skating during the snowy winters. Patrick had begun piano lessons in Tulsa. A neighbor who played in a jazz band continued Patrick's interest in piano by teaching him jazz as well as classical pieces. He joined a Boy Scout troop that camped in the snow. Lisa began violin lessons, using my father's old violin. The children walked to and from school with other neighborhood kids. Suzanne, six, walked home on her own because first grade recessed earlier than her siblings' classes. I watched eagerly, and a bit anxiously, for her to appear each day as she made her way through the wooded backyard toward our house. It seemed to take her a long time so I finally asked why she walked so slowly. Her reply surprised and thrilled me. She said, "Oh, I'm talking to my friends the birds." She loved our new home.

In 1971 Gene represented Cities Service on a U.S. trade delegation trip to Romania. He sadly observed how the Romanians were suffering under the harsh rule of Nicolae Ceausescu. Still, he was heartened to learn from the delegation's Romanian secret service escort that his mother was a devout Christian who attended an underground church in spite of the communist government's edict against such meetings. Obviously, the man did not report his mother to the authorities.

Gene returned to Romania several times and traveled to other countries with Cities Bill Allen, whose job was to negotiate oil contracts for the company. Gene also was responsible for reporting to Cities corporate management on their two large copper-mining operations in Arizona and Tennessee.

He was sometimes invited to eat in the executive dining room with the chairman, Charlie Mitchell, and frequently ate lunch with his immediate boss, Bob Sampson. He was getting to know the top Cities executives, and of course, more important from our point of view, they were getting to know him.

In the spring of 1972, Gene was approached by Jim Wood, a British-born Cities vice-president, who offered him an assignment in the exploration office in London. He promised to promote Gene to manager there in two years. Gene asked me if I was willing to go overseas again. I agreed as long as the company would move all our possessions with us, believing we would feel more at home surrounded by familiar objects.

My friend June accused me of having ice water in my veins because I wasn't in tears at the thought of moving again. I reminded her that had we not moved to New Jersey in the first place, I wouldn't have met her. Her retired parents stayed with our children while we flew to London to house hunt. With the help of an estate agent, we found a large Victorian-era flat in the borough of Kensington, an easy commute for Gene to his office in Knightsbridge. Located on the top floor of the corner building of a huge block of flats, it was light and cheerful. Each of the five bedrooms and three reception rooms had a coal-burning fireplace. The flats had been modernized many years earlier with central heating, but we discovered that it was much less effective than coal fires. The kitchen fireplace was now occupied by a "cooker" (range). There were also two full bathrooms and a "scullery" (butler's pantry).

Gene and the American who owned the flat shook hands agreeing not to "gazump" each other. This practice gave buyer or seller the option of backing out of the deal without penalty until the day the contract was finalized, which usually took several months. We agreed to pay the "key money" he wanted for the flat, ten thousand pounds, which granted permission to take over the lease and attached furnishings. Without the key money payment, the flat could have been stripped to the bare walls, and essentials like light fixtures, bathtubs and toilets removed.

Back home we began the moving process, which included selling the car and anything that would not fit in the flat. Lisa's fourth-grade teacher requested a meeting. Arriving that afternoon after school,

I entered confidently, knowing that Lisa was a sweet, bright and conscientious student. I was totally unprepared for his opening statement. "Mrs. Grogan, do you realize that you are destroying your child by these constant moves? You and your husband must stop dragging her from place to place!" He went so far as to say that Gene should change his profession. Shocked almost speechless, I tried to assure him that we loved our child and that what he was suggesting was not going to happen. Still, I was disturbed, although I never learned what Lisa had said to him or had done to prompt his dire prediction. I have often wished he could see the self-assured, happy person that she became.

All the same, I was concerned about how the children would adjust to apartment living in a big city and what effect these frequent moves would have on them and their education. Gene's grandmother, Jennie Southwick, had died in March at the age of ninety-six, leaving his mother, Thelma, retired and free, so we invited her to move to London with us. Thus began a happy arrangement where we had Grandmother Thelma in residence for several months of every year for the rest of her life. Having her with us was tremendously important to all of us but it especially gave the children a comforting feeling of stability. So once again, we left the United States, this time without a clue that we would live outside our native land for the next twenty-one years.

Five

LONDON TOWN,
HERE WE COME

London
September 1972 / December 1973

OUR PRIMARY GOAL for the family was to feel at home in our new country. London in 1972 was not a happy place. The euphoria of the 1960s was gone, and once again people saw little cause to be optimistic about the future. Evidence of privation was indisputable twenty-seven years after the end of World War II. Appliances such as electric refrigerators and washing machines did not exist in the average household. Renting a television necessitated paying the high license fee to turn it on, a luxury with only three channels. However, the British were avid fans of comedies such as *The Morecambe & Wise Show, Some Mothers Do 'Ave 'Em, Rising Damp, Fawlty Towers* and the venerable soap *Coronation Street,* which delved into the social and financial woes of the average Briton. Though the shows' dark humor helped make light of the situation for a few hours, low wages made people restive, especially union members who threatened to strike. The exchange rate was a drag on the economy at a staggering $2.75 to the English pound. High demand caused stress on the National Health Service, which offered free care to citizen and foreigner alike. Race and immigration issues were in the forefront as immigrants from former British colonies moved to Britain. Epithets like "dirty Pak" were commonly heard on buses and in shops, often uttered by genteel-appearing English women. Many resented American expats, who, with their foreign salaries and American company benefits, could live better than the locals. The WWII expression about Americans—"overpaid, oversexed and over here"—was resurrected. We were disappointed to discover that Conservative Prime Minister Edward Heath was completely out of touch with the plight of his people, concentrating instead on his two passions, sailing and music.

A dockworkers' strike held all our goods in port for weeks after our arrival. Gene had rented cots and purchased the essentials—linens, pots, pans and dishes. The former owner had sold us a kitchen table and six chairs. To our amazement and delight, the children, in spite of the Spartan conditions, thought flat living was marvelous. For the first time, they each had a bedroom. They loved the decrepit old lift (elevator) and the cheery, chain-smoking Irish doorman, and didn't complain about the weather although the sun didn't shine for almost two months. To them it was a great adventure. Suzanne did lament a couple of times that she "missed my woods" in New Jersey. Fortunately, we were living in Kensington on the west edge of Holland Park with an adventure playground, tennis courts, and plenty of wide-open spaces. During the month of August, the London Symphony Orchestra performed on a stage set in the shell of a manor house in Holland Park that had been bombed during the war. We attended a performance of the 1812 Overture dressed for winter, in heavy coats, hats and gloves, and with flasks of hot chocolate. When the cannons fired, the peacocks roosting in the trees took off, loudly protesting, which added drama to the performance. Everyone applauded for them and the musicians. Gene brought home a small book entitled *Hang Your Hat in London*. Written for Americans, it was an invaluable guide with chapters on weights and measures, manners and customs, and, my favorite, "Adapt or Die." That became our family motto.

Without refrigeration, most Britons shopped for food daily. We discovered that the Safeway supermarket on Kensington High Street was American in name only. The contents were all British, packaged in serving sizes for two people. In a street near our flat we found a greengrocer, a butcher, a news agent and an antiques dealer. The grocers were a cheeky pair who did not allow self-service, called me *luv*, and would sneak up behind me to grab a quick hug, something I was sure they didn't try with English matrons. With my basket on my arm, I persevered because their produce was excellent and their location convenient. Milk was delivered to the flat in small bottles. Grandmother and I traveled to Harrods for cheese and to other shops for poultry, bread and the like. The shop Panzer's specialized in expensive imported American and European food, and we occasionally indulged in uniquely American items like peanut butter and Fritos chips.

The children were enrolled at the highly rated American School in London. ASL was more demanding academically than the public schools they had attended. Patrick and Lisa were challenged and went to work. Suzanne had a more ambivalent attitude toward studying. Her third-grade teacher yelled at the children, scaring her—not a good start for a sensitive child. She did love music and theater. All three played instruments; Patrick played piano in the jazz band, Lisa played violin in a string group and Suzanne played clarinet. The girls joined the ASL Girl Scout troop and I became an assistant leader. On weekends, we prowled central London, visiting famous attractions like the Tower of London, the British Museum and the Tate Gallery. We never lacked for something interesting to see or do. The first year the girls rode a school bus for first- to sixth-graders, but Patrick, in seventh grade, had to find his way on public transport. The second year, the girls, nine- and eleven-years-old, begged us to let them ride the public buses as well. I was forced to let go and trust God for their safety, not easy sometimes when Patrick was robbed on the way home by British hooligans and Suzanne came home alone once when she was only nine.

Striving to feel at home, we determined to make English friends. Before we arrived, Gene had started attending St. Barnabas Anglican Church, located next door to our flat. Our children's presence created quite a stir our first Sunday, with people commenting afterward on their good behavior as if they were toddlers. With the exception of an American woman, Beverly Major, who was married to an English banker, we were the only Americans. The Majors had three children close in age to ours who also attended ASL. Most of the congregation's youngsters were away in boarding schools. The vicar, his wife, and members of the congregation were friendly, but for the first six months no one invited us to come around after church for sherry. When an unmarried curate arrived, the vicar announced that he needed accommodation for a brief period until his flat was ready for occupancy, and was astounded when we offered to take him. During the fortnight that Alex Murdoch lived with us, he became a member of our family. He was a tremendous sports fan with a boisterous laugh and a photographic memory. The children adored him and were happy when he started a Bible study class at church just for them. They were soon joined by the Major children.

Slowly but surely we were accepted by the congregation. Grandmother and I were invited to join a team of women chaired by the vicar's wife to plan a potluck supper. Each woman was asked to bring a certain dish—"Mrs. Brown, will you please bring your sausage rolls?" When they asked me, I suggested a cold dish of marinated green vegetables that instantly became known as "Grogan's Greens." I had to bring that for every dinner for the next six years. We were catering for one hundred people so at the end of the session the vicar's wife asked if someone would please bring one hundred cubes of ice. Suppressing laughter, Thelma and I volunteered. Wine and cider were served. The British consider water necessary for washing but certainly not for drinking. Shocked by the serving of wine at a church function, and because alcohol had never crossed her lips, Grandmother took the cider, not realizing it was hard cider. We had a good laugh at her expense but she surprised us by starting to accept sherry when it was offered. We were all changing and enjoying the experience.

Gene and I were longing for more spiritual depth and involvement with other Christians outside of the brief hour on Sunday mornings. The vicar's modus operandi was to preach a short sermon based on the headline in the Sunday Times that caught his attention over breakfast. We asked him if he would approve of our inviting our fellow parishioners to a Bible study/prayer meeting in our flat. He wasn't interested in promoting small groups but did not object. We soon had a lively group of American friends and a few British St. Barnabas members. Although we came from different cultures and Christian backgrounds, as we shared our joys and difficulties we developed close friendships. Lively discussions sometimes became heated but we grew to love and respect one another. Alex joined our group and always pulled a scripture from his photographic memory that led us closer to Jesus's example for living.

Fourteen families occupied our building, two on each of the seven floors. Directly across from us lived Stanley and Danie Meadows and their two young children. Stanley, an English actor, appeared on the London stage as well as in films. Having inherited a large commercial building near Heathrow Airport, he had the financial security to be choosy about his roles. Danie, a pretty, vivacious French woman, tutored our three in French and our kids occasionally babysat for the Meadows children. We socialized together frequently.

Ralph and Doreen Martin, in their late seventies, lived two floors below us and were members of St. Barnabas Church. Ralph, called Tubby, was a retired naval commander who had ships that were torpedoed during World War I and World War II. He was rescued from the sea both times. He was a charming raconteur and harmless flirt who adored Doreen. A member of the Irish aristocracy, she had been presented to Queen Mary at Court. Her personal maid, who was the same age as Doreen, had lived with her since they were children. Entering their flat took one back a century, with its heavy velvet curtains, old master paintings on the walls and a George III silver tankard gleaming in the candlelight. Tubby carved the "joint" (roast) on the sideboard and the maid served. They lived daily with the sorrow of the sudden death of their only child, Peter, from polio while he was a student at Eton in the 1940s. They had turned a family castle in Ireland into a children's hospital named for him. Doreen graciously taught me the finer points of good manners without making me feel that she was being condescending. They loved our children and the children loved them.

Celebrity sightings were frequent in our neighborhood. Historian Arnold Toynbee lived down the street. Actor Richard Harris owned a lovely old Victorian house about a block away and threw parties that sometimes ended late the following morning. One day coming back from the High Street, Peter Ustinov and Peter O'Toole had to step aside so we could pass, while Richard Harris in his stocking feet saw them into their limousine. The children took more notice when David Bowie bought Harris's house. We often saw famous people in shops, happily undisturbed by the other shoppers. There were celebrity children at ASL. Julie Andrews and her husband, Blake Edwards, both had daughters in our scout troop, as did Martin Landau and Barbara Bain. Lauren Bacall's son Sam Robards was in band with Suzanne. Rod Steiger and Claire Bloom's daughter and Fred Astaire's grandson were students there as well.

Oil companies and other concerns, such as the bankers, threw large cocktail parties that included people from many countries. Each month we received a stack of invitations, which we sorted into three piles: must go, want to go and no. We often found ourselves going out several nights a week. Long dresses were all the fashion in London in the seventies and I soon had a nice selection. We frequently entertained at home. Our children learned to be hospitable and meet adults with ease. I loved to cook but drew the line at feeding the constant stream of business visitors. Gene and I compromised by inviting them to the flat for drinks followed by dinner out. We worried that we left the children alone too much but it was easier when Grandmother was in residence. On weekends, Suzanne, eight, relished sleepovers in Grandmother's room next door to hers.

Eager to seize the opportunity to visit other countries, we made the most of every school holiday to take the family abroad. ASL also took the children overseas for music and academic competitions with other international schools and on ski and history trips. Our first trip taught us a valuable lesson. Instead of consulting a tour company or anyone else, we decided to spend Christmas in Paris. Booked into the Hilton Hotel, we traveled to France by train and ferry on December 23. The next day we toured the beautiful city on a bitterly cold day. Back at the hotel, the children's favorite entertainment became watching an old John Wayne film with a French soundtrack. They laughed themselves silly listening to Wayne speaking in high-pitched French. However, on Christmas morning, no surprise, everything was closed. The Hilton's main dining room had a Wild West décor with wagon-wheel chandeliers and waiters dressed in cowboy boots and jeans, a disappointing setting for us Okies. We used a travel agent for the next holiday.

Tragedy struck on Gene's birthday, March 13, 1973. He was in Houston on business when he received a call from his sister, Betty Hurst, in Albuquerque, New Mexico, with the horrifying news that Janet, twenty-two, the only child of Betty and her husband, Bill, had taken her own life. Following a brief, disastrous marriage Janet had attempted suicide once before but Betty had asked us not to share the attempt with her mother or other family members, so Gene and I were the only ones not totally shocked. Breaking such news to our children was devastating. The girls were too young to fully understand the tragedy but Patrick, thirteen, comprehended the horror. At bedtime, he knocked on my bedroom door and entered in tears. He cried, "How could she do that to herself?" I assured him that God loved her more than we did and she was safe in heaven but that we could not know how bleak her life felt to her. It was a desperate act by one who felt so alone. We sat and hugged each other for a long time.

But, like everyone who is close to someone who commits suicide, I asked myself what I could have said or done to have averted this tragedy. Gene flew immediately from Houston to Albuquerque for the difficult days leading up to and including the funeral. Fortunately, Grandmother had returned to Oklahoma shortly after Christmas and was able to stay with Betty and Bill for several weeks after the funeral.

A period known as the Troubles resumed in earnest in Londonderry, Northern Ireland, on Sunday, January 30, 1972, when thirteen unarmed protestors were shot dead by British soldiers, several in the back. The Provisional Irish Republican Army had begun a campaign challenging the partition of Ireland two years earlier, which culminated in this massacre. "Remember Bloody Sunday" became the rallying cry of the IRA thereafter. Eventually, direct rule from Westminster replaced control by the Protestant

Ulster Unionists inflaming both sides in the conflict. Most of the violence occurred in Ulster but London received its share; in March 1973 two bombs exploded at the Old Bailey (courts) and the Ministry of Agriculture in the City of London, the most ancient part of the city, where most of the government was located.

The IRA bombings continued during our six years in London. During 1974 alone, they bombed Madame Tussauds wax museum, Earls Court Exhibition Centre (not far from our flat), the Houses of Parliament, the Tower of London, Selfridge's and Harrods department stores, the Hilton Hotel and other places. Gene, dining in a hotel adjacent to the Hilton, heard the explosion and saw the smoke. Although there were few deaths, because the IRA usually gave a five-minute warning, there were many injuries including dismemberments, and damage in the millions of pounds. The only outward sign of security measures was the removal of all the sidewalk trash bins because the IRA had put bombs in them. Following the lead of our stoic British friends, we carried on as though nothing was happening. Their answer as to why they displayed no fear was, "Oh, my dear, we lived through the Blitz."

The government of Edward Heath was floundering. The Israeli Yom Kippur War in October 1973 sent oil prices skyrocketing when the Arab states initiated an oil embargo. The National Union of Mineworkers voted for a large wage increase in November. When they didn't get it, they walked out on strike, which led to the three-day work week to conserve power because most electric plants were run on coal. It was amazing to see shop clerks serving customers by the light of kerosene lanterns, outfitted in coats, caps and gloves.

We purchased a butane lantern for the kitchen table that provided 150 watts of light for the children to do their homework. Our lift only worked for short periods each day so, as we lived on the seventh floor, we planned our grocery shopping trips carefully. The combination of IRA bombings, strikes and resulting public unrest led to a hung parliament whereby no single political party had enough seats to rule. This forced the Conservative Party to call for an election in February 1974.

Escaping dark, cold England after Christmas, we left on a package tour to Morocco. Patrick's best friend, Mike Moraskie, joined us for this excursion. We were surprised to discover that this was the first time the tour company had included children. Ours were the only ones. Billed as a tour of the Royal Cities of Morocco, the stops included Rabat, Casablanca, Marrakesh, Fez and the Roman ruin at Volubilis. Our bus guide was a lively raconteur who kept us royally entertained.

But it was also an eye-opening experience for us and our children. For the first time we were approached by child beggars their age. In Marrakesh, while on an evening carriage ride, our horse stepped on a woman who dashed in front of our vehicle trying to keep up with her husband. As she lay injured, a hostile crowd surrounded us. Fortunately, a policeman materialized from the crowd and transferred us to an empty carriage whose driver took us galloping back to our hotel. We were all shaken by the experience.

A happier memory was our visit to the Roman ruin of Volubilis. A woman on our tour, a Latin teacher from Cornwall, had signed up just to visit this site. When we arrived she said to the children,

"Come with me and I will show you Volubilis." Gene and I tagged along. Her extensive knowledge and humorous descriptions of this ancient Roman city, its buildings and how its people had lived made the city come alive for us.

Another memorable day, we visited the religious city of Fez on Eid al-Adha, the Festival of the Sacrifice, a Muslim holiday that honors the willingness of Abraham to sacrifice his son as a submission to God's command. God intervened through His angel Gabriel to tell Abraham that his sacrifice of a ram was accepted. Each family who could afford to slaughtered a sheep and ate one-third, shared one-third with relatives or friends, and gave one-third to the poor. As we walked into the city center for lunch, people were washing sheep intestines in canals by the side of the path. Some of our group lost their appetites on the way in, but at a traditional Moroccan restaurant, seated on cushions around a low table with our freshly washed right hands, we ate with relish from a huge platter of couscous and lamb stew.

On the bus back to the airport, Gene and I were surprised and proud when our guide spoke movingly about the joy that the children had added to the tour and the entire busload cheered and applauded his comments.

Six

DEEP ROOTS

London
January 1974 / June 1978

OUR FAMILY was well settled in London at the start of 1974. With Grandmother again in residence, I flew home to Oklahoma to see my dad. My conscience and vague concern for his health caused me to depart London in the dead of winter. Summer visits with the children were chaotic, with no opportunity to give him the undivided attention that I believed he would welcome. He had often said he was lonely since Mama's death in 1970. I spent two weeks cooking his favorite food, buying him clothes and listening to his stories. One scene from that visit remains vivid. We were holding hands, sitting in the formal living room on an uncomfortable sofa. I have no idea how we came to be there. Rarely had my father touched me once I learned to read at age five and he no longer felt the necessity to read me the Sunday funny papers. He began to speak of his relationship with my mother, painting a picture of a happy marriage. He must have known I knew that wasn't true as he tried to construct a family history that made him feel better. Although his perpetual black moods and unpredictable temper had clouded my childhood, I just let him talk. A year later when he died of a heart attack, I was comforted to know that I had not contradicted him. It took me years before I was able to recognize Daddy as a flawed human being, as we all are, and forgive him.

On Sunday, March 3, Turkish Airlines Flight 981, bound for London, crashed shortly after takeoff from Paris's Orly Airport because of an improperly closed rear cargo door; all 346 passengers and crew were killed. Fearing that a Cities family was aboard, Dick Bradley, the London manager, asked if we would go to Heathrow Airport to find out. The names of Loren Hart, Cities' chief geologist in the London office, his wife, Joan, and their three children were on the manifest. With heavy hearts we returned home. A total of thirteen children and parents connected to the American School in London were on that flight. The next few weeks were filled with grief and mourning as we attended memorial services—including a mass funeral in Paris—cleaned out the Harts' apartment, hosted traumatized family members and comforted our own family. The following summer we traveled to Kansas to meet family members who had been unable to come to London. When we spent the night with Loren's parents, Mrs. Hart brought out picture albums; we listened to stories, cried and laughed together, hoping that our presence let them know how much we cared.

March brought the election of Labour leader Harold Wilson as prime minister. He was fifty-eight years old, a pipe-smoking alcoholic whose past record did not bode well for the country. Labor unions, sensing weakness, started striking. The miners were joined by sugar growers, bakers and dustmen, causing shortages of sugar, flour, yeast and salt, with garbage piling up in the streets. No bread in the shops or ingredients to make it. At some of the shops, good customers were offered small amounts of staples from under the counter at checkout. Earlier in the year, there was an acute shortage of toilet paper. The cause was never explained. Visitors to the U.K. or husbands traveling to Europe on business were asked to please bring in flight bags filled with squashed toilet paper rolls. Custom agents waved them through with understanding smiles. "The Great Run on Sugar" strike that began in May ended by autumn. Each Briton consumed an estimated 110 pounds of sugar per annum, mostly in tea. It was unthinkable that regional elections coming up in October could be held with the British drinking unsweetened tea. The Wilson government continued to struggle with inflation above 20 percent. Wilson's proposed amendment to restore a payment to pensioners failed but he did secure a 35 percent pay raise for the miners. However, due to the economic crisis, Wilson resigned after only two years in office. His legacy was an indecisive foreign policy, gross mismanagement of the economy and a Resignation Honors list full of scoundrels.

For spring break, we took the children and Grandmother to Italy. In Assisi on Palm Sunday we were awakened by pealing village church bells. From the balcony of our room, we watched the people parade along the street below us carrying olive branches. At the Monastery of St. Francis Assisi, we saw the marble floors of the monks' cells hollowed from centuries of bodies sleeping on them, and the monks at work in the surrounding fields. There we experienced an almost tangible sense of peace. Francis's life of simplicity and love for all of God's creation inspired us as it had millions over the years. Grandmother wrote a poem about our visit.

In April, we had an addition to the family, a gift from our friends Jack and Diane Van Dien in the form of one small Siamese kitten; we named her Zuli (for her lapis lazuli blue eyes). She was beloved in spite of some nasty habits such as consuming anything wool, escaping the flat at every opportunity, and nosily racing down the halls at midnight.

Patrick, a typical 1970s teenager with shoulder-length hair, frayed bell-bottom jeans and a passion for rock music (as well as classical and modern jazz), excelled academically and received standing ovations at school concerts as a fine jazz pianist. However, a pragmatist, he was not considering a career in music. With an interest in becoming a veterinarian, he volunteered on Saturdays for our vet, Mr. Butt. Instead of assigning him to clean cages, Mr. Butt took Patrick as his assistant and taught him the business. The experience solidified Patrick's desire to pursue that profession.

Lisa had a close-knit group of friends, worked hard at her studies and practiced her violin that she named Alfie. She was a quiet, confident girl and a voracious reader, and still played dolls with her sister. Suzanne had a nice group of friends, enjoyed playing piano and clarinet and reading Enid Blyton novels. She was thrilled to be in the school musicals, *Catastrophe* and *Madame Butterfly,* and made her film debut with a fleeting appearance in the first *Death Wish*. Of course, she couldn't see the R-rated finished product, but the father of Patrick's friend Mike Moraskie, a film distributor, clipped a frame from the film to make a photo for her.

We frequently had houseguests, so many in fact that we called our flat the Grogan Hotel. Although the children had to shift rooms, they welcomed the visitors and were uncomplaining about the disruption. However, when we started getting requests from friends of friends, we produced a list of reasonably priced hotels to suggest to them.

The charismatic movement that we had experienced in the sixties in America swept through Britain in the seventies. We sometimes attended Holy Trinity Anglican Church on Brompton Road, where charismatics packed the church in sharp contrast to the sparse congregation at St. Barnabas. We joined an organization called Post Green where we made friends with British charismatics, particularly June Evans, who became close. Patrick and Lisa occasionally rode their bikes to a Christian coffeehouse. Gene was the only American in a men's Bible study group that met for lunch at Boodle's, the venerable men's club in the City.

However, our exposure to the faith of Muslim and Hindu friends convinced us that God's love and guidance were available to all. We joined a British nonprofit organization whose members hosted teas in their homes on Sunday afternoons for foreign students attending universities in London. We met fascinating young people from all over the world, the best and brightest representatives of their countries. As they shared their family backgrounds and cultures, we and our children grew in knowledge, respect and tolerance for the rich diversity we encountered. Our commonality greatly overshadowed our differences. We all strove to love each other, live in peace and grow in faith, whatever that faith might be.

In May 1974, Gene became general manager of the Cities London office when Dick Bradley and his vivacious wife, Ruth, were transferred to Burma. With the nice increase in salary, we were able to pay back the money with interest we had borrowed from the children to buy the house in New Jersey. Gene's work load increased greatly and he hired young geologists and geophysicists from Imperial College as well as experienced Europeans like Swiss national Roland Schwab, who with his wife, Greta, and their daughters, joined the Cities family. Several American families transferred to London, and we were especially pleased to be joined by Frank and Louise Mytinger, whose children had been friends with ours since they were small.

On January 8, 1975, my paternal grandmother, Ida Mae Houtzer Rice—Mama Rice, as we called her—died at the age of ninety-eight. As editor of a weekly newspaper that published legal notices, she was respected by people in our town, but she caused a lot of unhappiness in our family due to her enmity toward her daughters-in-law and her demands on her sons. My father complained constantly about her but also revered her. Mama Rice was blind, bedridden and uncommunicative the last two years of her life. But surprisingly, before she died she had responded affirmatively when my two of my mother's prayer group friends called on her and told her that Jesus loved her. I had received a letter from one telling me that she believed Mama Rice was a Christian. Knowing how much he loved his mother, I sent the letter to my dad.

On March 15, my sister, Beverly, called with the news that Daddy had died suddenly at home of a heart attack. She found him sitting in a chair by the phone. He possibly could have called for help but he was afraid of being an invalid, so we believe he chose to die at home. Perhaps he also felt that he had no reason to live any longer now that his mother had died.

A Baptist layman, lawyer and family friend performed the service for my father as he had done for Mama Rice. We met beforehand, and he related a recent meeting with my dad. "One day in January, I arrived early at the office and found your father waiting for me. As I was not his attorney, I wondered why he was there. He asked, 'What do you think it takes for a person to be a Christian?' Picking up my Bible, I read him a relevant passage of scripture. At the end, I asked him if he believed in God and if he prayed. He said he did, so I firmly believe that your father died a Christian." Perhaps the letter that I forwarded to him had moved him.

Cities Service was a partner in the development of the oil fields under the North Sea and on November 3 the first North Sea oil flowed through British Petroleum's pipeline amid great fanfare when Queen Elizabeth II pushed a gold-plated button at BP's control center in Aberdeen. Gene, who went to Aberdeen several times a year for partners meetings, described the city, built of grey granite dug from a quarry in its center, as dark and dismal. Little did we know that in the future we would be calling Aberdeen home.

In less than one hundred years, Great Britain had gone from ruling "the empire on which the sun never set" to being "the sick man of Europe." With inflation still running at 16 percent, the International Monetary Fund was treating Britain like a third world country. Half of all Britons had a 1940s standard of living, lacking telephones and central heating.

For the fourth March in a row, trouble visited the Grogan household. After several episodes of tummy ache, I was diagnosed with appendicitis and entered the London Clinic for surgery. While I was in the hospital, we had a burglary at the flat. The fearless thief had entered by climbing down a drainpipe and crawling through a window. Had he lost his grip, he would have plunged seven stories to his death. Fortunately for us, some friends had arrived from the States and were sleeping off their jet lag. Hearing a noise, they started talking, which alerted the thief who fled with very little loot.

With famous patients like actor Elizabeth Taylor and numerous Saudi princes, the London Clinic was the premier hospital in the city. The food and care were excellent, but unfortunately the cleanliness was not. Discharged from the hospital after a week, I developed a high fever at home and our primary doctor, who visited me daily to drain the wound, insisted I remain bedfast. After many days without noticeable improvement, fearing that something serious had been discovered during the surgery, I confronted Gene, who assured me that was not true. Finally fever-free after three weeks in bed, it was glorious to see the trees in full leaf and flower boxes full of blooming plants. In June, to celebrate my recovery, Gene took me to the Continent for a few days. We spent the night in Luxembourg and then drove up the Mosel River Valley, stopping along the way to sip wine in riverside cafés. Spectacular fields of red poppies stretched as far as the eye could see. At one particularly beautiful spot, Gene pulled off the road, led me into a field of blooms and took my picture. Red poppies always lift my spirits since that glorious trip.

When Patrick was thirteen, he went with a group of mostly British students on safari to Africa. Sponsored by the World Wildlife Fund, they were accompanied by a film crew from Blue

Peter, a popular BBC television program for ages eight to twelve. When we met Patrick at Victoria Station upon their return, he strode toward us with his duffel bag in one hand and a long Maasai spear in the other. His first words were "Mom and Dad, we gotta go there as a family!"

After Christmas 1976, we joined a group of seven other people to spend ten days in Kenya and Tanzania. Leaving congested Nairobi we stopped at Lake Nakuru, where we ate lunch and photographed the bright pink ring of thousands of flamingos encircling the lake. Late in the afternoon, we arrived at Treetops, the famous and unique hotel where Princess Elizabeth had learned of the death of her father, King George VI, in 1952. A substantial tree house with fifty rooms for guests, located over a large waterhole, it attracted wildlife in abundance, especially during the dry season when we were there. Our next destination was the Maasai Mara, the Kenya section of the Serengeti Plain situated in the Great Rift Valley, a dramatic geological fault thirty-seven hundred miles long from Syria to Mozambique. The fertile valley was bordered on both sides by high escarpments where the lodges had been built to provide cool, comfortable retreats. Twice-daily excursions to view the wildlife on the hot valley floor, early morning and late afternoon, were broken by sumptuous lunches followed by a swim or nap. At the Lobo Wildlife Lodge in Tanzania we attended a New Year's Eve party that featured a disc jockey with a 45-rpm record player and a short stack of records. What he lacked in equipment he made up for in enthusiasm, wildly dancing by himself to each tune. We felt that his record of "Oklahoma Hills" was just for us.

The Ngorongoro Crater, a huge volcanic caldera two thousand feet deep and covering one hundred square miles, formed an ecosystem all its own with a population of twenty-five thousand animals, including the big five: rhino, lion, leopard, elephant and buffalo. They roamed through forests, swamps and plains and drank at freshwater springs. Our van driver expertly navigated the steep, twisting road to the valley floor that had been turned into a slippery quagmire by rain the previous night. At Lake Manyara Hotel we had a splendid view of Mount Kilimanjaro, snow-capped even at summer's peak. Patrick was right; it was an unforgettable holiday.

By 1977, although the Labour government had passed a plethora of acts to placate various constituencies, Prime Minister James Callaghan's government was increasingly unpopular. He stuck to his economic policy of "pay restraint" in spite of the fact that prices had increased by nearly 70 percent in three years. Strikes continued and spread, to include the firefighters union that struck for the first time in its history. The undertakers union struck leaving eight hundred unembalmed bodies unburied. The IRA bombings and a serial rapist nicknamed the Yorkshire Ripper, who had killed thirteen women by the time he was caught in 1981, added to the unrest.

The one bright spot on the horizon was Queen Elizabeth II's Silver Jubilee, the twenty-fifth anniversary of her ascension to the throne. Her extensive tour of the Commonwealth countries was covered in the media in exquisite detail. Because an assassination attempt by the IRA was a distinct possibility, she visited Scotland, Wales and Northern Ireland under heavy protection. Grandmother was thrilled to be with us, crammed as we were cheek by jowl along the parade route, part of the exuberant throng cheering as the Queen and Prince Philip passed by in a Gold State Coach followed by coaches and cars filled with the entire royal clan. No one did pomp and circumstance like the British.

Gene, with Irish partners, had organized an exploration company for Cities Service to search for oil in Ireland and I joined him on one of his frequent trips to Dublin. There I met John and Deirdre Pittock and Dusty Miller and his wife. They lived up to the national reputation for being gregarious and hospitable. Dusty's wife was an ardent Nationalist who plied us with tales of the atrocities the English had committed against the Irish through the centuries. Gene felt it was a good time to explore his roots. At the heritage arts shop he learned that the name Grogan was mentioned for the first time in the thirteenth century when a certain Mr. O'Gruagain was fined so many pence and told to "Keep peace with your neighbors hereafter." He decided that was sufficient research for the time being.

Patrick, sixteen, and his friend Bruce Bohr proposed a bike trip to Belgium over spring break. Taking the ferry across the English Channel, they spent a snowy week touring the country, staying in hostels. I had to marvel at the change God had wrought in my life over the past ten years. Not that I wasn't anxious about Patrick and Bruce's adventure but I surprised myself by agreeing to their trip. Gene thought it was a great idea.

Gene, Grandmother, Lisa, Suzanne and I drove to Devon and Cornwall to spend an equally frigid week staying in an unheated bed-and-breakfast near Plymouth. In spite of the cold, we had a marvelous time. The girls rode the farmer's tractor and got to hold newborn lambs. We visited the picturesque villages of Mousehole and St. Ives that clung precariously to the cliffs over the sea. We saw Roman ruins at Bath and drove the moors of Bodmin and Dartmoor, passing at a distance the notorious Dartmoor Prison that opened in 1809 and still housed Britain's most dangerous prisoners.

Grandmother and I took off for the Netherlands in May for a girls' weekend to visit the breathtaking Keukenhof Gardens of Lisse, southwest of Amsterdam. Established in 1949 on the grounds of the fifteenth-century Countess of Hainaut's castle, bulb growers of Holland displayed their spectacular planting of seven million flowers for a short seven weeks each spring.

The next winter Patrick took two ski trips, one with Mike Moraskie to Spain and another with a friend to Switzerland. Lisa proposed a trip with some of her friends to Ireland. When I balked, she reminded me that Patrick had been allowed to go on trips without adults. The children were growing up. I secretly asked the Pittocks to check on the girls, which they happily did, taking them on picnics and sightseeing. Fortunately, Lisa and her friends reveled in the attention and did not resent my intrusion.

Over the years we had established a tradition of celebrating Thanksgiving together with our American friends Jack and Diane Van Dien. Every year, Patrick wrote a pilgrim play that our children and the Van Dien children—Laurie, Roark and Wendi—performed for us. When their family was transferred to Paris in 1977, they invited us to come over for Thanksgiving. After a marvelous celebration, Patrick flew home with his sisters while Gene and I went to Normandy, where Gene was keen to visit the American Cemetery and Memorial located on the cliffs above Omaha Beach, overlooking the English Channel. The first American cemetery on European soil, it was established on June 8, 1944, two days after the D-Day landing. As a teenager during World War II, Gene idolized the men who fought in that war. Almost ten thousand Allied troops were killed in the invasion alone. Battered by a howling wind on a bitterly cold, snowy day, we walked what seemed like the entire 172 acres. We also visited the village of Bayeux nearby to see the amazing medieval tapestry housed in a small museum there. Hand-embroidered in wool, twenty inches wide by almost 230 feet long and completed in 1077, it depicted the conquest of England by William the Conqueror in 1066. It was a cogent reminder that Britain had had its ups and downs. We hoped that things would improve in the coming year.

In January of 1978, for the first time in five years, inflation fell into single digits, just under 10 percent. The pay restraint policy of Prime Minister Callaghan had been chipping away at inflation since its peak at over 26 percent, but unemployment reached a postwar high of 1.5 million while strikes and IRA bombings continued. Margaret Thatcher rose to prominence as leader of the Conservative Party, the first woman in British history to lead a political party. In January she struck a sensitive nerve, giving the Conservatives a temporary boost in the polls, with her remark during a Granada Television World in Action interview about Britons fearing being "rather swamped by people with a different culture." The Labour Party's coalition with the Liberal Party dissolved and the Conservatives began pressuring Labour to call a general election. Had Callaghan done so in the summer, Labour might have prevailed; but continuing strikes and a bitterly cold winter were his downfall. The lorry drivers union struck, causing disruption of oil supplies and other essential commodities. Callaghan had to put the army on standby to drive the trucks to avoid the complete shutdown of the country. Returning from a business trip abroad, in the middle of the strike, he told the press that the rest of the world did not see that Britain was in chaos. The Sun newspaper featured the famous headline "Crisis? What crisis?" In the general election, Margaret Thatcher and the Conservatives won; they would hold power through three elections covering eleven years.

At home, Patrick, eighteen, was eagerly anticipating graduation. He had been accepted at Oklahoma State University as a sophomore by taking exams that proved his competency in several subjects. The assistant dean of the School of Veterinary Medicine, a Welshman who listened daily via shortwave radio to the BBC broadcast, had warmly welcomed him and continued to mentor him through his years studying veterinary medicine. Gene and I and his sisters, while happy for him, were sad to part with him. We planned one last family trip for spring break.

On March 11, Palestine Liberation Organization frogmen swam ashore near Tel Aviv and commandeered a bus, taking its passengers as hostages. In the shootout with the Israeli Army that followed, almost fifty people died. Our assumption that our April tour would be canceled was incorrect. Two days before our departure, Gene had to fly to Houston for a meeting. Grandmother, Patrick, his girlfriend Stephanie Arzonetti, Lisa, Suzanne and I met Gene in Paris, where we were closely interviewed by an agent of Mossad, the Israeli secret service, before boarding an El Al flight to Tel Aviv.

Arriving at our hotel in Jerusalem, we discovered that the members of our tour, with the exception of a couple from London, were all Northern Ireland Protestants, including three Protestant ministers. Israel was swarming with military. There were tanks on the streets, heavily armed soldiers everywhere, helicopters circling overhead and sharpshooters on the roofs. In spite of the high alert, not one of the excursions on our itinerary was canceled, not even to the Arab cities of Hebron, Bethlehem, Nazareth and Nablus. The Garden of Gethsemane was packed with worshippers at sunrise on Easter Morning and we heard the familiar words from Matthew 28:6, "He is not here, for He is risen!"

We toured the country from the Sea of Galilee to Masada. Although being in the Holy Land was a dream come true for us, we felt bombarded by propaganda from our Israeli Zionist guide and, almost in counterpoint, a Presbyterian minister extolled the praises of Ian Paisley, the raging leader of the Democratic Unionist Party in Belfast. When Gene and I were alone we discussed our upcoming move—to Bogotá, where Gene had been offered the job as president of Colombia Cities Service. Although it was a substantial promotion for Gene, we would be taking our teenage daughters into a dangerous country. For us, it was not a relaxing holiday.

Immediately following our return to London, Gene and I flew to Bogotá. He got acquainted with the operation and his staff while

I went house hunting with an American expat real estate agent. Returning to London, we began intensive Berlitz classes in Spanish, each with a private tutor eight hours daily for six weeks. Grandmother ably took over at home. We bought a two-month-old Lhasa Apso dog we called Tuppy, for her coat the color of the British bronze tuppence coin. The cat treated the tiny dog with disdain. Following Patrick's graduation from ASL, plucky Grandmother agreed to take the girls and the pets to Garber for the summer. All our furniture and household goods traveled in shipping containers on Air France. Cities Service was willing to stand this expense because most everything entering Colombia by sea was stolen. On our last night in London, Charles Waidelich, Cities president, arrived from Tulsa to host a party for us and Gene's London replacement. He asked me if I was afraid to be moving to Colombia as kidnappings and murders were rampant in that unstable country. I assured him that I knew the danger but also told him that I expected Cities Service to quickly pay the ransom if Gene were kidnapped.

Gene and I went our separate ways. He reported for work in Bogotá and I flew to Oklahoma to help Patrick prepare to enter Oklahoma State University in Stillwater. We bought him a small VW Rabbit hatchback car. He had an Oklahoma driver's license but very little driving experience. With a lump in my throat, I handed him the keys to the car, gathered Grandmother, the girls and pets, and flew to Bogotá.

Seven

DANGEROUS BEAUTY

Bogotá
August 1978 / January 1981

WE ARRIVED at night. Gene, his armed driver, and a bodyguard with a machine gun were at the gate to meet us. Chaos reigned in the customs hall. We anxiously watched while agents rifled through our bags, searching for anything they wanted that they could confiscate for themselves. When we exited the terminal, the guards were on high alert for potential kidnappers. We girls, mute with shock, huddled together in the back of the car while Gene was sandwiched between the guards in front. The house, floodlit on all sides and guarded by a sentry with a rifle, had a very sensitive alarm system that planes flying overhead frequently tripped. We fell into bed feeling that we had just landed in a war zone.

Colombians tell the following joke: As God created the world, when he got to the last part of land that would become Colombia, he decided it would be his masterpiece. So God gave it three mountain ranges instead of one; wide and flowing rivers, brightly colored birds and butterflies, over three thousand varieties of orchids; jungles; beautiful beaches; and abundant natural resources, including

87

fabulous emeralds and gold. When He had finished, looking at its perfection, He became worried that the rest of the world would be jealous. So, He put the worst people there.

Spain controlled Colombia from the arrival of the conquistadores in the sixteenth century until they were ultimately driven out by colonialists in the early nineteenth century. Two factions formed within the country, the Federalists led by Francisco de Paula Santander and the Centralists led by Antonio Nariño and Simón Bolívar. Although constitutions were enacted from 1810 onward, friction between the two groups continued until all-out civil war erupted in 1948 among towns and communities that identified with one of the two parties. Known as *La Violencia*, in five years, one hundred eighty thousand Colombians lost their lives. In 1953, a truce created a National Front to govern jointly, alternating the presidency every four years with equally shared government posts. That policy continued while we lived there. However, the violence never ended.

The Marxist-Leninist people's army FARC, the communist liberation group ELN and the urban guerrilla group M-19 were the primary groups opposed to the government. These groups plus government forces, right-wing paramilitaries and drug cartels were each guilty of atrocities. The M-19, formed by members of the educated class to protest a fraudulent election on April 19, 1970, began with dramatic symbolic actions such as the theft of the sword of Simón Bolívar in 1974. However, they soon turned violent, kidnapping and executing a union leader in 1976. In 1979 they dug a tunnel into the Colombian Army weapons depot, where they seized over five thousand weapons. Gene, as president of a foreign oil company, was a prime kidnapping target by the M-19 for propaganda purposes as well as ransom. They did not hesitate to execute their hostages, while criminal gangs targeted the wealthy just for the ransoms.

Lisa and Suzanne entered Colegio Nueva Granada, a private college preparatory school with a student population 75 percent Colombian and 25 percent expatriate. Located on the side of a mountain at nine thousand feet above sea level, surrounded by a high barbed-wire fence, it resembled a prison. The first day of school, Lisa, not being adjusted to the altitude, fainted in class. Although classes were taught in English, the socializing was completely in Spanish. Our girls were on a steep learning curve as their second language was French. Lisa continued her French studies after school at the Alliance Française. She and Suzanne made a few Colombian friends but mostly socialized with Americans. We were all under a lot of stress trying to adjust to the climate, culture, danger and language, but the girls were troupers, not complaining or crying, although I am sure we all felt like it.

Through our real estate agent I hired a daily maid—a somber, shy girl. I doubted that she would stay with us but Mesalina turned out to be a loyal, happy member of our household. She and Grandmother could be heard chatting and laughing although neither possessed a word of shared language.

We joined the Episcopal Church, a small congregation that occupied the same building as the Protestant Church of Bogotá. An English vicar who had lived in Colombia for many years served as our pastor. Through friends at school, Lisa and Suzanne became active in a Baptist Mission Church's youth group. All three were English-speaking congregations and most of the members were

Americans. I joined the Baptist women's Bible study as our church had no small group meetings. Gene and I became friends with couples from all three churches. However, for the first time we did not have a couples' Bible study in our home because Gene's responsibilities made for long hours.

Bogotá was frequently cold and wet. Wood was delivered by donkey to supply the two fireplaces that provided the only heat in the house. A popular escape on the weekend was a trip to "hot country," out of the mountains. Gene's driver, Vicente Coy, always crossed himself when we started down the precipitous roads, marked at every hairpin curve by shrines to loved ones who had died there. We looked forward to outings at a coffee plantation where we dined al fresco, swam, played volleyball and enjoyed Christian fellowship with about ten families in relative security. These excursions formed our happiest memories of the years in Colombia.

We began to make Colombian friends through business and the neighborhood. English was spoken by most of the educated class but I sometimes found myself with Colombian wives who did not speak English. I enrolled at the Universidad Javeriana to increase my fluency. The social life was as hectic as it had been in London. Bogotá had good restaurants and people entertained lavishly at home as well. When we had a party, huge bouquets of a wide variety of orchids from guests arrived on the day, completely filling the house. Invitations were sent out for 8:00 p.m. but some people did not show up until 10:00 p.m. and I could not serve dinner until everyone had arrived. Standing and drinking for two hours while cigarette smoke filled the house was not for the fainthearted.

Gene's jogging habit ended abruptly when we arrived in Colombia. Our neighbor, a partner in Avianca, the Colombian airline, jogged with thirty bodyguards dressed identically as the neighbor. Because of the danger, he finally relocated his family to Miami, Florida, and commuted back and forth for business. Miami was becoming the refuge of many affluent Colombians. Protecting oneself in Colombia was futile. No matter what route one took between home and work, a person was vulnerable when arriving at either destination. The girls were guarded at the house until they boarded the school bus but were unprotected otherwise. We all carried pocket Bibles for comfort in case we were kidnapped.

I was asked by the U.S. Embassy staff for assistance visiting Americans in Colombian prisons. Bogotá prisons with the ludicrous names of Buen Pastor (Good Shepherd) for the women's prison and La Modelo (The Model) for the men's prison were perilous institutions with abysmal living conditions. When the Colombian representative for Amoco, a Cities Service partner, heard of my new activity, he insisted that I quit. After tense negotiations, I reluctantly agreed not to return to the extremely dangerous men's prison but continued to send in food and other items that the men requested.

As I continued at Buen Pastor, one of the women asked me to start a Bible study. With the warden's permission, I went into the interior courtyard each week guarded by one of the American prisoners—as there were about thirty M-19 incarcerated women who were hostile to my presence. The women I met there were no different from people I met in daily life, except for being confined where they remained, usually without trial, for years. Some in my Bible study were eager to change their lives for the better but others had developed demoralizing survival skills in prison. Sadly, my guard, who returned to the States after three years, rejoined her drug cartel gang and was murdered within months of her release. The one who requested the Bible study became a Christian while in prison, returned home after four years of brutal incarceration, turned her life around, married a Christian man and has been an inspiration to all who know her. I have been blessed to call her my friend for over thirty-five years.

On a Thursday in December, a Cities pipeline exploded in the jungle, sending a stream of fire through a village nearby, killing a number of people and destroying many homes. The villagers had been using the pipeline as a bridge over a stream, with their bare feet slowly corroding the metal. Gene flew by helicopter without security to the site, a dangerous move because the area was controlled by the FARC guerrilla group. The local priest helped to calm and comfort the mourning, angry crowd. That Saturday morning, the three-inch headline across the top of *El Tiempo,* Bogotá's principal newspaper, claimed that the president of Colombia Cities Service had been arrested. Although it was untrue, Gene expected to be taken into custody when he arrived for work Monday morning. When he was not, Cities attorneys recommended that he leave Colombia for a short period. Under Colombian law, the head of a firm could be held criminally responsible for accidents or malfeasance by the company. Gene and his American field manager, also a target for arrest, spent the night at an undisclosed destination. I was not even told where they were. While the girls and I were very tense, Grandmother appeared calm, perhaps not understanding the danger we were in.

The next morning, we each packed a small flight bag and prepared a picnic lunch to eat on the flight. We went with our driver, Vicente, and a bodyguard to the headquarters of the Departamento Administrativo de Seguridad (DAS) for our passes to leave the country. I had been told to be sure that we were not being followed. If we were, I was to call the office and the pilots and men would take off without us. I nervously glanced behind the car every few minutes on the long drive to the security office. At the airport, Gene and his manager were anxiously standing with the two pilots beside an eight-passenger Cessna plane. We landed in the northern port city of Cartagena, where the head pilot, Rudy Faccini, took a trembling Lisa with all our passports through passport control while the rest of us hid around the corner of the building. Once we left Colombian air space, we all started cheering, knowing there would be no Colombian Air Force jets forcing us to land. The pilots opened the beer they'd brought and we feasted on sandwiches and Christmas candy. We landed in Jamaica for the night. After a hair-raising ride to our hotel we sat in the garden drinking Mai Tais, and later fell into bed exhausted. I don't even remember eating dinner. Landing in Florida, we parted with Gene and his manager, who continued to the Houston office, while the girls, Grandmother and I went to Oklahoma to prepare for Christmas. When we returned to Bogotá three weeks later, I was consumed with dread knowing what the Colombian prisons were like. We were tremendously relieved that Gene was not arrested. Gene and I lived with the stress, trusting that God was with us but also aware that we were not immune from life's dangers or sorrows. We were very concerned about the effect this was having on our children but not as aware as we should have been. They were suffering silently. However, once back in the U.S. the girls both had nightmares that we had been kidnapped or killed. We fervently prayed for a more peaceful new year.

Our hopes for the new year rose as we watched the sky over Bogotá fill with thousands of *globos*, paper balloons filled with air heated by small paraffin lamps. Some were huge whimsical shapes that required a team effort to get them launched. Frequently they caught fire on the ground accompanied by groans of disappointment, followed by cheers when adults and children saw their beautiful *globos* successfully float away. The dangers of living in Bogotá temporarily evaporated with this peaceful, awe-inspiring sight.

A few intrepid friends ventured down to Colombia to see us. We were eager to have visitors and took them on tours of the city and into the countryside as well. In Bogotá, we visited the Museo del Oro, filled with fabulous pre-Columbian gold- and gem-encrusted treasures. In the countryside, we toured the colonial towns of Santa Fe de Antioquia, Popayán, Villa de Leyva, and the Salt Cathedral of Zipaquirá (a huge cathedral carved within a salt dome). Once, when Lisa's childhood friend Madeline Siefke was visiting, we drove up a steep track to see Guatavita, a volcanic crater lake that spawned the legend of *El Dorado,* which attracted the Spanish conquistadores in the sixteenth century. According to the legend, the Muisca Indian chief annually jumped into the lake coated with gold dust, accompanied by many items of pure gold, to appease Chie, the goddess of water. Standing beside the tranquil lakeshore, we spied three men rushing down the hill toward us. Guessing they had robbery on their minds, we rushed back to the safety of the car and our armed guards.

Life at home was enlivened by the addition of Mesalina's baby boy, Edgar. When he was born, we went to visit her in the hospital, appalled to find her sharing a bed with another woman and her baby, and a third woman and baby on the floor under the bed. Each woman clutched her clothes, purse and baby, afraid to sleep because of thieves. Although we lived with the possibility of violence, the average Colombian lived with the reality of violence every day.

A few months after our alarming flight out of Colombia, Rudy Faccini, our pilot, was murdered in a contract killing, shot in the head at close range as his horrified pregnant wife watched. Unbeknownst to us, he had been flying U.S. Drug Enforcement Administration agents around Colombia in search of clandestine airfields used by drug cartels. Evidently he was not killed for helping us flee the country, but knowing someone personally who was murdered brought the horror of violence and the reality of our own mortality very close.

In spite of that, we responded to Lisa's protest that she did not want to spend her vacation beside the pool in Garber by offering her a rather risky alternative. Introduced to us by a mutual friend, Betty Welch and Birdie West worked with Wycliffe Bible Translators, a Christian organization that helped people worldwide translate the Bible into their own languages. They lived in the Amazon village of Acaricuara, where they had spent many years learning Tucano, a trade language among Amazon villages in Colombia and Brazil, turning it into written form and producing a Tucano Bible. They had become great friends so I asked them if they could use Lisa as a typist and dishwasher that summer. Because she was under eighteen they needed permission from Wycliffe management; once they secured that, they said they would be delighted to have her. Lisa was ecstatic. Her friend Mary Butler pleaded with her parents to go too. In July our driver, Vicente, took the girls to the city of Villavicencio, where they were met by a Wycliffe pilot who flew them to Loma Linda, Wycliffe's base camp. From there, they traveled in a single-engine Cessna over the trackless Amazon jungle for four and a half hours to the village. For the next fortnight, they slept in hammocks, bathed in the river, ate fried ants and loved every minute.

They plotted a return visit. Betty and Birdie were eager to have a census taken of the approximately 250 people in the village, to discover their relationships, ages and other demographic informa-tion. Mary and Lisa, required as rising seniors at Colegio Nueva Granada to do a project the following spring, submitted a proposal to conduct the census. Their completed task won top honors. Capping their high academic achievements, Mary became the valedictorian and Lisa the salutatorian at graduation.

Following Lisa's trip to the Amazon, Gene, the girls and I traveled to the States together to take Lisa on a tour of East Coast universities where her friends also planned to apply. From there, we flew to Oklahoma to be with Patrick. His first year away from home had been stellar. His grades were excellent and he had been elected president of the Pre-Veterinary Medicine Club. That summer he lived with Grandmother and worked for the local vet, a summer job that lasted five summers. He formed a close bond with the vet and enjoyed working with the farmers even though he had to shave off his beautiful red beard to be accepted in that conservative community.

Patrick made his first trip to Colombia for Christmas. He was happy to see us but uncomfortable in a country where he couldn't speak the language and we were constantly in the presence of armed guards. We were also nervous for his safety. When he discovered that he could earn ten dollars every two weeks at the blood bank in exchange for his red blood cells, he enthusiastically added to his already adequate bank account but also created abundant needle punctures in his arms. His height and bright red beard made him stand out from the crowd. I worried that he would be grabbed at the airport, mistaken for a drug smuggler and carted off to prison. For that reason, Gene's bodyguard accompanied Patrick onto the plane, saw him safely into his seat, and remained on the tarmac until the doors closed and the plane taxied away. Although I didn't feel the knot of fear that I had experienced years earlier in Argentina, the stress of continually being alert to possible danger was taking its toll on each of us.

On February 27, 1980, seventeen M-19 guerrillas dressed as joggers stormed the Embassy of the Dominican Republic, which was filled with diplomats attending a reception to celebrate Dominican Independence Day. Taken hostage were ambassadors from fourteen countries as well as the papal nuncio to Colombia, along with Dominican staff and catering crew. Our neighbor, the British ambassador, fortuitously avoided being kidnapped because he was late for the reception.

The gunmen demanded $50 million ransom and the release of 311 jailed comrades. Thus began sixty-one tense and sometimes ludicrous days, while Colombia and the world were mesmerized by the news that trickled out. Diego Asencio, the U.S. ambassador, born in Spain and brought with his family as an infant to America, was one of the hostages. Bogotá was his first ambassadorial post. Gene knew him well because he was part of a team of wardens formed to alert American citizens quickly in case of danger. Diego was intelligent and friendly and had an infectious sense of humor. He began to build a relationship with the guerrillas, believing it would be more difficult for them to start executing the hostages if they had formed good rapport. He also worked with the Venezuelan, Mexican and Israeli ambassadors and the papal nuncio to organize the hostages and confer with their captors. Each one worked to keep morale high: the papal nuncio led Mass every morning, the Venezuelan ambassador sang, the Mexican ambassador cooked breakfast, the Israeli ambassador supervised the cleaning details, and Diego told entertaining stories. Diego also helped the captors negotiate with the Colombian government as they seemed to have no clue as to how to proceed. His aim, of course, was to get everyone out alive.

As the days passed, the guerrillas released all of the women and some of the staff and catering crew. One ambassador escaped by jumping out of a window; at the end of two months only sixteen hostages remained. The captors eventually reduced the random demand to $10 million with the release of seventy prisoners. In the end, ransom of $2.5 million was paid, the guerrillas and eleven of their hostages were flown to Cuba where the hostages were put on a plane back to Colombia, and the guerrillas were given asylum. The rumor was that most of the guerrillas returned to Colombia within two weeks. Diego was lauded as a hero throughout Colombia, and years later he wrote a book about the experience entitled *Our Man Is Inside*.

In April, Grandmother arrived from the U.S. in time to see Suzanne perform in the school musical *Once Upon a Mattress*. She made Suzanne a beautiful gown in time for the prom that both girls attended—transported by Vicente, with their dates, for their safety as we required.

In May, Gene and I were invited to a dinner party for the Colegio Nueva Granada headmistress, who was taking a sabbatical in the States for a year. I received a call from a friend of hers in Cali, where she had lived for many years, saying she was inviting ten people to a small farewell dinner party for her in Bogotá. Gene and I arrived at the location at the same time as two other couples. The house, built on a hillside, had a spiral staircase from the ground floor to the main floor. First in line, I rang the bell and entered to find our hostess had descended halfway down the stairs to greet us. I introduced myself and shook her hand. Two steps above her I saw a Colombian man. He didn't speak or extend his hand so I continued up the stairs, expecting to be introduced to him later. When we were all settled in the living room, I asked, "Where is the man I saw on the stairs?" Another guest replied, "What have you been drinking, Jan?" After a few minutes, our hostess went to the kitchen for hors d'oeuvres. In her absence, the others, who knew this woman well, began to chat among themselves about how she was adjusting to the death of her husband. The hairs on the back of my neck stood up. I spoke quietly to our vicar who was sitting next to me. Father Pat had known the couple as he was vicar of the Episcopal Church in Cali during the period when the husband was slowly dying of cancer. I described the man I had seen on the stairs as short, stocky, with a round smiling face, wearing braces (suspenders). "That sounds just like him," was his reply. I could barely follow the conversation for the rest of the evening. I wasn't actually afraid because he looked as solid as the rest of us, but I did become fearful that it could happen again when I was alone. Thankfully, it never has.

The next morning I went to church to speak with the vicar. At the time, seeing an apparition was not compatible with my Christian theology. Also, I couldn't understand why I was the only person at the party who had seen him. I wondered if the woman would be comforted or alarmed thinking her husband was hanging around six months after his death. I had never concerned myself much considering whether or not I believed in life after death, heaven or hell. To me the benefits of the Christian life were very much in the here and now. I was a happier, more confident person who believed that in my prayers I conversed with a God who was personally involved in my welfare and was helping me to become a more loving, caring person every day. Now, I was faced with what I considered to be incontrovertible proof of life continuing after death. In some way, I was comforted by this fact, although a lot of unanswerable questions remained. However, when anyone asks me if I believe in life after death, I answer strongly in the affirmative.

Over the years, I have developed an afterlife theology that I find satisfactory. I always liked the image Catherine Marshall used in one of her books to describe her late husband, the minister Peter Marshall. She dreamed that she saw him in heaven working in his garden. Hebrews 12:1 says, "We are surrounded by so great a cloud of witnesses." I picture a thin veil separating this reality from the next, that in the next we will also go about our daily lives here on earth. I don't know if those who have died have any ability to see us but it comforts me to think of loved ones, especially my dear mother, keeping watch over us.

The God I worship is not vindictive; therefore, I do not believe in hell as described in the Bible. The people who have caused terrible suffering in this world, I believe, will be deeply remorseful and forgiven in the next. I don't believe that God ever rejects any of His creation. While I have taken part in many thorny theological discussions, my theology is rather simplistic. I am at the stage of life where I have lost interest in trying to find theological answers. I want to spend my days learning to love God and others more and live at peace.

Over the years, all of our children sought a personal relationship with God. They saw Gene and me intent on living our lives as followers of Jesus. We prayed with them. They had no doubt that our faith was very important to us. When Patrick was twelve, he asked his dad at bedtime what he needed to do to become a Christian. Gene gently led him in prayer. God did the rest and Patrick began to study his Bible and follow Jesus's example in his young life. While we lived in London, the famous evangelist Billy Graham held a crusade at Earls Court Exhibition Centre, and we attended with the children. Afterward, the girls asked Gene to pray with them. Lisa experienced God's closeness and care from that time forward.

Suzanne was quite young and it wasn't until she was nineteen that she experienced God's presence—during a flight from North America to Kenya in 1983. Sitting in economy class with glasses of wine, we chatted about our lives. I told the girls my ghost story. Until that time, I had told no one except Gene as I felt that I would not be believed. When I finished, Suzanne began to cry, saying she wasn't sure she was a Christian. Lisa and I joined her in prayer. After that, Suzanne felt secure in her faith. That experience made me feel more confident in sharing my story.

In August 1980, we took Lisa up to Dartmouth College to begin her freshman year. Suzanne had flown to Colombia alone to begin school; Betty and Birdie stayed with her until we returned. We were all feeling quite sad but Suzanne especially suffered parting with her sister. We found living with armed guards became more onerous as time passed. Shortly after our return, Frank Mytinger arrived on Cities business. He told Gene that a contract had finally been successfully signed in Kenya awarding Cities Service the right to drill exploration wells offshore in the Indian Ocean. Gene said that he would be interested in the position. Frank passed the word back in Houston. I'm sure that our friends thought it was professional suicide for Gene to surrender control of a large operation, after less than three years, for a small operation in Kenya but we were ready for a more peaceful life.

Patrick and Lisa arrived for Christmas, thrilled to hear that we were moving to Kenya. Suzanne, on the other hand, wasn't eager to move again. She loved Colombia, had become immersed in the culture, preferred speaking Spanish with me and chose to move to Kenya with us because her only other option was to graduate early from Colegio Nueva Granada and enter university in the States at the tender age of seventeen. But, having been to Kenya, she was also excited about living there.

A month before our departure, a friend who had been a Roman Catholic missionary in Colombia for twenty years arrived at our house to join a party celebrating the release of one of the American women from prison. When I opened the door, she stood there shaking. She said, "Jan, I need to speak with you privately." The guerrilla group M-19 had given her a message to relay to me. The message was, "If you return to Buen Pastor prison, you will be killed." They backed up the warning by revealing knowledge of our family, where the girls attended school, Gene's position and our home address. This credible threat made it easier for us to leave our friends in Bogotá and face the initial loneliness and adjustment we knew accompanied every move.

Eight

EXOTIC BEAUTY

Nairobi
February 1981 / December 1981

OUR FIRST SIX WEEKS in Nairobi, we lived in one of the guest cottages in the garden of the famed Norfolk Hotel. Opened in 1904, the Norfolk was a haven for celebrities and big game hunters, the only escape from the choking red dust that engulfed the whole region. Offering hot and cold baths, restful rooms and Western meals, it became the focal point for British colonial social life in Nairobi. Nobility, aristocrats and adventurers, including Winston Churchill and Theodore Roosevelt, flocked to exotic Kenya. In 1933 Ernest Hemingway, with his second wife Pauline, came to Kenya for the first time. He spent many hours lounging in the Norfolk Hotel bar. Three works were inspired by this visit: *The Green Hills of Africa, The Short Happy Life of Francis Macomber* and *The Snows of Kilimanjaro*. On a second safari in 1953, with his fourth wife Mary, he stayed at the New Stanley Hotel, built in 1913 following a fire that destroyed the original Stanley. A giant thorn tree in the patio of the hotel served as a communication center with its trunk covered with hundreds of notes and constantly surrounded by people searching for friends and family. In 1981, years before e-mail, it remained popular to communicate this way.

Our cottage consisted of two bedrooms, sitting room, small kitchen and bathroom. Nestled among profuse flowering plants and an aviary filled with brilliant birds, it was an idyllic retreat from the bustling, noisy city. On December 31, 1980, a little over two months before we arrived, a bomb was detonated in a room rented by an enigmatic guest. We weren't told that it was a suspected terrorist attack by the PLO. I guess the hotel staff didn't want to alarm us. Reconstruction was in progress when we arrived. . While we were living there, Patrick flew out for spring break from Oklahoma State University. Having introduced the family to Kenya as a teenager, he was especially thrilled with our new posting. He would be spending his summer again working for the vet in Garber, so this was his only opportunity to visit us until Christmas.

When Suzanne and I arrived at the International School of Kenya for her first day, we were taken to the guidance counselor's office so he could introduce her to her classes. His first words were, "I just heard on the wireless that the kidnapped American missionary in Colombia was killed." Suzanne burst into tears. Betty and Birdie had stayed with Suzanne when we had been house hunting in Kenya. During that period, the wife and children of the Wycliffe hostage were at our house every day, being comforted by Betty and Birdie as tense negotiations for his release continued. Suzanne had become deeply involved in the ordeal, attached to the children, and prayed fervently to God for their father's survival. To receive news of his murder was heartbreaking. I took her back to the hotel. All I could do was try to comfort her. The age-old questions of why such trage-dies occur do not provide easy answers. There would be time to discuss how she felt about God, the murderers and what our response as Christians should be. For now, she needed time to mourn and heal.

In spite of this difficult beginning, Suzanne settled gracefully into her new school. The first classmates who invited her to eat lunch with them turned out to be involved with drugs. Although they did not become her closest friends, she always defended them and was grateful to them for their kindness. Set amidst picturesque coffee plantations, ISK consisted of numerous buildings designed to look like an African village. The school's six hundred students represented many nationalities due to the United Nations' headquarters for East Africa being located in Nairobi. The school offered both the American curriculum and the International Baccalaureate diploma. Suzanne's grades were excellent. At last, she wasn't being compared to her brother and sister and displayed the academic abilities that we always knew she possessed. She was quickly involved in their performing arts program, taking part in the school musicals and vocal and instrumental groups.

The attorney who had worked with Frank Mytinger on the Cities contract with the Kenyan government entertained us royally with his wife, and they introduced us to their friends in the British Kenyan community. He helped Gene get the office rented, staff secured and government contracts confirmed. Gene hired a young American from Kansas who was already working in Kenya as office manager, along with a Kenyan secretary and driver. Gene bought an old white Jaguar sedan as our personal car and a new Alfa Romeo for the office. When Grandmother Thelma visited with her friend Gordy Caldwell, they quickly became known as the Jaguar Mamas among our friends.

Like Colombia, Kenya held danger; street crime and home invasions were frequent. Our house was part of a neighborhood group consisting of ten houses, with a loud siren on each roof. Wearing distinctive vests, our staff would not be mistaken for the attackers when they ran to the defense of neighbors. With broad-bladed knives called *pangas*, bats, bows and arrows wielded by attackers and defenders alike, the contest was primitive and could cause harm although it hardly compared with the assault weapons and bombs of the Colombians. With gate guards around the clock, armed only with *pangas*, the atmosphere did remind us of the tension we had left in Bogotá.

Trained household help was in great demand in Nairobi. A new friend advised me to volunteer to fold the newsletter for the American Women's Association in order to get an advance peek to see who had staff available before the letters were sent out to the membership. I called a State Department wife who was listed as returning to the States. She said that John Maina was an excellent cook whom she had taught to make many American dishes, but she despaired of finding him a position because he had a wife and three young children he insisted on keeping with him in Nairobi. Men usually served as cooks, cleaners and gardeners with their families remaining in their home regions. When I went to meet John I liked him immediately, especially when he told me that he must have Sundays off because he was a Christian. I hired him on the spot. John called us Bwana and Memsahib, both terms of respect. Sometimes other Africans referred to Gene as *Mzee*, also a term of respect but meaning an old man, although he was not quite fifty. John became the head elder in a small church near our house, serving as its lay pastor.

A gardener, Mburu, hired by the house's owner, came with the house. He was Kikuyu, as was John, so I felt they would be compatible. The staff quarters behind our house consisted of two sections with two rooms each and a toilet/shower room in between. The staff cooked their meals outside over an open fire. I wondered how John and wife Beatrice, five-year-old son Job, three-year-old daughter Ruth, and infant Milka, plus a young cousin who would care for the children while John and Beatrice worked in the house, could possibly fit into two small rooms, but John assured me that the accommodation was good. Mburu lived in the other section and invited young Job to sleep in his extra room. In spite of being told by colonial friends that I was going to ruin the servants, I piped hot water into their quarters when we connected a new hot water tank to the washing machine.

Nairobi in 1981 had approximately a million inhabitants although no one really knew how large the population was because thousands were crowded into slums, attracted by the lure of jobs. Although independence in 1963 had removed the British colonial government from power, the Europeans living in the country were given Kenyan citizenship and remained the social and business elite. An Indian population, descended from indentured servants brought into the country at the start of the twentieth century, owned most of the small businesses. There was an Arab population, located mostly along the coast, descended from traders who settled there hundreds of years earlier. Of the approximately forty African tribes, the Kikuyu and the Luo were the most populous and powerful. By 1981, there was a fair amount of social integration among the various groups. We made friends across the spectrum.

The climate was sunny and dry with a constant cool breeze, thanks to the mile-high elevation. Bougainvillea covered walls and houses and climbed the tree trunks in a great variety of colors. In spring (October in the Southern Hemisphere) blooming jacaranda trees turned the city into a cloud of lavender. Modern and colonial buildings created an interesting architectural milieu. The streets were packed with vehicles of all kinds—pushcarts, *matatu* buses (small pickup trucks with shells on the back into which people crammed) and the ubiquitous Mercedes-Benz cars driven by UN personnel and Kenyan officials, who were jokingly dubbed "the Wa-Benze tribe."

The infamous red dust was everywhere due to the many roads still unpaved in the capital city. Decay of the infrastructure was already visible. Jomo Kenyatta, the first president, inherited a British-style civil service that rapidly became corrupt. Despite the corruption, Kenya had one of the most stable African governments. Under President Daniel arap Moi, it was expected to mature into an educated, prosperous country.

I found mingling with the pedestrians on the main thorough-fares fascinating. One could see the majestic *Maasai morans* (young warriors) dressed in their traditional red cloth and beads with their long, plaited hair caked with red mud. Their only alteration when coming to the city was to remove the blocks from their pierced ears and loop the large holes over the tops of their ears. They still carried their spears and had knives tucked into their belts. The Somali and Ethiopian women were tall, slim, long-necked and elegant, carrying themselves like queens. Kenya had many people whose loyalty to their tribes was first, and to the nation a distant second. Tribal enmity was rife. Tribalism was the elephant in the room that was never mentioned in polite company but affected everything.

Educated Kenyans spoke at least three languages: their tribal language, Kiswahili and English. Deference to white people was still evident, even after almost twenty years of independence. I was embarrassed to be pushed to the front of the queue in shops. My protestations that I would wait my turn were simply ignored.

Street crime was common. I quickly learned to put my handbag under my feet on the floor of the car and keep my arms inside with the windows partially rolled up. Yelling "thief" if one's purse was snatched on the street was hazardous because the thief might turn and call the accuser a thief. While we lived there, one incident of this practice ended with a crowd beating the innocent person to death before the police arrived to intervene.

When our household goods arrived, we moved into the cheerful, spacious home. The only heat was a large wood-burning fireplace in the living room. John laid a fire every evening before which we enjoyed our "sundowners" prior to dinner being served. Although I enjoyed cooking, I adjusted to having a cook with lightning speed. John was a good cook and adaptable, easily preparing dishes using my recipes as well as his own. It felt marvelous to say, "John, there will be ten for dinner tomorrow night; here is the menu," and to know that it would be perfectly prepared and served by John and Beatrice. The only time this failed was my fault. John made English short pastry and my attempts to show him how to make American-style pastry were unsuccessful, so when I wanted pie I made it. One day when we had guests, I made a banana meringue pie for dessert. After the main course had been cleared, John whispered in my ear, "Do you want the pie served in bowls, Memsahib?" When I asked if it needed to be served in bowls, he replied in the affirmative. Evidently, the bananas had liquefied when I put the pie briefly in the oven to brown the meringue so we had banana soup with floating pastry.

Every room had large windows and beautiful views of the blooming garden set among the tall trees. Frangipani trees near the house filled the air with perfume and provided hours of delight as we watched hummingbirds feed on the nectar. Our landlady had collected orchids from all over the world and placed many in the trees around our house.

One feature of this house was unique to Kenya. A steel accordion gate at the top of the stairs was to be closed and locked each night when we went to bed. It seemed like a fire risk to us but people who had lived through the Mau Mau Rebellion in the 1950s were adamant that we should use it to protect ourselves so that our servants could not murder us in our sleep. We thought that was ridiculous. However, after an attempted coup in 1982 when criminal elements replaced their *pangas* with guns, we began to lock the gate, feeling that it would at least slow down invading thieves while we set off the siren on our roof.

After visiting the Anglican Cathedral and the Presbyterian Church, which were both packed with standing room only, we chose the Lutheran Church, where the smaller congregation and its pastor were warm and welcoming. We learned that a Christian revival was sweeping through Kenya and adding converts exponentially. We had attended the Lutheran Church only a few weeks when the pastor asked us if we would like to have a house blessing. The congregation gathered at our house bringing potluck dishes. We stood in a large circle in front of the house while he spoke movingly and prayed for us and anyone who entered our home. From that day forward, we felt fully integrated into this loving, supportive community made up of American and Scandinavian missionaries, British Kenyans and African Kenyans.

Shortly after we had moved in, we were awakened by a loud boom, a crash, and Suzanne screaming that hot water was pouring into her bathroom. The hot water tank in the attic had overflowed, breaking through the ceiling with boiling water cascading through the hole. It happened to be a bank holiday; otherwise, Suzanne could well have been in the bathroom getting ready for school. Just the thought of it was terrifying. Gene rushed up the folding stairs into the attic and shut the water off. When we finally got a repairman to check it, he found that it was wired to bypass the thermostat. He repaired it and we cautiously turned it on. This was our first encounter with repairmen in Kenya. Fortunately, the man knew what he was doing. However, I soon learned that when a repairman told me he would have to go get a part, what it really meant was, "I don't know how to fix it and you'll never see me again." Well-trained people were in great demand but worth the wait.

Once we moved in, we went to the kennel to collect the animals, which we had left for boarding on our house-hunting trip. Tuppy, as always, was ecstatic to see us. Cats are not so forgiving; Zuli screamed at us when we arrived and told us of her displeasure at being left alone all the way home. However, in a few days, they both adapted to their surroundings. Zuli took charge of her new domain; in spite of the bell I put on her collar and her declawed paws, she was soon bringing us gifts of birds, lizards and the occasional small snake.

Kenya had two monsoon seasons, the long rains in April and May and the short rains in November. We were unprepared for the intensity of the rain. Just when we thought it couldn't rain harder, it did, producing a depression of spirit that I had never experienced before. Growing up in arid Oklahoma, rain was always welcome. However, this rain felt menacing even though it stopped abruptly at midday; the sun appeared, the tennis courts dried and we often played a round of tennis after lunch. About four in the afternoon the faucet in the sky opened again with another heavy downpour. I soon learned the necessity of the rain in Africa; if the rains didn't arrive on time and in sufficient quantity, the crops failed and people starved to death. Another dramatic event following the rains was the swarm of termites. Vital as they were to the ecosystem, they made a huge mess, flying around the outside lights. Removed each morning by Mburu by the shovel load, they were a great source of protein and a delicacy to the Kenyan people, sometimes eaten alive with the wings pulled off or fried with salt—but no oil—and stored as a food additive.

With the ground softened by the rains, two Kikuyu women were hired to plant grass to cover some bald spots in our shady garden. They arrived early, making the ten-kilometer walk from their village to our house carrying huge baskets on their backs filled with grass sprouts. These they planted one by one, bending from the waist with knees locked. They worked all day with rare breaks for a bit of food and water, singing and laughing as they worked. The

African spirit was truly amazing to us. No matter how poor or what tragedy occurred, they had a resilience and irrepressible joy that overcame adversity. Their generosity shamed the rest of the world. What little food they had they would share with anyone, even if it meant they went hungry the next day. We learned a lot from our African friends about giving.

We had some concern for our health as we moved to Africa. Before arriving in Kenya, we were given lots of immunizations as well as anti-malarial drugs. Plagued by a particularly virulent form of cerebral malaria, East Africa had a high mortality rate. Without screens, we closed the doors and windows at sunset. We used lots of insect repellent but did not sleep under netting at home. Tuberculosis was rampant. HIV/AIDS, recently identified, was still a taboo subject and poorly understood. Our American friend Dr. Mark Jacobson worked with an agency that approached churches to talk to their congregations about the disease and prevention protocols. We brought with us water filter systems, normally used on yachts, to install on the taps in the house to combat waterborne parasites.

Poisonous snakes were common; in our garden, Mburu killed several vipers. A grove of beautiful, rare, black bamboo grew across the stream that ran through our property, the natural home of the black mamba, which our Colombian friends would have called a two-step snake—one dropped dead two steps after being bitten. We never ventured to that part of the garden. A large crocodile emerged from the stream one day. Fearing for the children, Mburu chased it back into the stream brandishing his *panga*. A troop of handsome Sykes monkeys that regularly came through on their way to the forest were large and aggressive with no fear of women or children. They never approached the house except when a particular tree next to our dining room was full of fruit. During that period, we watched from inside the French doors as they stripped it bare in a matter of minutes. Africa provided adventures with just enough danger to make life exciting and give us an appreciation for our fascinating, complex world.

While Suzanne was at school and Gene hard at work preparing to drill his first exploratory well, I was active in several groups: a women's Bible study, the American Women's Association, a sewing group where we made simple dresses for poor women, and lectures at the museum. A prayer group of people from our church met weekly in our home.

On food shopping excursions, I bought staples from a small nearby Indian-owned supermarket where I applied for an account so I could pay my bill once a month—and also receive food items in short supply from under the counter. The day I received approval for our account, I heard the owner tell another woman that they were no longer making accounts. When she left, I asked him why then he had just approved ours. His reply stunned me. He said, "Oh, your husband's company is listed in the Fortune 500." For meat and produce we went to the central market, which comprised two floors teeming with vendors of produce, clothing, wood carvings and other tourist goods. I soon found my favorite produce seller, whose prices were fair with fruits and vegetables in good condition. I also became acquainted by name with the many crippled beggars who cruised around the floor on handmade skateboards. If I had change I'd pass it out; if not, they cheerfully said, "That's all right, Mama. We'll see you next time." In the butchery (butcher's shop), a separate room connected to the main market, the meat was hung in the open. Again, as in Colombia, we scrubbed and froze it before eating. My final shopping destination was a street where vendors sold enormous homegrown cashews, spices, pulses (peas, beans, lentils) and delicacies from other countries. The enticing, pungent aroma surrounded us as we got out of the car.

Due to the constant red dust, I had our Persian carpets washed frequently. The owner of the carpet shop was a devout Muslim. When I entered the shop and found him reading, I asked, "Is that your Qur'an?" "Yes," he responded. "If you have time, I would like to tell you about Islam." I accepted and, over the years, we had some wonderful talks about Christianity and Islam—without trying to convert each other. I appreciated people of other religions whose faiths were as satisfying to them as ours was to us, although I believe that Christianity provides us with a deep joy and optimism that is unique. My view of God, His love of all of His creation and creatures, was constantly expanding.

Also, my ideas about missionary work were changing. I had great respect for people who devoted their lives to serving others, using their skills whether in teaching, medicine, agriculture or other disciplines; they lived their faith more by what they did than what they said. I had less appreciation for those whose sole work was proselytizing. I always remembered a friend of another religion who became a Christian through her husband. She told me, "He did not knock down my house; he just built a more beautiful one next door, so I moved in."

We were invited to join the venerable Muthaiga Country Club, where we ate Sunday lunch and played tennis. The club also had a swimming pool, guest rooms and an excellent golf course that attracted international tournaments. The club was unchanged from its famous days as the playground of the Duke and Duchess of Windsor. Amazingly, some of their pals were still alive and seen weekly at the club. The women in their eighties would totter in on high heels, complete with hats and gloves for Sunday curry. When the television miniseries *Edward & Mrs. Simpson* was being aired in London, a copy was sent out to the club and we gathered in the card room each Tuesday night for six weeks. Gene and I chose the back row where we could watch the people as much as the TV screen. With cigarette smoke collecting against the ceiling, the crowd, absorbed in the story, drank as waiters kept their glasses constantly full. Occasionally, a deep voice would approvingly rumble, "Hear, hear."

Television, a propaganda tool for the government, offered nothing of interest so we spent our evenings after dinner reading or playing Scrabble. We listened to the BBC on shortwave radio and read the British papers, the *International Herald Tribune* and *Time* magazine, although the print media were regularly redacted by the government. We bought season tickets for plays at the Donovan Maule Theatre. Mostly British farce, the light entertainment was performed by professional actors from London in the leading roles. The theater was always sold out, the plays being wildly popular with the British Kenyans and expats who filled the house with uproarious laughter. Occasionally, the cast tackled a more demanding play such as an excellent production of *Equus*.

Getting to know the locals, hearing their stories and the gossip added immensely to our enjoyment of life in East Africa. We were especially interested in Ewart Scott Grogan. When we entered Kenya, the passport control officer asked Gene, "Are you related to Captain Grogan?" Gene responded, "Should I be?" The response was an emphatic, "No!"

In 1981 people at the club were still bewailing the act in 1967 of Captain Grogan's last mistress, known as the Cheshire Cat. "How could she have moved him to live in Cape Town? He had lived here for over sixty years!" He died in South Africa at the age of ninety-two.

Born in England in 1874, the son of a wealthy London wine merchant and schooled at the exclusive Winchester College, Ewart Grogan entered Cambridge in 1893. He was a brilliant scholar but his escapades and pranks during his two and a half years there led to his being "sent down" (British for expelled). In 1896, he embarked on an adventure that would define his life; he joined the British South Africa Company as a "bloody trooper," according to Grogan, to help put down a rebellion by the Matabele tribe. While there, he met Cecil Rhodes, a mining magnate and founder of the African territory named after him, Rhodesia, now Zimbabwe. Rhodes encouraged Grogan to develop British interests in Africa. He told him that a railroad route needed to be plotted from Cape Town to Cairo.

With the rebellion over, Grogan returned to England but was soon off on another adventure when his friend from Cambridge Eddie Watt invited him to go home with him to New Zealand. There he was captivated by Eddie's sister, Gertrude. She must have welcomed the courtship of this handsome, amusing sportsman because Grogan soon approached her stepfather to ask for her hand in marriage. He was, however, less impressed with Grogan. He asked the young man, "What do you plan to do with your life?" Frantically searching his brain for an answer, Grogan replied, "I'm going to map a route from

Cape Town to Cairo." "Fine," the man replied, "when you do that come back and we'll talk." I'm sure the Watt family, wealthy patricians, descendants of James Watt, the inventor of the steam engine, thought they'd never see this upstart again. They underestimated Ewart Grogan. Two years later, after surviving several episodes that should have ended his life, he returned to claim his bride. They settled in Kenya, where he became a highly respected and wealthy landowner. He and Gertrude had four daughters. He also had more children, all daughters, by various mistresses.

The incident that made him anathema to black Kenyans occurred in 1907. Three rickshaw drivers employed by Grogan were carrying his sister and her friends into town. Drunk, they terrified the women with their antics, refusing to stop and let the women out. At the time, Grogan was in an argument with the government over their lack of providing adequate policing and control over unruly servants. To make his point, he announced he would take matters into his own hands and whip the boys in front of the town hall. A crowd of colonials gathered to egg him on. Captain Grogan was feared by the Africans and a hero to many colonials from that time forward.

In 1982, local writer Leda Farrant's book *The Legendary Grogan* was published. I went to her book signing at the museum. When I asked her to inscribe the book to Gene Grogan, she looked up with a stricken expression. No doubt thinking of the illegitimate daughters, she asked, "Did I miss one?"

In April 1981, we received exciting news from Patrick via telex that he had become engaged to Dana Atchison. They were planning the wedding for August 1982 in Stillwater. Dana would graduate from Oklahoma State in May and was eager to begin her teaching career while Patrick finished his last two years of vet school. When our dispersed family gathered in Oklahoma over the summer, we all fell in love with Dana and looked forward to adding her to our clan.

In September, I was recruited to teach a class at the prestigious St. Mary's Catholic school for boys in Nairobi. The priest headmaster arranged classes for the non-Catholic boys during the hour each week when Mass took place. Taking charge of fifty eleven- and twelve-year-old Protestant boys was a daunting task. How could I possibly keep bedlam from breaking out? With trepidation, I prepared lots of activities and challenges to keep them too busy to get into trouble and actually found I looked forward to seeing these eager, happy faces each week. I felt that my class must be successful because soon I had a Hindu boy hidden somewhere in the room. Each week, the Guru would come to the door of my classroom and call out, "Come out, Vijay, I know you're in there," but he never found him. Teaching these children gave me the satisfaction that I had found in the prison Bible study in Colombia, but here Gene need not worry about my safety.

Preparing for Christmas seemed strange during the perfect summer weather. Lisa arrived after a grueling flight through West Africa. Patrick arrived from Oklahoma and the Meadows family from London. After Christmas, the Meadows family headed to the Maasai Mara National Park on safari. Our family went to northern Kenya for a few days to an area renowned for leopards. Afterward, Patrick flew to meet Dana in London to show her where he had spent most of his childhood. Happily settled in Nairobi, we looked forward to Suzanne's graduation from ISK and Patrick and Dana's marriage in the coming year.

Nine

WILD AND WONDERFUL SAFARIS

Nairobi
January 1982 / September 1983

AUSTERITY BIT HARD in 1982. President Moi faced a severe balance of payments deficit and so ordered all imports drastically limited. Almost all of Kenya's income from coffee and tea exports was used to buy imported oil, while the nation gamely searched for domestic sources. Gene's first offshore exploration well was a dry hole and he had been unable to secure a rig to drill a second well.

As the economic situation continued to decline, medical supplies such as x-ray film and anesthetics disappeared, as did luxury items like light bulbs and wine. Not surprisingly, the affluent managed to obtain what they wanted while the poor suffered without. The inequality did not go unnoticed. The Rhino Rescue Charity fund-raiser at an aristocrat's home in Karen, a Nairobi suburb named for the author Karen Blixen, flowed with wine and food for the huge crowd that attended.

In late March, Grandmother arrived for a three-month visit with Gordy Caldwell, a good friend of hers and the mother of my match-maker Theta sister Sally. Thelma, seventy-seven, and Gordy, eighty-one, were lively and ready for adventure. As soon as word circulated that they were in residence, they were included in all our social invitations and joined me in my activities. They sewed dresses for poor women and worked on the quilt kit that I had bought with them in mind. Gordy, with Mburu's assent, started working in the flower beds; thankfully, she did not encounter any snakes. They spent happy hours sewing on the terrace, watching the monkeys and birds pass through our garden into the Karura Forest. Sitting on the terrace with them one morning, as John gathered our coffee cups, I asked, "What's for lunch, John?" His reply, "Lice soup," made me laugh and the ladies gasp. Kikuyus, like Japanese, sometimes mix English l's and r's.

Suzanne's graduation on June 12 was held in the beautiful Kenyatta International Conference Centre's amphitheater. We had a bird's-eye view of the twenty-five students on the stage below us and were extremely proud when Suzanne was awarded the highest academic honor for the last quarter of her senior year. She had continued her piano lessons at the University of Nairobi with a kind but demanding gentleman from Goa and was recruited to accompany the International School of Kenya's string ensemble at graduation.

Madeline Siefke and Lisa had arrived in time for Suzanne's graduation. Afterward Grandmother, Gordy, Lisa, Madeline, Suzanne and I left on safari in a van with a driver. After visiting Lake Naivasha and Treetops, we turned west to the famed bird sanctuary at Lake Baringo. On the way our driver suggested a detour to another lake. There our van became mired in a deep accumulation of guano, and the driver's attempts to dig us out were unsuccessful. As the shadows began to lengthen, he left us on our own and went in search for help. We constructed a loo with *kangas* (ubiquitous lengths of cloth used for many purposes), inside which we each took our turn while the others kept a wary eye out for lions. The driver finally returned with a farmer who pulled us to safety with his tractor.

The next morning, we were awed by thousands upon thousands of birds circling over the lake. With a surface area of fifty square miles, Lake Baringo was a critical habitat for more than forty-five hundred species of birds, as well as being an important source of fish and home to a large herd of hippos, known to be one of the most aggressive and dangerous animals in Africa. Late in the afternoon, we boarded a small boat with a guide to see them, having no idea that our guide would take us right into the middle of their territory. Suddenly the huge creatures began to explode out of the water around us. It was thrilling and terrifying at the same time. Our intrepid elders were delighted and fearless. The lake was also filled with crocodiles. Between the hippos and the crocs, we were quite invigorated by the experience of feeling like prey.

Our next stop was Governors' Camp in the Maasai Mara. As we traveled the small road south along the Ugandan border, I became aware that our driver kept looking anxiously up the hill on our right. He finally confessed to me that the area was full of bandits. I joined him on the lookout with visions in my head of six naked women trudging along the road at night.

Governors' Camp was famous as the most luxurious tented camp in Kenya, boasting thirty-six well-appointed tents with a small breezeway separating each tent from a smaller one that contained a flush loo and shower. Before dinner, as we sat around a campfire sipping our Pimm's, we were entertained by a great storyteller and serenaded by a Kenyan quartet plus a pride of lions not far away. A delicious candlelit dinner followed in the dining tent. Before departing for bed, we were instructed in the use of the flashlights, which had a beam that would pulse to alert our Maasai guards in case of danger. We were also warned that there were dangerous Cape buffalos in the area.

Suzanne and I, occupying the last tent in a long row, were awakened at four in the morning by a bump on the side of the tent. I lifted the flap and came eye to eye with a huge buffalo. Cautiously, I tried to position my light to alert the guards, but to no avail. Suzanne wisely went back to sleep. At dawn I heard a guard outside go, "Shoo," and the buffalo trotted away. During breakfast the staff had a good laugh at my expense, telling me that was just old Bongo, who had become a familiar visitor to the camp. We spent our last day and night at Serena Lodge in Amboseli National Park. As we floated in a pool of cool spring water, we enjoyed the view of 19,600-foot, snow-capped Mount Kilimanjaro in the distance.

After bidding farewell to Madeline and Lisa, who left for the States, Gene, Thelma, Gordy, Suzanne and I traveled by train to Mombasa on the Indian Ocean. The charmingly seedy Victorian steam train still boasted white-glove service in the dining car and decent food. The track laid in the late 1800s cost many laborers' lives as the lions found the flimsy sleeping cars to be cafeterias on wheels for which the train earned its nickname, *The Lunatic Express.*

In 1982, our fellow passengers were a colorful mix of races and nationalities. We recognized a breathtakingly handsome *Maasai moran* who had appeared in *National Geographic* magazine; he relished the adulation of all the women as he slowly ambled down the train's aisles. The clacking of the wheels lulled us to sleep in our Pullman berths. We enjoyed a full English breakfast the next morning before pulling into the station in Mombasa.

Our favorite hotel, the Nyali Beach, was an idyllic setting in lush forested gardens. One afternoon, in our swimsuits and flip-flops, we explored the exposed seabed when the tide was out to discover the sea creatures trapped in small pools of water, and ogle the topless German tourists whose goal on holiday was to roast to a crisp. Grandmother Thelma and Gordy, who had never been to a topless beach before, were exceedingly entertained, especially as one very large woman startled Gene as he was drying his feet near a water tap. He raised his head just as she appeared right in front of him.

At the end of June, Thelma, Gordy, Suzanne and I flew to London and a week later flew on to America. Shortly after we left, Gene was awakened by the house guard running up the drive yelling. Thinking he was drunk, Gene reached for the call button to awaken John but fortunately also hit the alarm on the roof that brought the neighborhood vigilantes and their staffs descending on our house. Four men armed with bows and arrows were trying to steal the curtains from the transom windows in our sunroom. They escaped but the attempt showed how desperate poor people had become.

On August 1, after Gene had joined us in Oklahoma, a group of Kenya Air Force soldiers took over the Voice of Kenya radio station and announced a coup d'état. Although the effort was quickly put down, the rebels set off rockets from the forest behind our house, killing one neighbor. From that time forward, the government was on high alert as the rebels now possessed guns.

Patrick and Dana were married on August 5, 1982, at the First United Methodist Church in Stillwater, Oklahoma. The ceremony was conducted by two Southern Baptist ministers, Dana's mentors during her university days. The five attendants included their siblings. The Meadows family, our neighbors when we lived in the U.K., arrived from Paris and June Evans came from London. A joyful congregation of family and friends celebrated afterward in the Georgian Lounge at the OSU Student Union. When the couple appeared dressed for their departure, they were handcuffed together. Fearing that his friends were planning a shivaree to kidnap his bride, Patrick was taking no chances. He had arranged with Gene's cousin to fly them in his plane to Wichita, Kansas, where Patrick had stashed his car. They escaped, after a frantic race in Bill's car to the airport with revelers in pursuit.

Suzanne was as eager to join her siblings in America as we were sad to see her go. When Gene returned to Africa, she and I moved in with our friends Bill and Sue Montgomery in Tulsa. We shopped for a car and other things she needed for university. She entered Oklahoma State to study hotel and restaurant management, to which she subsequently added a second degree in accounting. The sadness of parting with her was cushioned for the time being when Lisa joined me to go to Kenya, escaping the frigid New England winter.

Angela Nesbitt enthusiastically welcomed Lisa's arrival. Both girls had been active in the Episcopal Church's Edgerton House at Dartmouth. We had met Angela the previous Christmas. She and Suzanne had become good friends and Lula, as she was known, quickly became an adopted daughter. She worked at the Commercial Bank of Kenya, where Lisa began a six-month internship. Lula's parents, Jim and Mary, both had Kikuyu mothers and British fathers. Jim, a physician, accepted us into his practice. Knowing the Nesbitts brought us deeper into the local community, making us feel more at home in Kenya. While in Nairobi, Lisa took night classes in Arabic at the cultural center operated by the governments of Kuwait and Saudi Arabia. She continued Arabic studies for the next seven years.

In the autumn Gene began to hear rumors of a possible merger between Cities Service and Occidental Petroleum (called "Oxy"). Cities Service Oil Company, founded in 1910 by Henry L. Doherty, was a family-friendly company that hired young engineers, trained them carefully, and expected to keep them for life. Doherty, a brilliant self-made man, left formal schooling at age twelve to go to work for Columbus (Ohio) Gas Company. By the age of twenty, he was their chief engineer and, over his lifetime, accumulated 130 patents for his inventions. By the age of thirty-five, he began to buy utility companies. Several located in Oklahoma produced oil, one with the evocative name of the Indian Territory Illuminating Oil Company. He consolidated his holdings under the name Cities Service. By 1982, leveraged buyouts were popular among predatory entrepreneurs. T. Boone Pickens was the "buyout king" who made a run on Cities Service without success. However, from that point forward, its sale seemed to be inevitable. When negotiations with Gulf Oil Company failed, Occidental began talks with Cities' top management.

With all three children at universities, Gene, now 50, was concerned that he might be forced into early retirement. Once we realized that by depleting our savings we would be able to pay their expenses, we tried to stay calm and await the outcome. In December, Suzanne and the Meadows family arrived for Christmas. Patrick and Dana did not join us; Cities Service's policy paid for the children's flights home for a maximum of four years, which Patrick now exceeded. We felt their absence keenly but decided that paying their fares for a short holiday trip was unwise with education bills looming. Aware that we might once more be moving, we treasured each day in this beautiful country.

In early 1983, without a drilling rig at his disposal, Gene was idling his days in the library reading the brief history of Kenya's search for oil. Cities Service had an oil platform in operation offshore in West Africa, not far from Lobito, Angola, about 120 miles south of its capital, Luanda. An international crew worked 28/28—twenty-eight days on the rig followed by twenty-eight days off. However, the manager had no leave unless the company could find a replacement, so Gene was asked to travel to Angola to relieve him for six weeks. When Gene arrived, he found the streets of the capital full of soldiers.

Cuban troops occupied the north of the country, supporting the Angolan socialist regime that was engaged in a raging civil war that had begun with independence in 1975. There was little active commerce in Luanda. Gene said he couldn't even buy a pencil or a piece of paper. All the supplies for the men, including food, were imported by air from Portugal. In spite of the unrest, oil production continued with little disruption. Once a week, Gene flew by helicopter from the office in Luanda to the rig and called us in Nairobi via satellite connection to an operator in Connecticut. On those low-flying trips, he saw huge stingrays fifteen feet in diameter, pods of dolphins, and bluefin tuna twelve feet long.

In February, Grandmother Thelma fell and fractured her hip. This was our first indication that she was aging. Fortunately, she recovered well. Suzanne made the dean's list for the first semester at Oklahoma State. She invited her roommate to come with her to Kenya in May. Of course, I began to plan a safari. Patrick was deep into his second year of vet school and Dana was reveling in her first teaching assignment at a country school in Sumner, Oklahoma, not far from Stillwater. She taught a class of bright and lively first and second graders.

Our cook John invited us to make a trip to Nakuru to meet his parents. With Lisa, Beatrice and me in back, Gene in front and John driving the Jaguar, we went north through lush barley farms and rolling hills. We passed several roadblocks on the way up and back due to rumors of another possible coup. John's parents came to the car to greet us when we pulled into their five-acre farm. They were formal but friendly. Their house was built of wood planks set on a painted concrete floor with a tin roof. It consisted of two bedrooms, a living-dining room and kitchen with a wood-fired cookstove. There was no electricity; kerosene lanterns hung from the ceilings. Water was carried from the river. There was a privy a good distance from the house. The living room had overstuffed furniture, festooned with antimacassars; family pictures and Christian plaques covered the walls. The windows had wood shutters on the inside with chicken-wire screens on the outside of a gauge so large they could only be there to discourage thieves. Everything was immaculately clean.

John's parents took us on a walking tour of their farm and neighborhood, introducing us to everyone along the way. Half of the land was planted with potatoes and kale. On the other half, John's father had built a long, low building with eight rooms. He had reserved two for married sons and families when they visited; the other six were rentals. On the farm were three milk cows, chickens and a turkey incubating a clutch of eggs. With Egerton College located nearby, the rooms were in great demand from families who accompanied their students to school. John's father had purchased another small plot on which he was building a second set of rentals. By African standards, John's parents were prosperous. His father, the ruling elder in his church, directed the construction of a large new church building. All of John's five brothers and two sisters graduated from college with the entire family contributing financially. The family also held fund-raising parties, *Harambees* (Kiswahili for pull together), to raise more money from extended family and friends.

John's mother had prepared a delicious lunch of boiled chicken, *irio* (a Kikuyu staple dish of mashed potatoes, corn and peas), fried cabbage, carrots, onions and chapatis. We had oranges and bananas for dessert. After lunch, we began our farewells. An hour later, we pulled away from the farm, the car loaded with one hundred pounds of potatoes and a trussed live chicken at my feet. This was a high honor because chicken was the most expensive meat available in Kenya. Our admiration of this principled, hard-working family continued to grow as it does to this day. They live their Christian faith in a humble, loving way, caring for themselves, their friends, and those less fortunate.

During a party at our home in May, Gene received a call from the States. After the party, as we were on our way upstairs to bed, he casually asked me, "How would you like to live in Aberdeen, Scotland?" When I replied that I would love it, he said, "Good, because they offered me an excellent position and I said yes!" While we wouldn't move until late summer, we began to think about the next stage of our lives with great relief.

This move was complicated because Occidental had a weight allowance for possessions. We sold and gave away some items. Other things, including our boudoir grand piano, were sent back to the U.S. for storage. When we announced our transfer, Elisabeth and Godfrey Dawkins, our friends and neighbors, asked John and Beatrice if they would work for them. John accepted their offer and worked as their cook for almost twenty years until he fulfilled his dream: Attending university at night, he graduated with a degree in theology. He became a full-time Africa Inland Mission pastor with a ministry for women and children in Nairobi's "Deep Sea" slum.

When Suzanne and her roommate arrived, we left on safari (absent Gene who was once again in Angola). Joined by Angela Nesbitt, three Dartmouth students in an environmental studies program and an Anglican priest friend of one of the students, we hit the usual spots, Treetops and Keekorok Lodge in the Maasai Mara. It was a terrific safari with excellent animal and bird viewing and jolly companions. It was also bittersweet because we expected it to be our last safari before we moved to Scotland. However, Suzanne and I had just said farewell to her friend when we were surprised and thrilled by an invitation to join Richard Leakey, son of the famous paleoanthropologists and archeologists Louis and Mary Leakey, at his camp in Northern Kenya with a party of about twenty.

At Koobi Fora on Lake Turkana, Richard had made significant discoveries of hominid remains. In Nairobi we boarded a DC-3, one of the reliable workhorse planes built in the 1930s and 1940s. We landed on a dry lake bed and transferred to an open flatbed truck with a roof to protect us from the blistering sun for the hour-and-a-half ride. As we bounced along the rutted road, we were entertained by the driver and guide, members of the Gabbra tribe. These nomads roamed this territory and were employed by Richard as guides and guards. About halfway to our destination, our driver stopped, got out, and conferred with the guide. He had spotted three armed men on horseback on a hill a mile away. Fearing bandits, he told us to put all of our valuables out of sight and remain quiet. As we anxiously watched them approach, they were indeed a fearsome-looking trio. The driver and guide spoke with them at length. Although it seemed like an hour, only a few minutes passed before they turned and slowly rode away. We were told that Richard had agreements with various elements in the area not to harass his guests.

At Koobi Fora, we were met by our genial host with cool water and fruit. Located right on the lake's edge, the main building was actually a large veranda decorated with colorful rugs, cushions and comfy deck chairs. A constant wind blew across the lake, moderating the extreme heat. Richard began his conversation with a strong warning. Although it was very hot and dry, he told us that, amazingly, we would not be thirsty but it was essential that we drink constantly. A few years before, he had lost both kidneys from dehydration and was alive only because of a kidney donation from one of his siblings. Since Lake Turkana was a saline lake, all the drinking water was trucked in to his camp. We would bathe in the lake, but he assured us we were in no danger from the lake's huge crocodiles because of the abundance of tilapia fish. Two animals that we did need to watch out for: the cobra and a large scorpion. Both were plentiful in the camp. I had begun to wonder at the wisdom of joining this outing when he assigned us our quarters. Similar to the building that John's father had built as rentals, there was a long stone building with individual rooms. The windows were just large holes in the walls so the wind was not impeded from keeping us cool at night. I noticed that some of the windows had heavy large-gauge wire over them, but the one Suzanne and I had did not. I asked Richard why. His answer was unsettling. He said that sometimes he brought families to the camp and that a pride of lions in the area would come into the camp if they heard children's voices.

Since Suzanne was so thrilled with this trip, I stifled my apprehensions and began to enjoy listening to Richard's fascinating stories and to relish the delicious meals his staff prepared. After dinner, we were invited to wash off our travel dust in the lake. I told Suzanne that we should enter the lake only when everyone went in and try to stay in the middle of the group. I worried that the crocodiles might decide to vary their diet. I also told her that once inside our room, we should use the plastic wash basin as our potty at night rather than venture out where the snakes and scorpions might be roaming, even though they could easily come in.

The next morning, we began our first trek to one of Richard's hominid sites. I discovered that, at forty-five, I was the oldest person in the group. As a fair blonde, I turned beet red with the exertion of walking in the heat but I felt just fine. However, Richard, who could lope like a gazelle back and forth from the front to the end of the strung-out line of walkers, appeared frequently at my side asking if I was okay. Would I like to stop and rest? I began to feel very old indeed but to my great relief made the trek without incident. By the end of the day of trekking, I slept like a baby even with the lions serenading us as we drifted off. Returning home on the third day, dirty and disheveled, we rejoiced that our last safari in Kenya had been such an unusual and memorable one.

Gene, Suzanne and I boarded a Kenya Airways flight for the first leg of our journey to America via the Far East. After almost three hours in the air, as we circled the Seychelles islands preparing to land, our pilot announced that the hydraulic system had failed and we would return to Nairobi. It was a very quiet flight back as we had three hours to consider our fate—and then we skidded to a stop against a fence at the end of the runway. Not allowed to enter the terminal but transferred immediately to a plane that was fueled, staffed and ready to go, we went back to the Seychelles, safely landed, and rented a Mini Moke (a vehicle resembling a golf cart) to drive around the lush, hilly island. We spent a blissful few days in this paradise, lounging on the sparkling white-powder beaches, snorkeling, touring the spectacularly beautiful island and eating at fabulous Creole-French restaurants. We stopped in Hong Kong and Taipei for a few days to visit friends and tour those fabulous cities.

Then we arrived at our principal destination. Gene had served in the Korean War in 1953 and wanted to visit the country thirty years later. He and his jeep driver during the war, Woo Bok Kee, had maintained their friendship. We flew to Seoul, changed planes, and landed at night in the port city of Pusan. While we were unloading our bags at the hotel, a man stepped out of the shadows and said, "Grogan?" Woo Bok Kee had come to Pusan to be sure everything was satisfactory and also to give us our itinerary for the next three days. The schedule was challenging, broken into fifteen-minute intervals, with almost no time to rest on this whirlwind tour. The next morning we took a bus to his city, Taegu.

Woo Bok Kee was a Christian in 1953, a time when Christians were stoned in the streets in Korea. After the war he had opened a bicycle shop, which Gene said was equivalent to being a Chevrolet dealer in the States. His family lived above the shop. With nine other successful Christian businessmen, he formed a group who pledged to build ten churches in the Buddhist villages around Taegu. They were working on number nine when we arrived. We toured the villages as well as two assembly plants owned by his friends; one built organs, the other television sets. One morning Woo Bok Kee collected us at the hotel at 4:00 a.m. We went to his church for a prayer meeting where we sat kneeling with our feet tucked under us for two hours listening to the fervent prayers of about twenty people. This was a daily ritual. At six thirty we left to eat breakfast and by eight o'clock, the men were in their shops at work. Through such dedication, Korean Christians followed Christ's example in their worship and sharing of God's love in their daily lives. It was no surprise to us that Christianity had spread like wildfire across Korea.

After visiting family in the U.S., Gene and I proceeded to Aberdeen, Scotland, where he started work immediately and I started house hunting. We bought a house and I returned to Nairobi to supervise the packing. John and Beatrice had everything in perfect order at home but told me that our cat, Zuli, had stopped eating two days before I arrived; she had terminal cancer and we tearfully said good-bye to the dear old girl.

When Gene arrived, several friends and organizations entertained us and it was with great sadness that we left such wonderful people and our easy life in Kenya. We were, nonetheless, grateful that our future seemed secure; the intervening months of uncertainty had given us time to reflect anew on the precarious nature of our material life and the enduring nature of love, trust, and support of family and friends. As we looked forward to Scotland, we felt a kinship with those we knew in Colombia and Kenya whose futures were more uncertain than ours had been. Their faith and optimism inspired us.

FAMILY ALBUM

Bride and groom: flanked by my parents Wilbur and Lucile, and Gene's mother, Thelma, in Lawton, Oklahoma, December 7, 1957

At war: Gene in Korea, 1953

Our honeymoon hideaway, 1958

Gene and Jan, Price Tower, Bartlesville, Oklahoma, 1958

Still at home in Garber, 1963: Gene, Patrick, Jan,
Grandma Southwick, Grandmother Thelma and Lisa

The children, in 1964: Patrick at five, Lisa, three, and Suzanne nearly one

On the beach: near Comodoro Rivadavia, Argentina, 1963,
Lisa, Jan and Patrick

A pumping unit, Texas,
1959

Argentina, 1963

In London, 1972: Lisa, Suzanne and Patrick

In Kenya, 1982: Suzanne, Patrick and Lisa

Above, Scottish ships; Christening
the *British Amethyst*

Right, Jan aboard the schooner
Malcolm Miller

Opposite, Gene and Jan
in Scotland, 1984

Suzanne and Jay, 1994

Lisa and Jim, 1990

Patrick and Dana, 1982

Lisa and Jim Sams with James and Claire, 2001

Suzanne and Jay Lipscomb with Lisa, Maggie and Will, 2005

Three generations of Eagle Scouts: Patrick, Michael,
Clay and Gene Grogan, Tulsa, 2003

Dancing with mom, 1994

Gene and Jan on our 50th anniversary in Costa Rica, 2007

Together: Jan and Gene at Copper Ridge,
Gene's last residence, in 2013

Jim and Lisa, Patrick and Dana, Suzanne and Jay in 2005

Nana and grandchildren in 2013: Courtney and Clay Grogan,
James Sams, Nana, Michael Grogan, Will Lipscomb,
Claire Sams, Lisa and Maggie Lipscomb

Ten

BONNY SCOTLAND
AND A WEE DRAM

Aberdeen
September 1983 / December 1984

GENE AND I WERE unusually quiet as we boarded the plane for Scotland. Although we were grateful that he had a job, we were leaving the perfect weather of friendly, exotic Kenya for cold, wet Scotland. We had been happy in Kenya. We believed that we had contributed positively to the lives of others and we were continually inspired and challenged by the faith-filled lives of our friends. However, the last year in Kenya, Gene had been bored and frustrated not being able to drill the second well. I sometimes fretted about being so far from the children, especially when both Lisa and Suzanne had bouts of illness.

Our mood was not lifted upon arrival when no one met us at the airport. In the dark we collected a rental car and drove to the flat that Oxy provided. When we began to unload our bags, we were surprised to be greeted by a cheery Aberdonian. We had heard that the locals were dour and chary of strangers—most everyone south of Edinburgh. This gentleman carried the bags upstairs with Gene, offered to help us get settled and invited us to visit him and his wife next door. That encounter made us feel a bit better, but I was already apprehensive about how Gene would be accepted into the Oxy community.

With two thousand Occidental employees in the Scottish region, Gene was the first former Cities Service employee, and many must have wondered why he was brought in as engineering/safety manager when there were capable Oxy men in place for promotion to that high position. Fortunately, Americans Joe Snape, the general manager, and Dan McReynolds, the production manager, welcomed him warmly. I hoped the other employees would follow their example.

The next morning, Gene called from the office to tell me that Margery, the wife of Jim Farquharson, the human resources manager, was coming to take me out. I opened the door to a smiling petite, blonde Aberdonian who charmed me with her lovely accent and friendliness. Only much later, when we had become close friends, did she reveal the fear and trepidation she felt when Jim gave her the assignment of entertaining the new American. She drove me around the city pointing out with pride the major landmarks as well as important shops for food and other essentials.

This area was settled over eight thousand years ago, a fact confirmed by remains of prehistoric villages that were found on the banks of both the Don and Dee rivers that bordered Old Aberdeen. The city received royal "burgh" status from Scottish King David in the twelfth century. In 1319, Robert the Bruce issued the Great Charter that transformed Aberdeen into a property-owning, financially independent community. From that time forward, in spite of wars that left the city sacked and burned numerous times as well as devastation from plagues, Aberdeen grew in population and wealth. Before the discovery of oil in the North Sea in the 1970s, the city thrived on fishing, timber, shipbuilding, textile mills and paper making. By the time we arrived, most Aberdonians had decided that the oil industry was good for the city.

The terraced house we had purchased was located on Gladstone Place, a pleasant, wide street in the heart of town. Constructed shortly after the turn of the twentieth century, built of large hand-hewn granite blocks from the quarry nearby, it was twenty-one feet wide and three stories tall with a slate roof. Most of our neighbors had lived there for thirty years or more. The houses had double entries, with a small vestibule between them where one could get some relief from the wind. The doors were bordered by stained-glass windows on the sides and top, the design paired with the house next door. Our house, however, had been modernized in the 1950s to let in more light, so one of my first jobs was to find a stained-glass artisan to copy the design of my neighbor and restore our house to its original glory.

A week after we arrived, Lisa flew in from Hanover, again escaping the New Hampshire winter. Although Aberdeen, at fifty-seven-degrees north latitude, was fourteen degrees higher than Hanover, it was tempered by the Gulf Stream. We discovered that in spite of the bitterly cold wind, the well-built home was warm and cozy compared to our former London flat.

Lisa was a boon companion; she helped me buy a car and locate contractors for renovations to the house. At the University of Aberdeen she found a Palestinian woman professor who agreed to give her private instruction in Arabic twice a week, ending each session to Lisa's delight with a belly-dancing lesson.

We remained in the flat for two months while the contractors installed a beautiful new kitchen, new floors downstairs, an antique marble fireplace to replace the modern one in the dining room, and a shower in the original coal cellar behind the kitchen. The workmen, a cheerful bunch, were eager to introduce us to local habits and customs. Aberdonians speak an English dialect known as Doric. When they talked to each other, we rarely understood a word. One morning, one of them said, "I'm going out for *rowies*. Do you and Lisa want one?" When I responded with a blank look, he laughed and assured me that we needed to try them. He returned with hot pastries that literally dripped with butter. They were delicious, but it didn't take long to understand why the Scots have the world's highest rate of heart disease. Their diet and penchant for smoking were a deadly combination. Counting on Scotch whisky to "clear their pipes" obviously didn't work.

Shortly before American Thanksgiving, we moved into the house; our young friends Mike Colby, one of the Dartmouth students we met in Kenya, and Angela Nesbitt arrived to spend the holiday with us. They were quickly put to work unpacking boxes. The first piece of mail put through our mail slot was an invitation from the neighbors next door, Daphne and Michael Boyle, to join them for Hogmanay, the Scottish New Year's celebration. They also invited us in for "a wee dram," the Scottish version being a tumbler full of Scotch straight up, no ice or water. We were expected not to be wasteful but to drink it all. We met the Boyle children—Maureen,

John and wee Michael—who were near in age to our children. Again, we were amazed at the friendliness and hospitality we received.

We began visiting churches within walking distance of our house. Arriving at Rubislaw Church between services, we were greeted by a smiling woman who was tidying the sanctuary. She walked us down the street one block to the Church Centre, served us coffee, and introduced us to various members who were enjoying a social hour. We were beginning to understand that the dour reputation of the Scots was undeserved—unless one was English! One older couple, George and Jessie McLennan, quickly became friends, which was quite surprising when we later learned from George that he had a strong antipathy toward Americans. He had been a prisoner of war in Germany during World War II. His camp was liberated by American soldiers at the end of the war and then abandoned when they heard a troop of German SS soldiers approaching. Although George and his fellow prisoners escaped by hiding in a barn he found it difficult to forgive the Americans for fleeing and leaving them defenseless.

Suzanne arrived for the holidays, joined by Angela Nesbitt's brother, Sidney, who was a student at Trinity College in Dublin, and a friend of his who was also not making the long journey to Africa. We attended a service on Christmas Eve. I had asked one of the church elders if the midnight service would be a candlelight service. He hesitated and then without elaboration gave me a very cautious, "No." I did not query him further. When we walked through the door, the reason became evident. The sanctuary smelled like the inside of a brewery. One match would have blown the roof. As the pub across the street closed just when the service was beginning, the balcony overflowed with inebriated young people. However, stern looks from the pastor kept them quiet and ushers carefully removed those who passed out.

Our first indication that this New Year's celebration would be vastly different from ones we had experienced elsewhere came when Lisa called to reconfirm her trip home. She had booked her flight on January 1, but was informed that no flights left on that day because all Scottish airports would be closed. On New Year's Eve we ate a large family meal, fortifying ourselves for the beginning of "first-footing" festivities at midnight. Just after twelve o'clock, we stood outside the Boyles' door with Gene in the lead, because tall, dark-haired men were favored as "first-footers." Blonds were considered to bring bad luck. He had a lump of coal in his hand indicating his wish that the Boyles' hearth would be warm all year. Their house soon filled to capacity with friends from our street and surrounding areas. After much drinking and eating and being hugged and kissed by everyone, we formed a large ring, held our neighbors' hands, and sang the many verses of "Auld Lang Syne." Thus began a parade from one house to another with more Scotch offered at each home. Around 4:00 a.m., we arrived at a house where they served most welcome steaming bowls of soup. At that point, Gene and I said goodnight, with our new friends teasing us for being wimps; our gang swept up with the Boyles children and their friends, arriving home near dawn. Most of the men went to play golf at the Royal Aberdeen Golf Club at 8:00 a.m. They napped in the afternoon; by night, the process of first-footing began again. Often the festivities continued for several nights, until every friend had been visited. For years after we left

Scotland, the Boyles called us on New Year's Eve, in the midst of the revelry, and wished us Happy New Year followed by Michael Boyle singing "The Northern Lights of Old Aberdeen" and his hometown song, "The Song of the Clyde."

Our introduction to life in Aberdeen had gone better than we expected. However, we once more moved home for ourselves and our children. When asked, "Where are you from?" they had difficulty answering, responding with, "At what time in my life do you mean?" The move to Scotland was our thirteenth since we married in 1957. Fortunately, the effect of this transient life bound our family closer every year and gave us the confidence to face whatever we individually encountered, knowing we always had strong family support.

In early January of 1984, we experienced our first Aberdeen blizzard. When I casually tossed a dry pine branch onto the coal fire, a noise like a jet engine filled the room and fiery chunks of coal dust began falling on the hearth with sparks flying onto the carpet. Because power and telephone lines were downed in the high winds, we were unable to call for help. We ran between the kitchen and living room with pails of water. Our neighbors told us we had "lummed out" (*lum* was Scottish for chimney). Graciously, they didn't accuse us of trying to burn down the neighborhood.

After advertising for a housekeeper, I interviewed Betty Hardie, a small, assertive woman who began our conversation by telling me all the things that she would not do; she would not wash windows, nor iron, nor cook. It seemed that I was the one being interviewed.

Desperate for help after being thoroughly pampered in Kenya, I hired her anyway. It was the best decision I could have made. She was dependable, thorough, and taught me the mores of the lively Scottish working class. She had an apt Doric saying for every event of life, greeting me with *Fit like?* (How are you?), to which the proper answer was the understated *Chavvin* (I'm doing okay). Other favorites of hers were: *Ne'er cast yer clout ere May be oot* (Never take off your coat until May is over) and *There's noutt sa queer as fawk* (There is nothing as strange as folk).

Scottish hospitality ran deep. Daphne Boyle hosted a coffee morning for me in January that started at ten o'clock. She served delicious home-baked treats with the coffee, bringing each offering to us individually, hot from the oven. Amid much laughter, the social-izing continued into the afternoon. I was beginning to think that, as the honoree, perhaps I was supposed to leave first and was just about to stand up when Daphne produced the sherry bottle and glasses. This was nothing like a coffee morning "down south." We parted around two o'clock, well filled and, perhaps, a bit tipsy.

The neighbors seemed to entertain constantly. We were delighted to be included in all of their festivities as if we had lived there for thirty years. We reciprocated serving buffet style, definitely not up to the Scottish standard, but they seemed to adjust gracefully to American ways. Gene redeemed us a bit by always jumping forward to light the ladies' cigarettes, a courtesy not generally extended by their husbands. They loved and teased him. We were soon being introduced to our new friends' friends, such as Sir Maitland Mackie and his charming and outspoken American wife, Polly. Mike, a dairy farmer and widower, had met her when he was on a cattle-buying trip to the U.S. He was head of the family-owned Mackie's of Scotland ice cream company, as well as chairman of the Milk Marketing Board. Polly, a rancher and every inch a Texan, must have been a shock to his Scottish friends, but she soon won them over with her devotion to Mike and winning personality. They became great friends of ours. Queen Elizabeth II had chosen Mike to be Lord-Lieutenant of Aberdeenshire, her representative in our area; she knighted him for his services to the crown and for his many civic and philanthropic activities.

During our years in Aberdeen, we were invited to several weddings where we took part in ceilidhs (pronounced kay-lees), which are similar to American square dances but much more boisterous. One reel, "The Dashing White Sargent," was performed at terrifying speed. Our friends never missed a beat and just grabbed our hands and tossed us from place to place in the dance.

We joined a Bible study group at Rubislaw Church that met weekly in homes. We became close friends with this small group of about ten people. Scott Hutchison, our pastor, was an indomitable man who had contracted polio while at university, which left this great athlete on crutches for life. At six-foot-four, with the powerful upper-body strength necessary to lift his weight, including heavy metal leg braces, he was an eloquent spokesman for the disabled in Britain. Gene and I were invited to become elders and were inducted to serve on the church session (governing board), a lifetime position. As elders, we each had districts of approximately ten homes where we visited quarterly to inquire about the health of the members and see if they had needs that the church could address. In this patriarchal society, women elders were an anomaly but the Scots in my district accepted me into their homes and served me tea. An elderly woman in Gene's district read him passages by Robert Burns, laughed uproariously when he did not understand a word, and relished translating them for him. As a lonely shut-in, she eagerly looked forward to his visits.

Aberdeen was a handsome city with remarkable ancient sites, museums and theaters, but the Scots were truly passionate about their mountains, hills and glens, fleeing the confines of civilization at every opportunity. Hill walking was possibly the most popular sport in Scotland. While it sounded rather tame, nothing could be further from the truth. The trails were narrow with precipitous drops. When a sudden fog reduced visibility to the end of one's nose, it wasn't unusual for fatal falls to occur. This fact never deterred our friends, who seemed to be renewed physically and spiritually from their sojourns in their spectacular countryside. Gene and I found glen walking more to our liking although it was really considered more an activity for old people with their "sticks" (canes).

Aberdonians' wry humor exposed the truth of their climate, such as, "I missed summer this year because I was in the loo." Of the six years we lived in Aberdeen, we had only two summers when it was possible to sit comfortably out in the garden. Some years, the rain was so unrelenting that the swollen rosebuds never opened, and fell rotten on the ground. Due to the cold, bedding plants were not put in until the middle of June. Because of the long days, they soon caught up in size to blooms of those "down south," with the city of Aberdeen winning the *Britain in Bloom* contest many times. There were some days when the sun seemed not to set at all. Golfers were able to play through the night due to the twilight conditions. The sun shone brightly until 10:00 p.m. and rose around 3:30 a.m., so I bought curtains with blackout linings for us to be able to sleep.

In winter, the wind off the North Sea was strong and penetrating. The shortest days provided only seven hours of light and often the sky was overcast and forbidding. People got grumpy. Many escaped to the tropics for respite. We were relieved when the days began to lengthen in late February. One delight during the dark winter was the astonishing display of the aurora borealis, the northern lights. By March Aberdeen was clothed in yellow with millions of daffodils planted on every inch of public ground from the parks and verges along the streets to the hills that flanked the highways out of town.

The Grampian region of northeast Scotland was dotted with castles, some dating from the eleventh century and many of which had been owned by the same families for hundreds of years. We were delighted when our American friends Bob and Ann Cooper, whom we had first met in London, invited us to stay in a castle leased by Bob's employer, Dowell Schlumberger. A meticulously restored tall, round stone edifice, it had slits for light as well as for slinging hot oil and shooting arrows at invaders. A steep circular stairway hugged the inside of the outer wall with rooms on each of several levels and a kitchen on the bottom floor. Amenities, such as bathrooms, kitchen appliances and heating installed under the stone floors, had been added, but the realities of what it was originally greatly dampened the fairy-tale idea of living in a castle.

Eagerly anticipating Patrick's graduation at Oklahoma State with his degree in veterinary medicine and Lisa's graduation from Dartmouth College with a bachelor's degree in government, I flew to Oklahoma in April, stopping as I frequently did to visit my cousin Marilyn Stephens Bailey in Washington, D.C. The daughter of my mother's beloved younger sister, Maudalee, and her husband, Roy Stephens, Marilyn was like a sister to me. During those visits, I fell in love with the beauty and graciousness of Washington.

Gene arrived just in time for Patrick's graduation. We were proud of Patrick, who had completed his education in a record six years. He had been offered a job in an outstanding practice in Tulsa, the Woodland Animal Veterinary Hospital, having spent his internship there earlier in the year. From Oklahoma, Patrick, Dana, Suzanne, Grandmother Thelma, Gene and I flew into Boston and drove to New Hampshire for Lisa's graduation. Lisa planned to attend law school but she decided to take a gap year before continuing her education.

From Boston, the seven of us flew to Britain. We were especially grateful that we would have several weeks together as it took a least at week before we were completely comfortable with each other. The children had to adjust to being with their parents after years of independence as we moved from the parent-child relationship toward a more equal adult one. It was easy to fall back into old habits like, "It's very cold. Aren't you going to wear a hat?" Such comments, initially met with vexation, quickly morphed into laughter. Although the children had been abruptly ejected from the family nest when they began their studies in the States, we had been pleased to watch them handle their new freedom responsibly. Communicating by post was frustratingly slow; in their letters, they did not share any difficulties they might be experiencing and we rarely spoke by phone because of the expense. We gave them lump sums for each semester plus a credit card in case of emergencies. We were thankful that Patrick and Suzanne had Grandmother Thelma close by and Lisa was blessed to have Fred and Jean Siefke, her friend Madeline's parents, who accepted her like another daughter, inviting her home for every holiday. However, being separated from them for months at a time was a heartache that made our times together precious.

Patrick and Dana returned to Tulsa in July to start their new lives. They bought a small house, acquired Barney the dog and Tattoo the cat, and joined John Calvin Presbyterian Church. Dana had thoroughly enjoyed teaching while Patrick completed his training, but she did not look for a teaching position in Tulsa as they planned to start a family.

When Lisa returned from Scotland, she settled in Tulsa and went to work on the campaign of Frank Keating, a Republican running for Congress. Although she enjoyed being in town with her siblings, working closely on a political campaign was disillusioning. She eventually returned to Hanover and worked for a publishing firm while she awaited law school responses.

In the fall, Mati Snape and I were invited to christen two new ships for use in the oil industry. We arrived at the Aberdeen Harbour jetty on a sparkling, clear day. We had been warned that it was bad luck if the bottle didn't break when it hit the ship's hull on the first try. Mati successfully christened her ship. Following her lead, I swung the bottle with all my might, relieved when it smashed the side of the new *British Viking*. The crew cheered their approval from high on the upper deck. We then climbed aboard to enjoy a champagne feast. Our photo made the front page of the *Aberdeen Press and Journal* the next day.

We had a full house for Christmas. In addition to our girls, Lisa brought a friend from school and Angela Nesbitt's brothers, Sid and Nik, joined us. This year we began Hogmanay by first-footing the McLennans. We arrived as the clock struck midnight in order to be present to hear George serenade Jessie with his bagpipes, beginning at the bottom of their garden and working his way slowly to the back door. He was rewarded with a tumbler of whisky followed by fruit-cake, an annual ritual for this pair of elderly lovebirds. We ended 1984 grateful for our family and friends, excited by Patrick and Dana's news of the expected arrival in June of our first grandchild, and feeling very much at home in Scotland.

Eleven

WARMTH IN THE COLD

Aberdeen
January 1985 / December 1986

DURING OUR YEARS in London, Gene was occasionally invited to
go bird shooting, a sport at which he excelled and one he enjoyed
immensely. Wives were sometimes included and entertained with
sightseeing or shopping outings. We were never invited to shoot. At
large country estates, the accommodations were luxurious, the food
sumptuous and the service impeccable. On driven shoots, beaters (men
with dogs) drove the pheasants through a wood with the shooters
poised on the far side to blast away as soon as the birds were flushed.
In Scotland Gene purchased the proper attire: plus fours (knee-length
trousers), long wool socks and shooting gloves; but he balked at the
tweed jacket and tie, opting instead for the warmth of his heavy sheep-
skin coat. His favorite outings, however, requiring no fancy garb, were
Saturdays spent with his friend Norman Calder, a retired physician,
rough shooting on a farm west of Aberdeen. They would tramp through
the woods and fields enjoying being outdoors with Norman's faithful
black Labrador retriever, Kate, flushing the game. After a long afternoon in the cold and wet, tired and happy, they would retire to the

farmer's house for rusty nails, a warming combination of whisky and Drambuie liqueur. They each brought home a brace of pheasants (a cock and hen) and, sometimes, hare or grouse, leaving the remainder of their birds for the farmer to sell. I took the game to a poulterer in George Street for cleaning and freezing. In later years, after I became suspicious that I was receiving older game instead of what I had brought in, our housekeeper Betty Hardie's cousin, a recently retired gamekeeper, was happy for the job of cleaning Gene's kill.

Norman's wife, Barbara, who was English, became one of my closest friends. Her father had been an eminent obstetrician and gynecologist to the aristocracy. A keen sailor who taught Ba to sail, he was part of the flotilla that rescued the British army from the French coast following the disastrous Battle of Dunkirk. As a young mother, Ba passed the tests to become a ship's captain and navigator. In 1967 she became the captain of the *Malcolm Miller*, a tall ship with an all-female crew. She took me on a tour of this vessel when it visited Aberdeen. Ba had multiple sclerosis but didn't want people to know. She said it wouldn't have been good for a doctor's business to have an ailing wife. She pushed a bicycle around the west end of Aberdeen, collecting her shopping in a basket, but never actually rode it. A devotee of the Psalms and a woman of strong faith, she possessed an infectious sense of humor. In addition to our faith, we shared a love of history.

In March 1985 my friend Ann Cooper arrived home from the Mayo Clinic, where she had gone for routine surgery. Five days after her first operation she had been rushed back into surgery again. Her return was bittersweet because of her frailty. Thus began several months when her family and local friends put faith and friendship into action to help her recover. By September, she was ready to celebrate. Her mother-in-law flew to Aberdeen from the States. With a friend from London, we four drove to the west coast of Scotland where we island-hopped by ferry to Iona.

A small island near the town of Oban, Iona had been a center of Christian worship since the monk Saint Columba and twelve companions fled there from Ireland in the year 563. This community played a crucial role in the conversion of the Picts of Scotland and the Anglo-Saxons of Northumbria. Iona became an even more prominent Christian center in the ninth century when the Kingdom of Alba was formed. We visited ruins of Benedictine and Augustine nunneries founded during that period. In the stillness, broken only by the wind and calls of gulls flying overhead, we spoke softly as if we were in church. In this famed center of learning and art, the Celtic cross was first designed and made, and several examples of the tall stone symbols remained on the island. Iona Abbey, begun during the thirteenth century, was still supported by a strong Christian community. In 1549 a burial inventory was made of the cemetery at the abbey that listed forty-eight Scottish kings, eight Norwegian kings and four Irish kings. We could have stayed at the abbey, but decided that a local hotel would be warmer and more comfortable. We had our meals there, and followed the tradition of helping with meal preparation and cleanup. Automobiles are not allowed on Iona and hiking over the rugged terrain was one of the delights of being there. Guided walks were led by members of the abbey staff with time for prayer, devotional recitation and scripture reading. During our visit to Iona, we were deeply moved by the fact that our dear friend had survived her ordeal with cancer and thanked God for this miracle in our midst. We experienced such peace on Iona as well as a connection to the countless Christians who had lived and worshipped on this small dot of land.

In May, Gene and I flew to Zurich, then drove to Liechtenstein and to Innsbruck, Austria, before turning south into Italy. In Bressanone, we stayed at the Hotel Elephant, famous as the inn where Hannibal had stabled one of his war elephants when he crossed the Alps in 218 BCE. Years later, a local artist, who had never actually seen an elephant, painted a mural of one on the side of the hotel to commemorate the story. His elephant with a very long tail and a very short trunk was the farcical result.

We headed to Venice where we spent three blissful days and nights touring this treasure, mostly by foot. Our final stop was Lucerne. We arrived in the early afternoon, found a charming old hotel, and spent the rest of the day walking the famous bridges over the Reuss River. Dating from 1333, they were painted with dramatic scenes of the city's history, including grotesque pictures of plague victims.

As we traveled through Europe, our thoughts strayed to the States, where our grandbaby was due soon. When Gene stopped to buy petrol for the car, I approached passersby and asked, "Could you please direct me to the central telephone exchange?" Frustrated by the common response, "No English," I finally resorted to Spanish and was pleasantly surprised to discover in their eyes and smiles the light of understanding. The next hurdle was to understand the directions in Italian. Fortunately, with the similarity in languages and reconfirmation by me in Spanish, we were able to find these handy places where we could talk as long as we pleased and pay at the end.

Michael James appeared on the fourth of June. Patrick had taken time off following his birth so I did not have to arrive until June 17 to begin my duties. I reveled in my new role and chose the name Nana, the most common title in Scotland for grandmother. Granddad Gene made a quick trip over to meet his new grandson.

Lisa had received three acceptances to excellent law schools after Christmas. Duke's new double degree program appealed to her. By starting classes in June rather than September, and taking extra courses during her three years there, she could graduate with a master of laws in international and foreign law (LLM) as well as the juris doctor degree (JD).

Suzanne was attending summer school in Stillwater. Her two degrees, in hotel and restaurant management and accounting, required five years plus one summer session to complete. After summer school, she visited us in Scotland and helped entertain foreign guests.

While this hectic life kept me quite busy, I still felt lonely without the children around. I had mentioned to Gene that I would like to return to university someday. At the University of Oklahoma I had completed the course work for a bachelor of science degree in medical technology but had never completed the laboratory internship.

The University of Aberdeen, founded in 1495, the fifth-oldest university in the English-speaking world, was renowned for its high academic standards and superb research facilities. Its biblical motto was: "The fear of the Lord is the beginning of wisdom." In 1983, the university began to accept mature students, characterized as anyone over twenty-five, and Gene urged me to take advantage of this opportunity. In September, I was accepted as a part-time student taking a course in early modern history. Several of us mature students became friends: Scots Margery Farquharson and Sally Ann Mathieson, Dutch national Hanna Andriesse, American Marilyn Brumfield and I formed a close-knit support group.

Becoming a student again after almost thirty years was challenging, especially since I had never written an essay, an exercise every British child learned in primary school. Also, the essay exams held in June that determined whether one passed or failed were terrifying to contemplate. Walking the campus with books in my arms, having coffees with my friends and soaking up the interesting lectures made me feel like a teenager again. Gene patiently helped me with my writing and did not complain about the quick meals or hours spent studying. He was genuinely interested in what I was learning. Essays that I printed on our first home computer made a good impression on my professors. Concerned that he might be transferred before I graduated, Gene encouraged me to become a full-time student the next year.

Amy Kennedy, a venerable member of Rubislaw Church, died in early December. Nearly one hundred, she had suffered terribly with crippling arthritis that bent her legs so that she could barely walk. But she never missed a service, attended the weekly Bible study, and always had a smile and hug for everyone she met. She had been married to a university professor and had hosted many students for tea in their home. She rolled bandages for the Red Cross during the wars, but said she had never accomplished anything considered significant. All the same, several hundred people packed the large sanctuary on a cold, dark, wet day to pay tribute to her. It was a demonstration to all of us that living a simple life filled with love and service to others was more important than attaining great fame or fortune. Of the many people we knew over the years, she remains a shining example to me of an exemplary human being.

Suzanne and Lisa arrived for the holidays, joining us for the annual, non-candlelit, midnight Christmas Eve service at Rubislaw Church. This year, we decided to begin our Hogmanay celebration by viewing a ritual that had been resurrected at the turn of the century but had its roots in ancient pagan worship, supposed to ward off evil for the coming year. In the coastal village of Stonehaven, strong men paraded up and down the High Street of the Old Town from the ancient Mercat Cross, where weekly markets were held, to the harbor, swinging heavy burning tar balls over their heads. The tar was encased in mesh with a chain and handle attached. It took great strength for the men, and courage for the spectators, as chunks of the burning tar sometimes flew off into the crowd. After about an hour the men, exhausted from the effort, flung the nearly consumed balls into the sea, which caused a loud hissing sound as they hit the icy water accompanied by the cheers from the crowd. We returned to Aberdeen to first-foot our friends, grateful for the blessing of living among the Scots and being accepted so completely into their community.

Burns Night suppers are an annual event wherever Scots reside. Held on or near Robert Burns's birthday, January 25, the meal is a dignified black-tie occasion with much humor and, of course, heavy consumption of Scotch whisky. Our host welcomed us and led us, standing, in the Selkirk Grace, a popular blessing given at many dinners:

Some hae meat and canna eat,
And some wad eat that want it;
But we hae meat, and we can eat,
And sae let the Lord be thanket.

We remained standing as a piper piped in a huge haggis carried aloft by the chef on a heavy silver platter, accompanied by much approbation by the guests. The "Address to a Haggis," a poem by Robbie Burns, recited by a man well versed in the dialect, was followed by many toasts. We were served ample helpings of haggis (a mixture of offal, suet, oatmeal and seasonings encased in a sheep's stomach), tatties (mashed potatoes) and neeps (mashed swede turnips) washed down with more whisky. After a dessert of sticky toffee pudding, we settled down for a long night of speeches and poetry readings, each ending with another toast. These recitations can be serious or light. However, the "Toast to the Lassies" is invariably hilarious, answered by a woman giving a "Toast to the Laddies" in the same vein. At the end of the evening, a designated guest expressed our thanks to the host and we joined hands to sing "Auld Lang Syne."

The Berkeleys and the Wintours became some of our closest friends. Physicians John and Muriel Berkeley had served for years as missionaries in the Himalayan Kingdom of Bhutan and also in Yemen on the Arabian Peninsula. In Aberdeen, John was in charge of geriatric services for the Grampian region, a large area of northeastern Scotland, which included a hospice facility called Roxburghe House. Muriel was a pediatrician and professor. David and Joyce Wintour were also in the medical profession. David had a family practice and served the oil industry as a doctor specializing in treating emergencies of offshore divers. Joyce was a nurse psychologist. They were in our Bible study/prayer group and also elders at Rubislaw Church. We served on various committees together. Both families inspired Gene and me with the strong faith that they practiced daily in their commitment to God and their fellow man.

In fact, everywhere we lived we found people who shared our faith in God. To us the Bible was a living document. We learned through its stories how to love extravagantly—even those people whom we might normally have considered our enemies. We learned that no one was outside of God's loving embrace and should not be outside of ours. Sometimes behaviors masked our common humanity but with time and patience we could find good in every person.

In March, Gene and I met our friends Fred and Jean Siefke in Yorkshire on their annual visit to Britain. We stayed in the Black Swan Inn in Helmsley near the medieval walled cathedral city of York, where archaeological evidence attested to human habitation by the eighth millennium BCE. York became a major trading city on the navigable River Ouse for the import of goods from Europe and the export of raw materials such as wool, timber and grain. The Great North Road, originally built by the Romans, facilitated commerce to other parts of the island.

York had a turbulent history, invaded and conquered many times. Many of the ancient sites had been excavated, making it a major tourist attraction in the north of England. The wall around the city, which we walked in spite of the cold, wet weather, sat above the original Roman wall, and York Minster, the eleventh-century cathedral, was built on top of ruins that probably dated from 180 when Christian missionaries from Rome arrived. From the fourth century onward churches were built on that site.

In April we flew to Istanbul, where we began a two-week coach tour of western Turkey seeing places that the Apostle Paul visited on his trips to Asia Minor. Of the thirty people on our tour, Leo and Norrie Murphy from Canberra, Australia, became great sightseeing companions and longtime friends. The Topkapi Palace was built by Mehmet the Conqueror after he had led the Ottoman Turks to conquer Constantinople in 1453, ending the four-hundred-year spread of the Byzantine Empire. The Ottomans amassed immense territory and incredible riches, such as a throne of pure gold that weighed 550 pounds and the Topkapi dagger decorated with diamonds and emeralds the size of golf balls. Hagia Sophia's Cathedral, completed during the reign of the Christian Roman emperor Justinian in the sixth century, was a huge domed edifice without interior supporting pillars, a masterpiece of engineering for its time. We marveled at the interior of the Blue Mosque, whose walls were decorated with over twenty thousand blue Izmik tiles.

As we strolled through the ancient ruins of Troy, located on a bluff overlooking the Dardanelles (Hellespont, as this strait was known in antiquity), we were warned by our guide not to pick up any pottery shards or ancient coins as this was punishable by incarceration in the notoriously grim Turkish prisons. One day we were approached by a man on horseback holding out a handful of coins for sale. We quickly waved him away, concerned that we would be in danger of arrest even being seen with him.

The first Christian site of our tour, the ancient ruins of the Basilica of St. John, located near the city of Selçuk, was also built during Justinian's reign. It replaced an earlier church where it was believed that the Apostle John was buried. According to legend John had fled Galilee with Jesus's mother, Mary, following the crucifixion and settled near the bustling city of Ephesus. We visited Mary's House, a modest stone structure with a healing spring, carefully tended by an order of nuns. At the basilica, we met a group of teenage Turkish schoolgirls on an outing. They were singing and dancing and invited us to join them, which we did. We were frequently approached by young people eager to practice their English.

Walking up the steep ancient thoroughfare into Ephesus gave us the same awesome view that visitors must have had in the first century. A settlement dating from the Bronze Age, it became a rich, sophisticated port city under the Greeks and Romans. The library, now carefully restored, had been one of the great repositories of learning in the world. From Kusadasi, we turned east toward Cappadocia (the ancient kingdom of Phrygia), driving up the Meander River valley through an Eden of flowering fruit trees on both sides of the river.

In the evenings a group of us would leave our hotel in search of a local restaurant, where invariably we would be greeted warmly by the staff and other patrons. Turkish food revolved around fish, fresh vegetables, fruits and local wine. The food was simply prepared and delicious. The cost of meals was so reasonable as to be embarrassing. Turkish hospitality made us feel exceedingly welcome in their country.

At Hierapolis (Pamukkale), we swam after dinner in the natural pool fed by 118-degree calcium-loaded springs that flowed over the edge of a cliff down into a deep ravine. The calcium formations of rippling white cascades sparkled in the light of a full moon. Over the centuries this area had been controlled by Hittites, Lydians, Persians, Greeks and Romans. By the twelfth century CE, Anatolian Seljuks controlled the region that later became part of the Ottoman Empire until the modern state of Turkey was born when Mustafa Kemal Ataturk led an uprising that resulted in Turkish independence in 1923. Cappadocia was famous for the impressive rock formations made of tufa, a type of soft volcanic rock that was subject to wind erosion. The pillars and minaret-like forms were natural but people also carved into them to make houses, churches and monasteries. In the town of Göreme, dating from the Roman period, people occupied some of these houses until the 1950s when the Turkish government evicted them because of the danger of collapse. Some chapels remained, decorated with beautiful frescoes still bright due to the arid climate.

Kaymakli was one of over two hundred underground cities that were begun three to four thousand years ago but were last occupied by Christians in the first century to escape persecution from the Romans and later the Ottomans. Some of them were four levels deep and protected by a maze of narrow tunnels, air vents and huge stones levered over the entrances. As many as fifteen thousand people lived down there. The crude electrical system, installed for tourism, failed twice while we were underground. Our guide carried a flashlight and gave one to Gene as we were at the end of the single-file line. We could stand up in the rooms but in several places we had to crawl through the claustrophobic tunnels.

The city of Konya, known as the religious center of Turkey, was a fitting final destination, site of the tomb of the founder of the Sufi sect of Islam, Jalal al Din Muhammad Rumi, a Persian poet known as Mevlâna. The Sufis, commonly called the Whirling Dervishes, are reputed to be the most spiritual Muslims. They took a vow of poverty and performed a meditative ceremony to induce ecstasy called the *sama*. We quietly entered the museum that surrounded the tomb, with our shoes removed, and waited patiently as the men appeared and performed this ritual.

In the hinterlands of Turkey, we occasionally saw images of President Reagan on televisions screens. Only when we returned to Istanbul did we learn that the United States had bombed Tripoli, the capital of Libya. The Muslim world was up in arms at this outrage but we fortunately experienced no repercussions while in Turkey.

Back in Aberdeen we attempted to reproduce some of the delicious dishes we had enjoyed using a cookbook in English. Of course, the Scots were always ready to party. One neighbor arrived sporting a fez. Not surprisingly, Gene had to grill the kebabs outside the dining room door holding a large umbrella in the downpour. When the party ended well after midnight, we knew it had been a success and probably a boost for Turkish tourism.

In 1986, uncontrolled oil production by non-OPEC countries produced a glut, which precipitated a 46 percent drop in the price of oil and lower demand worldwide. OPEC (the Organization of

Petroleum Exporting Countries, composed of thirteen mainly Middle Eastern states), attempted to stabilize the price of oil by agreeing to control their joint production, but others like Russia and Mexico did not cut back. The effect on the oil industry reverberated through the world economy. Occidental management in Los Angeles sent out orders to trim operations to the bone. Gene was faced with giving notice to men who had families; it was one of the few times I saw him truly distressed. Cities Service had rarely fired employees even in times of austerity and he was shocked by this management decision.

Following my university exams in June, a childhood friend of mine and his wife came from the States for a visit and Grandmother Thelma and Gordy Caldwell arrived at the same time. We six attended the famous Royal Edinburgh Military Tattoo, a dazzling performance of military bands and fife and drum corps. Other popular outings included the Clydesdale horse and horticultural show and the Braemar Gathering Highland games, which the Queen always attended, as had her grandmother, Queen Victoria. Astonishingly strong men in kilts and sneakers competed in the various contests, such as putting the stone (throwing a 28-pound rock) and tossing the caber (the size of a telephone pole).

Our Scottish friends had recommended that we join the National Health Service. We had used private doctors in London after hearing of long waiting times in the public system. The Scots assured us that the NHS was excellent so we signed on. A young doctor whose office was walking distance from our house accepted us into his practice. He was knowledgeable and prompt. He made a house call when I had a bout of flu, and sent me to a highly regarded pulmonary specialist in town who diagnosed and treated me for asthma. During our six years in Scotland, we enjoyed good health care at almost no cost and became fans of the equitable single-payer system.

Suzanne and Lisa were progressing well in their studies. Suzanne was scheduled to graduate with two degrees in May. She also found time to pick up some extra money and experience serving at Oklahoma City banquets hosted by the governor at his mansion. Lisa was wearing out a computer and her eyes at Duke Law School but she was successfully managing the heavy load for her double degree. She was named to the Deans' Advisory Council, an honor recognizing the esteem and trust of her teachers and fellow students.

Patrick, Dana and year-old Michael were thriving as well. When the vet practice began expanding with satellite clinics in other parts of Tulsa, Patrick was put in charge of one of them where he successfully added a loyal clientele of pets and owners.

One Sunday Gene was part of a three-man panel that spoke at Rubislaw Church on the topic "How Does Your Christian Life Relate to Your Business Life?" A number of professional women in our church were not included on the panel but the minister, Scott Hutchison, was moving them gradually into positions of authority. He asked me to serve as representative on the Presbytery of Aberdeen, a body that had governing power over the Church of Scotland churches within the city. It was shocking to think of having a woman representative, and to appoint an American was just asking for trouble to my way of thinking. With a twinkle in his eye, he told me that's why he wanted me to serve. I agreed but assured him that

I had no intention of speaking in that august body. I could feel the chill in the air when I took my seat for the first time in the historic building. It turned out that I wasn't the only woman in the room; there were two or three others, all older. Keeping my mouth shut was easy. It was enough to withstand the withering looks from my fellow presbyters. I did not enjoy being an icebreaker but faithfully attended the meetings, took notes and submitted my reports at our church's session meeting.

Twelve

FLYING THE NEST AND
A NEW HATCHLING

Aberdeen
January 1987 / July 1988

MY CLASSES IN ENGLISH literature and classical civilization were
intense and fascinating, but the reading and essay assignments were
heavy, leaving little time for anything but studying. However, I was
happily immersed in books that I doubt I would ever have read on
my own. Ba Calder's suggestion that we fly south for a few days in
Sussex and Kent in April gave me the opportunity to visit Roman
ruins that I had read about, and to take a much needed break. We
escaped cold, damp Aberdeen to the wonder of spring in Sussex, a
paradise of color with the fresh lemon-green willows, blooming bulbs
of every kind and snowy lambs frolicking on deep-green fields. We
stayed at the charming fourteenth-century Angel Inn in Petworth.

Two Roman sites stand out in memory. Fishbourne, located just
west of Chichester, was reputed to be the residence of Cogidubnus,
King of the Regni tribe before the Romans arrived in 43 CE, when
he became viceroy. His palace, with superb mosaic floors, continued
to be occupied through the second and third centuries. Bignor, on
the edge of the Downs, one of the largest Roman villas in Britain,
covered over four and a half acres.

When we entered the next county, we began to see the hop barns for which Kent was famous. They were distinctive and graceful, topped by cone-shaped cupolas over the drying kilns, with curved metal vents jutting into the air. Hops were imported into Britain from Europe in the sixteenth century. Used in brewing beer as a flavoring agent and stabilizer, they also had an antibacterial effect that allowed the yeast to thrive. With the addition of hops to the barley already grown in Kent, the village of Maidstone on the Medway River became a center of the brewing industry.

Sissinghurst Castle, our last stop before I took Ba to her destination, was an important home from the Middle Ages. King Edward I visited there in 1305 and Queen Elizabeth I spent three nights there in 1573. However it had become a ruin by 1930, when the author and gardener Vita Sackville-West and her husband, the diplomat and memoirist Sir Harold Nicolson, bought it. They restored it to new glory where it became famous, not only for the residents but for the magnificent gardens that Vita designed and built. Organized into a series of "rooms" that opened onto each other, creating changing views, the gardens provided pleasure around each corner as we walked through. Also, looking up at the aerie built overlooking the garden where Sackville-West did her writing and held her assignations, we speculated on the life and times of this vivacious aristocrat.

I took Ba to Bede House, an Anglican convent of the Sisters of the Love of God, near Staplehurst, where she planned to spend ten days in silence and contemplation, as she did on a regular basis. Ba planted the seeds of the value of spiritual retreat that germinated in my life in later years.

Gene, who had been in London on business, met me at Gatwick Airport. He was waiting for me at the top of the escalator with my ticket and a bouquet of flowers. Over the years, my dear husband had turned into the romantic man I pined for in my youth.

Back in Aberdeen, we were surprised by the news that our beloved pastor, Scott Hutchison, had announced his plans to retire. Although with determined effort he remained mobile and able to stand in the pulpit until he was sixty, he felt he could not serve the congregation as well from a wheelchair. Gene was asked to join the search committee for what would be a year-long work involving applications from prospective ministers, travel across Scotland to surreptitiously listen to them preach, and end with a detailed report and recommendation. Although it was a heavy time commitment, Gene was honored to be included on the committee, and the members became close comrades over their months together. Stories of their usually vain attempts to sneak unnoticed into churches in small, close-knit villages were very entertaining. The unanimous choice, Andrew Wilson, served ably as Rubislaw's minister until his retirement in 2012.

The first weekend in May, the family gathered in Stillwater, Oklahoma, to celebrate Suzanne's completion of her years of study. Her first graduation ceremony at the College of Home Economics with a degree in hotel and restaurant administration was followed by her diploma in accounting at the Spears School of Business. We barely had time to race in the heat from one place to the other. We were immensely proud of her accomplishment of two degrees while remaining on the dean's list. And she immediately started her new job at the upscale Excelsior Hotel in Tulsa as the reservations manager.

Earlier, Gene had flown to London to make a presentation to David Martin, president and CEO of the international division of Occidental Oil and Gas Corporation. It was well received but we had no idea that it was more than a normal report. To our surprise, in June, Gene was notified that he was taking over the North Sea operation for Oxy, to succeed Joe Snape, who was being transferred to London to assist John Brading, chairman of United Kingdom Occidental. Gene's new responsibilities at work, and the social obligations connected with this position, made an already crowded schedule hectic at times. However, there were also delightful experiences, such as being invited to attend the annual Garden Party that Queen Elizabeth II held at Holyrood Palace in Edinburgh. The palace, built in the 1670s, was the official residence of the Queen in Scotland. We were blessed with a beautiful sunny day albeit accompanied by a chilly breeze from the sea. The Queen and other members of the royal family walked around in a roped-off section of the garden for about an hour where they met various guests pre-chosen for the honor. The Queen's colorful regiment of archers, with their bows, arrows and feathered hats, served as her guards.

Gene became a member of the Institute of Directors, which was made up of people who owned or directed businesses in Aberdeen. He also was invited to join the Royal Northern and University Club, founded in 1854, a men's club where women were permitted as guests only in the dining room. When we traveled, we took advantage of its reciprocal privileges with some of the finest private clubs in the world. British Airways moved him to VIP status, which included private escorts in airports and usually an upgrade to first class. When British Telecom had a service outage that blacked out all of Aberdeen, our phone was restored immediately because his business was considered vital. All this superb treatment reminded us of the Ash Wednesday mantra from Genesis 3:19, "Remember you are dust and to dust you shall return."

Lisa flew to Toronto, where she had secured an internship with the law firm of Fasken and Calvin. She had been invited to stay with a good friend's aunt who lived in Toronto's western suburb of Oakville. Lisa found her room well stocked with Georgette Heyer novels and settled in happily. She thoroughly enjoyed the summer and found the firm to be a congenial work environment. She was also impressed with Toronto and its beauty, cleanliness and culture. By the end of the summer, she was seriously considering a career in Canada even though it would require another university year studying Canadian law. Before she returned for her final year at Duke, the law firm offered her a job.

Meanwhile, Gene got a most unusual call at the office—from Suzanne. She tearfully poured out her despair over her situation at work. The hotel's general manager required his employees to work long shifts and never told them in advance when their next day off would be. She was exhausted and could make no plans to visit family or friends. She told her dad that she was going to look for an accounting job. While he tried to soothe her, he also advised her not to abruptly quit her job until she had secured a new one. Within a week she called with the good news that she had found a position as an accountant. Fortunately, she was able to come to Aberdeen for a rest before starting work. Later she learned that the manager of the hotel had been fired and that she had been the tenth junior manager to quit due to his draconian methods.

In the autumn, Occidental's chairman David Hentschel, his wife Clydella, and president David Martin with his wife Sally arrived from California on a short visit. John and Peggy Brading and Joe and Mati Snape came up from London. With Dan and Anne McReynolds, Gene and I made detailed plans to entertain them. We booked suites at a small luxurious country house hotel west of Aberdeen on the Dee River. Anne and I entertained the wives while the men were in meetings. Gene and I stayed at the hotel to ensure that everything went smoothly, which it did—though I was concerned for their safety because all the men were commuting in one helicopter between the office and hotel. I doubt that would be allowed today. We took the women sightseeing and on the third day we flew with the men to the Orkney Islands. The weather was atrocious, cold with a fierce, driving rain and high seas. While they toured the huge Oxy oil terminal where petroleum from the North Sea platforms arrived in pipes that crisscrossed the sea floor, we women braved the elements to see some excavated Stone Age ruins. It had been a successful trip but I'm sure the visitors were happy to get home to warm California.

When the university adjourned for the holidays, we flew home to Tulsa and the entire family gathered to celebrate. We had a glorious Christmas together, being awakened each morning by Michael saying, "Hi, Nana and Dad-dad," and watching the wide-eyed excitement of the two-and-a-half-year-old as he discovered the sock with his name on it filled to overflowing by Santa. Patrick and Dana had a surprise for us as well with the news that Michael would have a baby brother or sister by summer. With a new grandbaby on the way and Lisa's graduation from Duke Law School coming up, we joyfully anticipated 1988.

Gene and I met each evening for sundowners to recap our busy days. With a student in the house, most evenings we both were back at work by 8:00 p.m. In March, during a spring holiday, we met Fred and Jean Siefke near Hadrian's Wall at Farlam Hall Country House Hotel in the English county of Cumbria. Constructed during the reign of Roman Emperor Hadrian around 118–119, the wall was built to protect Roman territory from the Barbarian hordes to the north that the Romans never succeeded in pacifying. We walked an exposed section of the wall that was originally eighty miles long and sixteen to twenty feet high with forts at intervals for the soldiers stationed along it.

Suzanne, prospering in her new job at Memorex, had already received a raise. Patrick and Dana were looking forward to the arrival in late July of a sibling for Michael. We rarely heard from Lisa, who was preparing for final exams before graduation in May. Grandmother, eighty-three, didn't appear to be slowing down, her fractured hip a distant memory.

Gene and I flew to North Carolina in May for Lisa's graduation. Suzanne had already arrived and we were immediately immersed in festive events, some hosted by the law school and others by parents of Lisa's friends. The dean circulated through the throng after the graduation ceremony, complimenting each of the graduates with personal remembrances. As she had been dean for less than a year, we were impressed that she knew each graduate so well. After Suzanne flew back to work, Gene, Lisa and I began a celebratory trip through the Carolinas and Dawsonville, Georgia, where Gene's father, Deane, had been born. We returned to Scotland leaving Lisa to close her apartment and plan her return to Toronto, where she would start work as a lawyer with Fasken and Calvin.

In 1979, the Conservative Party handily won the election, making Margaret Thatcher, as leader of the party, the first woman prime minister in British history. She inherited a country still in recession with increasing racial tension and high unemployment. Attacking the problems head-on, Thatcher cut spending on social services, education and housing. She restricted immigration, especially of Asians, and vowed to break the stranglehold of unions. She demonstrated her toughness by allowing nine Irish Republican prisoners on hunger strikes to die while in custody. To put it mildly, the public was wary of her. However, her determination to restore Britain to its former glory was solidified in 1982 when Argentina attacked the Falkland Islands (known in Argentina as the Malvinas). Within three days, Thatcher responded by dispatching the Royal Navy to retake the islands. In only two and a half months, the Falklands War ended with a complete victory for Britain. The economy began to recover, inflation went down from 18 percent to 9 percent, and mortgage rates also declined.

In 1984 the National Union of Mineworkers went on strike. Although the mine workers were suffering terribly, Thatcher refused to respond to their demands and, after a year, the strike collapsed without any concessions by the government. She privatized the "family jewels": gas, water and electricity. In 1987, she had again lowered taxes but introduced the "Community Charge" that became derisively known as the poll tax, a level tax on every adult resident. Scotland was the first part of the realm where this highly unpopular tax was collected.

By 1988, into her third term, Thatcher's popularity rating was at its lowest. Her policies hit close to home when universities throughout the country were told, as a cost-saving measure, to streamline their curricula, specifically to cut the humanities. The University of Aberdeen gave notice that its classics and art departments were being closed or greatly curtailed. My classics professor was being transferred to another university and my history of art professor was terminated. The following summer these two fine teachers took their own lives. Maggie Thatcher, a chemist, was obviously blind to the value of producing well-rounded graduates and heartbreaking human toll was the result. Students and faculties who protested throughout Britain were ignored. Once more, she justly earned the sobriquet "The Iron Lady."

While she was recognized for her success in rescuing Britain from economic ruin, decisions made during her long tenure had lasting effects for both good and ill. Never popular within her own party for her autocratic rule, the resignation of her deputy prime minister, Geoffrey Howe, caused people within the Conservative Party to mount a campaign to unseat her. Facing a second ballot in an internal election, she finally resigned and left 10 Downing Street in tears.

Patrick and Dana asked me to be in Tulsa before the birth of their second baby to take care of three-year-old Michael. I flew to

Oklahoma, where Clay Andrew was born a week later on July 27, 1988—a beautiful, healthy brother for Michael. But shortly after his birth, he was rushed back to the hospital with viral meningitis. Although we knew this was not unusual in newborns, still it was a relief when he returned home in a few days fully recovered. Gene was able to stop by to meet his new grandson in early August following a trip to Oxy's office in Bakersfield, California.

With Dana recovered, I flew to Toronto to meet Lisa before returning to Scotland. She had been accepted to study Canadian law for a year at McGill University but there was a problem. A law pending before the Canadian Parliament would require anyone practicing law in Canada to take Canadian citizenship and renounce any other. Distressed by this possibility, she decided to return to the States and search for a job in Washington or New York, where she had taken the bar exam. She secured a position in international law at the Internal Revenue Service, and lived with my cousin Marilyn in Washington for several months.

I returned to Aberdeen, my joy at becoming a grandmother again and my pride in Lisa overshadowed by feelings of dread and mourning. The reason: When I had reluctantly left Scotland, Gene was enduring the single greatest crisis of his career, and the hardest period of his life: the disaster called Piper Alpha.

Thirteen

HORROR AND HEARTBREAK

Aberdeen and Piper Alpha
July 1988 / October 1999

ON JULY 6, 1988, between Lisa's graduation and Clay's birth, Occidental's oil platform in the North Sea blew up. This was the worst oil-field accident in the history of the petroleum industry. One hundred sixty-seven men died in the explosion and its aftermath. It is impossible to put into words the horror the victims, their families and the British nation experienced. Gene was in charge of Occidental's North Sea operation when it happened.

When the phone rang a few minutes after ten that night, Gene and I were sitting in our living room with Jim and Margery Farquharson enjoying a nightcap following a hilarious performance of *Scotland the What?* at His Majesty's Theatre. Gene returned from the call ashen with the news that there was a fire on Oxy's North Sea platform Piper Alpha. This platform, located 120 miles northeast of Aberdeen, was a collection hub for gas and oil pumped from two other platforms, Claymore and Tartan A. Gene, Jim and Margery ran to their cars and sped to the office. Jim, head of human resources for Oxy, and Margery, like him an Aberdonian, would spend weeks answering phone calls from distraught family members.

After the first explosion, a large semisubmersible firefighting ship, *Tharos*, constantly on standby as a safety measure, moved close to the platform and began spraying the fire in an attempt to open a way of escape. The *Tharos* crew launched a small speedboat that pulled six men from the sea, but a huge explosion killed them and the two men rescuing them at about 10:20 p.m. *Tharos* was then forced to pull away because of the heat. From that time forward, there was no hope of putting out the fire, which was being fed by fuel pouring through pipes coming from the other platforms. Many of the 228 men on the platform found shelter in the fireproof accommodation block; others, some of them badly injured in the initial blast, jumped into the fiery sea in hopes of saving their lives. At 11:50, the accommodation block fell into the sea. Fifty-five minutes later almost the entire platform was gone. Of the 228 men on Piper Alpha, only 61 survived.

The next morning, Joyce Wintour and a young pastor from Rubislaw arrived at the house and spent the day with me. We cried, prayed and drank many cups of tea. Gene appeared before the press on TV but it never occurred to me to turn it on and my friends did not suggest it. Perhaps they were trying to shield me from the horror everyone, including Gene, was going through. Suzanne, watching the news in Oklahoma with friends, suddenly cried out, "That's my dad!" The children called but I had no information. For several days Gene came home only to shower and change, too traumatized to talk. He slept in snatches on the sofa in his office.

On Thursday, Dr. Armand Hammer, corporate chairman of Occidental Petroleum, arrived from California and Prime Minister Thatcher from London. Both were kind and stalwart. Gene appeared on

TV with them as did John Brading, chairman of Occidental Petroleum UK.

Mrs. Thatcher asked Gene if the men working on Piper Alpha had torches (flashlights) by their beds in the living quarters. Recalling the IRA bombing of her hotel in Brighton in 1984, she said she had felt the explosion, grabbed her torch from the bedside table and went to the door of her room. When she opened it, there was nothing on the other side—instead, she saw a chasm three stories deep. If she hadn't had her torch, she could have fallen to her death. Gene assured her that the men did have torches.

We began to attend memorial services in all parts of Scotland. There were Oxy executives at every service. A team arrived from California to take over the internal inquiry into the accident while Gene continued running the day-to-day operations. The Bradings came up from London frequently. Peggy and I went to Aberdeen Royal Infirmary to visit the survivors.

Thirty-seven of the survivors were rescued by a fast rescue craft driven by coxswain James Clark, who received the George Medal, the second-highest civil decoration in Britain, for his bravery. Eighty-seven bodies were recovered when the living module was raised from the seabed later in the year. We then attended funeral services for many of the men whose families had held memorial services earlier. Frequently, Gene and I were welcomed into their homes and treated as members of the family. John Brading was amazed at the way we were treated in Aberdeen; he told us that in London, people turned their backs when he entered the room, leaving him feeling rejected and isolated. Perhaps our deep roots in the Aberdeen community shielded us from the anger directed toward him. Of course, we never knew what actions our friends were taking for us but felt surrounded by love and concern in spite of the horror we all felt at the loss of so many lives.

Three weeks after the accident, the famous oil-well firefighter Red Adair arrived with his team to extinguish the fire still blazing on the remains of Piper Alpha. Gene said that at seventy-three years of age, he was still a strong, impressive man, confident of his expertise and the competent crew he headed to get the job done. He was also sensitive toward the Oxy employees who were under so much pressure and grieving as well.

Lord William Cullen, a Scottish judge, was appointed to convene an inquiry into the Piper Alpha accident. He spent the next year gathering information. Gene and Dan McReynolds, the operations manager, were among the last to testify in the autumn of 1989.

In the weeks leading up to their appearance before Lord Cullen, the pressure of testifying began to build. Oxy's legal team met with the men who would face the inquiry and tried to prepare them to defend the company's procedures and actions. Several contracting firms also faced intense scrutiny. Insurance companies representing the various entities were leveling charges and countercharges. Gene's ambivalence as the inquiry date drew near caused him great distress; he believed that the company had followed safety procedures common to the oil industry and trusted the contractors to do the same, but there was no clear culpability. In his testimony, he spoke the truth as he believed it to be. The lawyers were lavish in their praise for his ability to respond effectively to the prosecutors but he was given no opportunity to speak of his anguish or the guilt that he carried for being ignorant of needed reform.

A year later, Lord Cullen issued his report. It was a devastating indictment of Occidental and the North Sea petroleum industry in general. The causes were both a systems failure and human error. Lord Cullen made 106 recommendations for wide-ranging changes, starting with the removal of petroleum industry oversight from the U.K. Department of Energy to the Health and Safety Executive. The Department of Energy's prime interest in the profitability of oil production conflicted with its oversight of safety measures. The design of Piper Alpha was determined to be seriously flawed, and as a result a Norwegian oil platform in the designing stage was radically changed to make it much safer. New safety regulations were adopted throughout the industry world-wide. Gene read the long report thoroughly and took personally his failure to recognize the dangers that had been exposed in Piper Alpha's operation. He was never able to speak of the accident without crying. We both could never hear the Royal Navy Hymn, "Eternal Father, Strong to Save," played as it was at every funeral service we attended in 1988–89, without reliving the agony of this tragic loss of life.

When the report was published in 1990, Gene and I were living in Muscat, capital of the Sultanate of Oman, where Gene had been named president of Occidental Oman. All of the Oxy expatriate employees who had been directly involved in company operations before Piper Alpha had been transferred out of Scotland. This decision gave the employees a fresh start elsewhere and helped the company's image as well by removing anyone who could possibly have been considered implicated in the accident.

Knowing that 1989 would be our last year in Scotland, time spent with dear friends became all the more precious. "Kitchen lunches" in Norman and Barbara Calder's home were a highlight of many Sundays, as were "sherry natters" with Ba at our house on Wednesdays. Other friends were sources of tremendous support and comfort. At the end of January we joined a large group from Rubislaw Church for an Elders' Retreat at Crieff Hydro Hotel in Perthshire. Built in 1868, this huge Victorian complex boasted a premier health spa set on nine-hundred lush acres, with activities for all ages: golfing, fishing, horseback riding and the like. Gene was at last able to talk and pray with close friends, and to rest. Like most of the Occidental staff, he was at the point of exhaustion. The company physician had predicted that many of the people deeply involved in Piper Alpha would suffer poor health following the shock they had endured. Now it might be called post-traumatic stress disorder. John Brading, the U.K. Oxy chairman, had already been critically ill and Gene suffered from a painful inflamed eye for months.

Following exams in June, I learned that I had passed and would graduate. My outstanding history lecturer Jennifer Carter told me several years later that I was ranked first in her class. Graduation was scheduled for July 5, and Lisa flew to Aberdeen to join us for the ceremony. I was eager to see her in person because we had noticed that a certain "Jim" was appearing regularly in her letters. She had dated several men since settling in Washington but had always identi-fied them by their occupations. When I asked her to tell us about

Jim, her reply took my breath away: "Would you like to meet him? He can fly over next week." Before Jim appeared, his youngest sister, Victoria, who was sightseeing in Britain at the time, arrived by train. Gene and I were charmed by this engaging young woman and eagerly awaited her brother.

Jim captivated us with his self-deprecating humor and quick wit. Also an attorney with the IRS, he was one of the people who had interviewed Lisa for her job. Jim's Druze grandparents had emigrated from Lebanon to the United States in the early twentieth century. Lisa's résumé had listed Arabic language studies; perhaps that had triggered his interest in her. We didn't have a ticket for him to attend my graduation ceremony but he joined us for the champagne and strawberries reception in the university gardens afterward.

Gene was so proud of me. We both got teary when he commented that my mother, who had died in 1970, must surely be celebrating with us. At last I had the university degree she had desired for me.

A few days later Gene hosted a party at the Atholl Hotel to celebrate my graduation. At lunch, there were toasts and not a few tears because it also was a farewell party. We had never left a place with such a sense of loss. We had been through times of great joy and deep sorrow with our friends. Two friends had recently died. In February, our neighbor Edna Anderson had succumbed to pancreatic cancer. She had attended a neighborhood coffee morning at my house two weeks before her death. Barely able to walk, she had crossed the street leaning heavily on her husband's arm. Unable to eat, she came to say good-bye to her dear friends. Jill Hutchison, our pastor Scott's wife, died from a brain tumor at the hospice facility. Her lively spirit and strong faith sustained her to the end.

I flew home to Oklahoma shortly after the party. Grandmother Thelma, after years of gastric discomfort, had finally been diagnosed with a malignant tumor. Gene joined his sister, Betty, in Oklahoma for their mother's operation. Betty spent many weeks caring for her as she recovered. I went to relieve her and be with Thelma during her six weeks of radiation.

In August John Brading called Gene to London to offer him the position of Occidental president in Oman. However, the new job presented a rather delicate situation. A team of auditors led by Sam Dominic from Oxy's Bakersfield headquarters had been dispatched to Muscat to examine the books of Occidental Oman's current president. The head of finance in Oman and one of the engineers had alerted the home office to irregularities within the operation. When the president learned of their reports, he physically threatened the men. The audit revealed serious breaches in the way contracts had been awarded; one contract that supplied oil-field workers in the desert was suspect, and another contract covered the sale of used oil-field equipment from a firm employed by the president's son-in-law. John Brading was reluctant to take action against the president because he had been successful in developing the field during his years in Oman and seemed to have a good relationship with the Ministry of Petroleum. However, when the president rejected the audit's findings, Brading decided to take action. He told the officer that he could either take early retirement or be fired.

When Gene took over, the contractor supplying the oil-field workers offered to reduce fees by 25 percent if Gene would renew the contract. Instead, he put the contract out for bids and secured another contractor for almost 35 percent less. And before we left Oman four years later, Gene had to replace the miles of used pipe in the field as it was defective and leaking.

We made our first trip to Muscat in September. Gene found most of the employees were scared and unwilling to talk to him. He recognized that restoring trust and good morale was going to take time. Surprisingly, the ousted president's wife appeared friendly and helpful to me. She knew of a gated group of eight houses on a hill overlooking the coast to the south and near the mountains to the north. Owned by one of the Omani ministers who was also a cousin of the ruler of Oman, Sultan Qaboos, these palatial homes were new and two were still unoccupied. The front doors opened into a spacious reception room two-and-a-half stories high and finished in white marble surrounded by a gallery on the second floor with a windowed cupola at the top. Between the reception room and the living room were very tall, beautifully hand-carved, painted doors in Omani Arabic style. We happily signed a lease and I returned to Aberdeen to begin preparations for the move.

The housing market in Aberdeen had not rebounded from the downturn in 1986 so Gene and I were concerned when we listed our house for sale. In Scotland, attorneys control the real estate business, and follow a curious protocol: they accept sealed bids, and in due course set a closing date. When I returned, our solicitor invited me to his office; as he opened the bids and read out the proffered prices, we both became quite excited. Earlier in the year Conoco had announced it was closing its London office and moving all its employees to Aberdeen. The company had engaged a local real estate entrepreneur to bid on homes chosen by Conoco employees, buy the houses, and lease them to Conoco for a set number of years, at the end of which he would take control of his property. The high bid on our house was more than double our total investment in it. For the first time in our long experience of losing money on the sales of our houses, we recouped all the earlier losses and then some. Several of our neighbors put their houses up for sale when they learned of our success, welcoming the opportunity to downsize for their retirement years.

Occidental held a farewell party for Gene and me in the company's large gym. Through many speeches, toasts and gift presentations, we were given a tremendous send-off. Gene was recognized for the warm Christian gentleman that he was, respected by the employees for leading the company safely through a challenging and difficult period. Dan and Anne McReynolds graciously held another farewell party for us with our closest Oxy friends.

We sadly left Aberdeen knowing that in Muscat we were facing challenges within the company added to the usual ones, once more, of adapting to a new culture and building friendships anew.

Fourteen

COLD IN THE DESERT HEAT

Muscat
October 1989 / January 1990

WE ARRIVED IN MUSCAT in October and moved into the Intercontinental Hotel until our household goods arrived. Various oil-field service companies held joint farewell/welcome parties for the retiring president and his wife and for us. However, there was tension in the air. The ex-president and his wife remained in Muscat hoping for an audience with the sultan as he was known for his generosity to departing executives. We had no idea how people were feeling about them or us. We suspected that sides had been drawn both inside and outside of Occidental. Gene was hard at work trying to assess the situation while keeping the operation moving smoothly in the field. A testament to the fear of appearing to take sides was evident from the few Occidental wives offering to entertain me. The ex-president's wife took me out one day but soon became openly hostile, turning her back when we arrived at parties. I assumed it was because she had not shared the reason for their departure with others and was afraid I would do so. It was a lonely time. One American woman whispered to me that if I was feeling isolated I should know that people thought Gene and I were "a breath of fresh air." I was very grateful for her comment.

I went out a few times in Gene's car with his driver to see the area, the supermarkets, the modern mall, old town and the ancient covered souk (an Arabic bazaar of small shops where one could buy almost anything). However, I wanted the freedom of a car of my own. I found a beautiful Audi 80 and although Gene was required by Omani law to put his name on the title, it was mine and I could drive. I quickly learned that there were few restrictions for women. Dress was expected to be modest but there were no *mutawwa* (religious police) as in Saudi Arabia. Most expats were pleasantly surprised by the welcoming attitudes of the Omani people; they were not only friendly but exceedingly hospitable. For example, not long after we arrived, I was invited by a woman I'd met at one of the parties to join a group of American women on a sightseeing trip to the interior oasis town of Nizwa in search of an ancient kiln where pottery was made as it had been for hundreds of years. As our caravan of several SUVs pulled into town, the driver of the lead car stopped and asked a man for directions. He kindly pointed the way but before we arrived at the kiln, we saw this man standing outside of his house motioning for us to stop. He explained that he would like to give us refreshments. We entered his house to find a lavish display of fruits, cheeses, olives and juices spread out on a long cloth on the floor with cushions sprinkled around for us to sit upon. He brought his young children in to meet us. I soon learned that he was not unusual in displaying such phenomenal hospitality.

Early one November morning, Gene and I were collected at our hotel by Mohammed Ishmael and his wife, Kensie. Mohammed's company did business with Occidental. They took us to the interior of the country to attend a camel race where Gene was the honoree. When we arrived at the racetrack, we were met by Mohammed's brother, the banker in a nearby village. A large group of Bedouins were already seated on tall sand berms bordering the packed track, with men on one berm and women on the other. I was seated on the men's side next to Gene.

Although the Omanis were famous breeders of racehorses, camels were just as highly prized for their speed and were a source of great wealth for the Bedouins who populated the Omani interior. The races were serious business because it was not unusual for winning camels to sell for a quarter-million dollars. Before the first race, the announcer on the loudspeaker tried valiantly to pronounce Grogan without success; however, as the only man in Western clothes, Gene wasn't difficult to spot. Everyone cheered, probably because that meant the races would at last begin. Camel jockeys were young boys, five to seven years of age, used because of their light weight. They were stuck into the saddles with Velcro, and then also tied in. A terrified, screaming child caused the camel to run faster. Camel bridles have no bits so swift grooms waited at the finish line to dash out and grab the reins to stop the animals. There was a huge trade throughout the Middle East in poor boys from India, Bangladesh and other countries, who were either kidnapped or sold by their parents as camel jockeys. At this race, however, the boy who rode the winning camel was the son of the owner. He was ecstatic and showed no sign of fear. In addition to a share in the prize money, according to Mohammed's brother, the lad would also receive a percentage of the proceeds when the camel was sold. The price was paid in gold bullion, which was deposited into the bank in peacetime but withdrawn and buried in the desert during times of unrest.

After the race, Mohammed suggested that we drive up a wadi (dry river bed) to look at some caves while his wife and her sister-in-law prepared a meal of roast goat and accompanying dishes. On the unsurfaced road to the wadi we passed only one sign of habitation, a small general store. We entered the wadi and bumped our way over small boulders as far as we could, then walked the rest of the way to the beautiful, water-filled caves. Oman is blessed with more underground water than most desert countries. On the way back to the car, I was following Mohammed down a large smooth rock, with Gene several yards behind me, when my feet began to slip. Unable to keep myself from falling, I threw out my right arm to brace myself and came down hard. Although Mohammed was close enough to catch me, I'm sure it never entered his mind to touch me. I knew at once that I had seriously injured my arm. We got back to the car and started the excruciating journey back down the bumpy wadi. Mohammed's brother called an Indian medic, the local doctor, who said he didn't think my arm was broken but gave me some pain medicine.

The Omani women did not speak English but Mohammed told me they had planned to bathe me and dress me in Omani clothes before we ate. I was in such pain that I declined their offer. Because of the heat I had brought a change of clothes, so Gene helped me shower and dress. We then ate the sumptuous feast and began the two-and-a-half-hour drive back to Muscat. Arriving at the hotel around eight o'clock, Gene placed a call to Ahmad Kharusi, an Omani hired by Occidental as an expeditor who facilitated approval of necessary documents such as licenses. All I wanted to do was go to bed and have an x-ray in the morning. However, Mohammed told Gene he would do some checking. In about twenty minutes, the hotel desk clerk rang with the news that Mohammed and his brother, Dr. Wahid Kharusi, were on their way to our room. Wahid, the chief orthopedic surgeon in the country, had trained in Britain. Not a believer in coincidences, I already felt better believing that God was caring for me. Wahid drove us to the hospital where an x-ray revealed four breaks at the top of my upper arm, two of them through the top of the bone. Fortunately, there was almost no displacement so Wahid folded my arm across my chest and bound it to my body. He cared for me between his flights to the sultan's mother, whom he was treating for a broken ankle at her home in the city of Salalah in southern Oman. A week after my fall, we moved into our house. Wahid came to the house several times to check my arm and waited patiently while Gene gave me a shower. After six weeks, I graduated to a sling. Over Christmas, I rested while Lisa and Suzanne were visiting. In January, I began extremely painful therapy to break the frozen shoulder and elbow joints loose. When the therapist concluded that the job was 40 percent completed, I was released to finish my therapy in the swimming pool. What a relief it was to get into the water, where I slowly regained full range of motion.

While still in the hotel, I started looking for a couple to hire as cook and housekeeper. We had such success with John and Beatrice in Kenya and I hoped to do the same in Oman. An Indian agent produced a roster of résumés and I chose Patrick and Felcy Menezes from Bombay. Patrick had worked as a cook for ten years in an oil camp in Saudi Arabia and spoke several languages. He and Felcy had been married for five years but they had never lived together. I hired them sight unseen. Occidental arranged for their visas as no worker could enter the country without company sponsorship, including us. I told the agent that I didn't want the couple to have to pay a fee (bribe) for the privilege of being offered the job but, sadly, learned from them that they did indeed have to pay dearly. What a relief it was when they arrived in December, as I had felt quite insecure with my broken arm on the slick marble floors. Patrick, a charming fellow and an excellent cook, could read a recipe in English and follow it. Felcy was well educated, having attended two years of college beyond secondary school. Both were eager, hard workers. When the girls arrived for Christmas, everything was running smoothly.

The house was beautiful but the ground behind it was a rock-strewn wasteland that dropped off steeply to a high wall. Between our house and the barren mountains, everything was brown, a most depressing sight. Around the hotel grew lush gardens and I determined to have the same at home, having no idea what an expensive and difficult job it would be. I hired a company to clear the rocks and install topsoil. Dump trucks arrived, but the only way to get the earth into the back was one wheelbarrow load at a time, which was dumped over the wall. The men then terraced the garden into several levels with steps between the levels. It took days of backbreaking work. When it was completed, we seeded the ground for a lawn, added bougainvillea on the back wall, three banyan trees next to the patio to provide shade, fig trees and other bushes. Patrick watered everything twice a day because of the extreme heat. The result was lovely. When Mohammed and Kensie brought their six children for visits, they squealed with pleasure as they rolled down the grassy hills. The American Women's Group Oman, made up of all nationalities, had their holiday party in our garden. A door at one end of the living room opened onto a graceful fountain, which provided the pleasant cooling sound of splashing water. The landlord had the entire compound fogged every Saturday morning by Indian laborers using DDT (and not wearing masks) to eliminate mosquitoes. Some things were not easy to dwell on as I'm sure those poor men had short lives. The difference between our expatriate living standards and theirs made me uncomfortable. I also felt guilty when I thought about irrigating our garden in a country where water was more valuable than oil. But sitting on the patio at night with a cool breeze under the brilliant starry sky was an awesome experience.

In 1889, Dutch Reformed Church missionaries arrived from the United States to live and work in Oman. Although not allowed to proselytize among the Omanis, there were no restrictions against evangelizing non-Muslim workers. The missionaries built the only hospital and school in the country. When we arrived in 1989, the church was celebrating its centennial with Don and Eloise Bosch, Reformed Church missionaries, being honored for their thirty-five years of service there. Don, a surgeon, had served in the hospital and teacher Eloise had operated the missionary school. Although they were officially retired, the sultan encouraged them to continue to make their home in Muscat. He built a beautiful house for them with a large patio for square dancing. He also provided household staff, car and driver, and airline tickets between the States and Oman for family and friends to visit. The Bosches' square dance evenings were prized invitations, and skillfully mixed the international community with local Omanis. Eloise served a delicious buffet and Don was the instructor and caller for the dances. These evenings did more to break down cultural barriers than official diplomacy ever succeeded in doing. Here the most dignified ambassadors, oil company employees and Omani men boisterously laughed over their awkward attempts to master the square dance steps. Lasting friendships were forged on those evenings.

The sultan gave the Christian community ten-acre parcels of land divided between the Roman Catholics and Protestants upon which to build their churches and homes for staff. Since the weekend in Oman was Thursday and Friday, Christian services were also on Friday. Nineteen congregations, organized according to denomination and language, had services in our facilities each week, including the Eastern Orthodox Church. When we arrived, the English-speaking congregation, the Protestant Church of Oman, had two ministers, John Hubers, a Reformed minister from Iowa, and Ray Skinner, an Anglican priest from Britain. Both of these fine men and their wives were sensitive and caring pastors. Later, Chuck and Donna Johnson replaced the Hubers and Rob and Philippa Fieldson replaced the Skinners. All of them worked well with each other and led us admirably.

The English-speaking congregation was made up of approximately thirty nationalities with an especially large contingent of Christians from South India. Potluck meals at our church were not to be missed. We had never belonged to such a diverse and tolerant congregation, even with our differences in Christian practices or interpretation of scripture. In the Bible study group I attended there were women from Nigeria, Japan, Britain, the United States, India and Sri Lanka. We shared our personal concerns and prayed for and helped each other. Our friendships have lasted over time and great distance.

Archeologists have uncovered remains of human habitation in Oman from the Stone Age. Since prehistoric times the people living in this area built sailing vessels and rode the currents south along the eastern coast of Africa as traders and conquerors. A reed boat was unearthed in Oman that was forty-five hundred years old. In an annual phenomenon, the currents of the Indian Ocean reverse with the seasonal monsoon, allowing the sailors sailing downwind to return home. The Omanis were renowned for their shipbuilding and navigational skills. In the eighth century, the Omani sailor Abu Ubayda Abid Allah bin al Qasim al Umani, known as Sinbad, sailed from Oman to China. The Omani dhows, hand built in the city of Sur, were reputed to be the best in the Arab World.

By the last millennium BCE, the Queen of Sheba, claimed by both Oman and Yemen, became fabulously wealthy from trading in frankincense, a gum extract of a tree that grew in the area. The bark of this tree was as valuable as gold. Still sold in the souks, the price varied with the quality and was used by Arab women as the base for their incense mixtures. The women in each family had their own secret recipes. My new friend Kensie Ishmail gave me a jar of her special mixture, a small brazier to heat it in and a tripod over which I could drape my clothes and linens, just as the Omani women did, to absorb the luscious scent.

In the seventeenth century Oman was an independent empire and by the nineteenth century it controlled an area that extended across the Strait of Hormuz to Iran, Pakistan and as far south as Zanzibar. Omanis were among the first people to convert to Islam when the Prophet Muhammad sent one of his followers to the land around 630 CE. Three-fourths of Omanis were Ibadis, a conservative sect that dated from sixty years after the Prophet's death and dominated the interior of the country. Although Ibadi was the state religion, most coastal Omanis in the cities were Sunni with a small number of Shia as well.

By the twentieth century, Oman's power declined as the British Empire's influence grew. In 1913, the country split into warring factions; the interior was ruled by a powerful imam while the coast was under the control of a sultan. The sultan gradually gained more control of the interior and by the time he abdicated in favor of his son, Sultan Said bin Taimur in 1932, the country was unified and secure economically. The belief that there was oil in Oman triggered a new rebellion in the interior in 1954. In 1955, Cities Service Oil Company drilled the first exploratory well in the Dhofar region of Oman and made the first discovery, striking oil with the Marmul 1 well in 1956. When Gene reported for work in August 1957 as a geological engineer, he was offered a position as a geologist in Dhofar or as a petroleum engineer in the United States. Families were not allowed to go to Dhofar so Gene, about to become a married man, decided on petroleum engineering.

Sultan Said continued to rule Oman as a feudal state. There was no electricity except for one generator at the hospital. Don and Eloise Bosch lived in Iraq for three years while learning Arabic before they arrived in Muscat in 1955 with their three young children. Don joined the esteemed Dr. Thoms, also a Reformed Church missionary, as a surgeon in the hospital. The walled city's gate was locked at sundown by a watchman carrying his lantern and a huge key. No one could enter or leave until the gate was unlocked in the morning. Because of the extreme heat, the Bosches slept on the flat roof of their house in a mesh cage to keep the mosquitoes out. Beside each bed was a bucket of water in which Don and Eloise soaked towels to spread over the children and themselves in order to sleep. They had to get up during the night several times to rewet the towels.

Encouraged by the British, the sultan did agree to send his son, Qaboos, to England for secondary school in the early 1950s, followed by Sandhurst, the British military academy. Thus exposed to the modern world, he returned to Oman with "radical" ideas of trans-forming Oman from a fourteenth-century fiefdom into a twenti-eth-century modern state. Enraged, the sultan placed him under house arrest in Salalah. He made a fatal error, however, because he gave Qaboos's friends unfettered access. When oil extraction began in 1967, the sultan banked the revenue, refusing to use any of this new wealth for the betterment of the populace. Qaboos, with the help of the British, began to plot a coup. In 1970, the palace was attacked at night. A palace guard shot one of the intruders and the sultan shot himself in the foot as he removed a pistol from the table beside his bed. That was the only blood spilled. Qaboos ordered a plane to fly both men to England for treatment. Sultan Said spent the rest of his life living in the Dorchester Hotel in London.

With the new oil wealth, thirty-year-old Sultan Qaboos started to modernize his country. He began a huge electrification project throughout Oman, and built hospitals, houses and schools. He allowed newspapers and magazines from Europe into Oman, although when we lived there they were still heavily redacted. When our belongings arrived in Muscat, everything was delivered to the house except for our large library, which was delivered months later. All books with any reference to Israel or Jews, except our Bibles, were covered in black ink. Fortunately, we used a courier service that supplied uncensored material. When my *Vanity Fair* magazine arrived at the Oxy office with the naked photo of the very pregnant actor Demi Moore on the cover, it caused quite a stir in the mailroom among the Omani secretaries. Television was also censored but that was easily bypassed. The minister of information lived in a mansion not far from us with a huge satellite dish that received programs from Europe, which were then scrambled and rebroadcast within the country to the sultan's ministers and selected Omanis. They were provided with little black boxes that unscrambled the signals. Indian entrepreneurs did a brisk business in pirated boxes, which all of the expats purchased. We were thus able to watch uncensored news from CNN and British Sky TV.

Sultan Qaboos continued to be an absolute monarch but he was wise in slowly allowing more participation in the political system.

At least once a year, he and his ministers went on a driving tour of the country. When he stopped along the way, tents were pitched and the people came to speak to the sultan and his ministers about their local concerns. This contact with his subjects was unprecedented in the Middle East and he was loved for it. While we lived there, he formed the Consultative Council with representatives from all parts of the country. At first they were appointed, but in recent years they were elected from their districts, though the sultan always had the final word on any decision. In 2002, all citizens twenty-one years of age were given the vote and in 2004 he appointed the first female minister. There were clouds on the horizon, however, in the rise of fundamentalism, the decrease in oil reserves that accounted for 95 percent of the country's GDP, and the lack of jobs for the increasingly well-educated and restless youth.

Fifteen

NEXT DOOR TO WAR

Muscat
January 1990 / April 1993

AFTER CELEBRATING CHRISTMAS in Muscat with Lisa and Suzanne, Gene took us to Oxy's field camp in the vast Rub al Khali, the Empty Quarter of the Sahara Desert. A four-and-a-half-hour drive by SUV brought us to Safah, near the border with Saudi Arabia. Not far from the Muscat suburbs we left the smooth, paved highway for a road that was almost indistinguishable from the surrounding desert. Made of caliche (or hardpan), the road was a combination of calcium carbonate, sand and other local materials. Rolled out and watered down, it hardened into a surface that was suitable for driving. The final part of the journey was over trackless desert. Although Gene had made the trip several times, we wondered if he could actually find the camp by dead reckoning with only a compass. We were greatly relieved when it appeared in the distance and Gene laughingly assured us that it was not a mirage.

The camp consisted of a large building that contained offices, a gym, a game room with pool tables, a canteen and two dining halls, one for Muslims and the other for everyone else. This was surrounded by

American-built air-conditioned trailers for the approximately 250 employees. Alcohol was forbidden in the camp. The working conditions were challenging with temperatures that sometimes exceeded 120 degrees. The expat workers' schedule was 28/28—twenty-eight days in Oman and twenty-eight days anywhere in the world equivalent to the distance to their home country, with business-class tickets from Oxy. Although it was not an easy life, with excellent salaries plus adventure there seemed to be no shortage of American and European men eager to sign on.

Hundreds of miles of high dunes, spectacular sunsets and brilliant night skies with stars that looked close enough to touch gave the desert a unique beauty. Desert sand occurred in a variety of colors that, captivatingly, changed according to light and weather conditions. All the same, danger lurked everywhere. Sandstorms were truly terrifying, their size, speed and duration in the Sahara legendary. Getting caught out in one could be a death sentence. Bedouins, of course, knew how to survive and thrive in the desert. They often passed through the camp by camel or, more commonly, in very small pickup trucks driven with reckless abandon, often with a camel reclining regally in the back.

The desert also boasted some very unpleasant creatures. The camel spider—an arachnid of a different order than a spider and without venom—was an ugly critter with a body about six inches in length and long, hairy legs. Carnivorous, it could run ten miles an hour, jump high, and inflict a nasty bite. When it appeared to be chasing a person, it was actually trying to get into the person's shadow to cool off. There were also huge scorpions and poisonous snakes. The men seemed to thrive on the dangers of their work and the surroundings. They loved to tell tall stories of their adventures, which were easy to believe although they probably grew with the telling.

Suzanne, Lisa and I were pleased to see the camp but, after one overnight visit, were delighted to get back to the city comforts of Muscat. Too soon, the girls returned to their lives in the States, no doubt with tall tales of their own to entertain their friends.

Social life in Muscat was cyclical. Temperatures above 100 degrees combined with high humidity from May to September were the norm on the coast. The social season, crammed into the winter months from November to January, revolved around garden parties at homes and hotels. Most were cocktail parties around the hotel pools where we stood balancing plates of hors d'oeuvres and glasses of wine while making small talk for a couple of hours with the same people night after night. These became trials to be endured more than enjoyed.

Thankfully, we were also invited to the homes of Omani and expat friends, where the hospitality and food were outstanding and the conversation stimulating. We learned the true meaning of opulence. From the outside, Omani homes were attractive; inside they were awesome. A wing of the house or a separate building on the property was reserved specifically for entertaining. The room where we had cocktails in one home featured a dazzling Waterford crystal chandelier; returning from the dining room after dinner, we watched the chandelier open like a lotus blossom to reveal disco lights, converting the room into an Aladdin's cave for dancing. Another home had a snow machine in the ceiling and gently falling snow kept the dancers cool.

One of the most coveted invitations was to a home where our host—a doctor, entrepreneur and close friend of the sultan—led us into a huge room with numerous seating areas. He separated couples, thoughtfully placing us during the cocktail hour to meet people new to us. When dinner was announced, a wall silently slid open to reveal a dining room and enormous round table with seating for twenty-four. A stunning flower and candle creation about ten feet tall dominated the center of the table, cascading down onto the table-cloth. Twelve liveried servants stood behind our chairs. Each course was served under silver domes that were simultaneously lifted by the servants. A harpist played during dinner. Then we were led into the lush garden where we sat under the stars and listened to a small orchestra play both classical Arabic and Western music. On one occasion a famous Moroccan singer performed, and we were always impressed by our host's meticulous and superb planning.

A few of the Omani men we knew had more than one wife but polygamy was not the norm. The Qur'an states that if a man has more than one wife, each wife must be treated equally, so it was a financial investment that only moderately wealthy men could afford. We knew one man who had one wife in Saudi Arabia and another in Muscat; he took them together to London on shopping expeditions where they appeared in Western dress. We were shocked and saddened when two older men whom we knew took thirteen-year-old girls as second wives. However, our closest Omani friends were monogamous. The women's dress varied greatly. In the capital area, most women dressed conservatively but colorfully, with head scarves that covered hair but not faces. In the interior and the conservative southern part of Oman, many women only appeared in public in purdah (covered completely in black).

One must not make the mistake of believing that Muslim women were all downtrodden. The social norms in their societies were laid down and enforced primarily by devout women, not by the men. Omani men revered their mothers, who frequently chose their wives and exerted strong influence within the family structure. In Oman, the sultan decreed that education was as important for women as for men. Through secondary school, education was segregated by gender; at the university level, although the women sat in an upstairs area in the lecture halls, like the men they qualified as doctors, lawyers and economists and became government ministers. The ultimate proof of the culture's acceptance of the sultan's decision, of course, was that the bride price that Omani men paid for educated wives was much higher than that paid for those who were not.

Being entertained was delightful; entertaining at home was work. Gone were the days of casual dinners with homemade food and random seating. Formal invitations were sent out to His Excellency So-and-So and frequently had to be followed by a discreet phone call to inquire if the gentleman planned to attend. Determined to entertain at home as often as possible, I visited several hotels where I sampled the food and got to know the chefs and catering managers. I learned seating protocol from embassy experts. Using our large reception room as well as the balcony area above it and the outside patio for seated dinners, the caterer could set tables for eighty. We invited a mix of Omanis, Oxy employees, other business associates and Christian friends we had met at church.

Our first entertaining on a large scale, in January 1990 at the Intercontinental Hotel, was a cocktail party for Occidental's president of the international division, David Martin, and a group of Oxy executives from Bakersfield. The sultan's cabinet ministers, other government employees, the expatriate business community and Oxy employees were all invited with spouses. Gene and I spent many nights before this affair memorizing the names and titles of the guests. In the receiving line, the Oxy executives were pleasantly surprised by our ability to introduce our guests by name as we had been there such a short time. Of course, they didn't know how many cocktail parties we had attended in November and December. Still, we were pleased that our memorizing paid off.

Gene booked visitors into the Al Bustan Palace Hotel. Built by Sultan Qaboos on a magnificent cove, it is one of the most beautiful five-star hotels in the world. The top floor was reserved for the sultan's guests, such as potentates from the Gulf countries when the Gulf Cooperation Council convened in Oman. The main elevators did not go to that floor. It was rumored that the elevator to the top floor was large enough to hold a limousine so that the ruler would not have to leave his car until he entered his suite. The rest of the hotel itself was spectacular; guests could choose a Western or an Arabic style room. We highly recommended the latter with its walls beautifully covered in exquisite Arabic tiles.

Dubai, 270 miles from Muscat, was a tempting weekend destination. The four-lane motorway, smooth, flat and straight, encouraged high speed. A grave hazard, one that actually cost the life of one of Gene's young engineers, was hitting a camel. Dubai, more cosmopolitan than Muscat, had superb hotels, restaurants and shops. We took an ice chest to pack with pork because it was much more available and less expensive in Dubai than Muscat. An estuary running through the city, the Dubai Creek, was lined with huge dhows laden with goods from Iran, India, East Africa and elsewhere. Smuggling was rampant; the dhows looked ancient but they each sported the latest in radar to elude police ships. Gene was invited to a sheik's home for dinner. Afterward, asking Gene if he would like to see some carpets, the sheik took him to a large room where hundreds of carpets were stacked to the ceiling. He told Gene that he bought them by the dhow load from Iran.

A Canadian friend told us of a carpet shop in Sharjah, the emirate adjacent to Dubai. Carpet shopping with the owner, a gregarious salesman, became an almost irresistible habit during our years in Oman. We arrived by appointment because we knew that the process of drinking numerous cups of tea or Arabic coffee while looking at many dozens of carpets required at least three or four exceedingly enjoyable hours. We were encouraged to take our choices home on approval and pay on our next trip if we decided to keep them.

On one particular trip, carpet shopping was not the highlight. Returning to our room after a leisurely Valentine's Day dinner, we received a phone call from Lisa and Jim in Washington. Jim asked Gene for Lisa's hand in marriage as he had proposed to her that evening. There was an intense discussion about the bride price: Just how many camels was Jim offering to pay for her? Once that banter was over, I wanted to know if they had set a date. When September was mentioned, I knew I would have to leave right away to secure a venue for the reception and deal with a myriad of details.

We left in early March, and Gene spent a few days in Washington before proceeding to the office in Bakersfield. Planning a wedding in an unfamiliar city was daunting, so I was thrilled when Jim's mother, Betty, offered to assist me. Within a few days we had the arrangements made and I happily departed for Oklahoma, rejoicing that Lisa was joining such a loving and hospitable family.

I visited our family in Tulsa and Thelma in Enid, where she had entered a nursing home fifteen miles from Garber due to deteriorating health. Typical of Grandmother, when I arrived I found her cheerful, making friends and adapting to her new environment.

Returning to Muscat we welcomed our friends Johnnie and Mary Kay Heck, recently arrived from Pakistan as Johnnie became operations manager. His arrival completed the transition of the staff from the former president's to Gene's. Finally, he had a cooperative group whose trust in each other was restored.

"Omanization"—the hiring of Omanis for positions in private businesses—was encouraged by the government. Gene hired several women as secretaries and Omani men who were petroleum engineers. All of the women were Zanzibari Omanis, outgoing, eager to learn and not intimidated by working in an office with expat men. The archipelago of Zanzibar, located in the Indian Ocean off the coast of Tanzania, had been under the control of the Sultanate of Oman from 1631 to 1890, when it became a protectorate of Britain. Zanzibari Muslims had maintained their long relationship with Oman and, during the late twentieth century, many families moved to prosperous Oman during a period of instability in Zanzibar.

Most expatriate families departed Oman as soon as school was finished in May to escape the stifling heat. Gene gave his employees with children priority vacation dates and operated with a skeleton crew in the office. Although two commercial-sized air-conditioning units kept our house cool, we tried not to become house bound. We moved our tennis matches to 9:00 p.m. All the same, we were drenched with sweat before the first ball was served. We swam every evening in the ice-cooled pool. We had a water tank on the roof because, as in Argentina, precious water did not flow at all hours of the day. Oman began conserving water as early as 2500 BCE using an irrigation system called a *falaj*, brick- or tile-lined canals and cisterns where the scarce rainwater and mountain snowmelt were collected and then dispensed among the population in an equitable fashion. Some three thousand of these ancient systems were still in use when we lived there. In modern times, desalination plants were added out of necessity to supply the growing population.

In July, Suzanne and I flew to Michigan to represent our family at the wedding party in Jim's grandmother Hajar Hamady's beautiful home in Flint. Hajar, a kind and accomplished hostess, made us feel completely at home while unobtrusively providing for our every need. Her exquisite garden filled with Michigan relatives who welcomed us warmly. For many, this was their first time to meet Lisa. My attempt to discover how each of them was related to the others was greeted with bemused responses. Cousin seemed to suffice for most.

Gene arrived in Washington a week before the wedding to help us with the final preparations. The festivities were many: a barbecue on Thursday at Jim's Aunt Nonnie's home, the rehearsal dinner at

Jim's parents' home, the wedding on Saturday in the inspiringly beautiful National Presbyterian Church, the reception at the Weston Hotel in Georgetown, and brunch on Sunday at Cousin Jeanne Richard's home. Gene and I felt that not only Lisa but the entire Grogan clan had been adopted into this wonderful family. We were sad that Grandmother Thelma could not travel to be with us but our close friend Robbie Robinson called her during the reception to give her a full description of the weekend.

Escaping the doldrums, inevitable after such a glorious celebration, Gene, Suzanne and I flew to Crete, rented a car, and drove to a small hotel on the north coast. From there we spent an idyllic week basking in the warm, sunny climate and touring the island. Suzanne's two remaining vacation days were spent with us in Athens and Delphi. Gene and I completed the holiday by driving to see the ruins at Olympia on the western side of the Peloponnese peninsula.

Iraq had invaded Kuwait over a border dispute on August 2. By the time we returned to Muscat in October, Kuwaiti refugees filled camps inside the Omani border while the hotels in Muscat bulged with the upper crust of Kuwaiti society. The Middle East was on high alert fearing that Iraqi President Saddam Hussein might invade Saudi Arabia as well. Everyone waited for President George H. W. Bush, in conjunction with the UN Security Council, to respond. American ships and planes poured into the area. Near the Muscat airport, Americans constructed a field hospital. The U.S. Embassy enlisted American women to serve as volunteers. Gene doubled the length of the runway at the Oxy oil camp in the desert to accommodate large jets to evacuate Oxy families and employees, if necessary. American pilots, living in the Intercontinental Hotel, dubbed it a Five-Star Foxhole.

In spite of the uncertainty, life went on quite normally. Gene and I flew back home for Christmas with the family. However, when we returned in early January, the atmosphere was tense with dread. We arrived in Dubai on the last British Airways flight into the UAE .When we disembarked to catch our flight on to Muscat, members of the flight crew told us we were crazy because there was a huge crowd at the airport anxious to escape on any plane with a seat available. Perhaps we were, but Gene was determined to be with his employees and I was just as determined to be with Gene. We wondered what 1991 held for us and the world.

The Gulf War, code-named Operation Desert Storm, began on January 17, 1991, with a coordinated strike by a coalition of thirty-four nations led by the United States. Most of the troops were from the U.S. and used American materiel. In Oman we were eight hundred miles from the battle but we had a front-row seat—like everyone else in the world—because we watched it on CNN and listened to the BBC. Kuwait paid $36 billion of the $61 billion cost to drive the Iraqis out of their country. One could say they bought an army, 540,000 strong. The Saudis paid about $10 billion, as nothing separated Iraqi troops in Kuwait from Riyadh, the capital of Saudi Arabia, except 435 miles of sand, through which a superb motorway conveniently ran. The coalition nations were motivated by knowledge that Saddam Hussein could hold the world to ransom if he controlled the Iraqi, Kuwaiti and Saudi oil reserves.

An intense aerial bombardment prepared the ground for the invasion on February 24. From our patio, we watched tanker planes take off from our airport on their way to refuel the fighter jets in midair. In only four days, the coalition forces drove the Iraqis out of Kuwait and deep into their own territory. Estimates of the casualties on the Iraqi side were staggering: over a hundred thousand civilians killed, twenty thousand to thirty thousand soldiers killed, and seventy-five thousand soldiers wounded. On the coalition side a total of 358 died, 190 of them killed by Iraqis, the remainder by accidents or friendly fire, and 776 wounded.

Before they were pushed out of Kuwait, the Iraqis set seven hundred oil wells on fire. The smoke drifted over Oman, which brought the conflict closer home to us. Although Sultan Qaboos was firmly on the side of the coalition, some thought that many Omanis were not. Iraq's large army formed a strong counterweight to powerful Iran, the country most feared by its neighbors. The U.S. Embassy, through the warden system, advised Americans to keep a low profile, be aware of their surroundings, and not engage in political discussions with Arabs.

Gene and I continued our habit of walking on the beach at sundown. One evening we came upon some messages etched in wet sandbanks, written in Arabic and English, that said, "No Kuwait, Yes Saddam; Israel No, PLO Palestine Yes; Beat them Saddam with chemicals." Two Omani girls, completing the last slogan, took off running when they saw us. We had some sympathy for their position when it was revealed that the Americans had bombed a shelter containing hundreds of Iraqi women and children. Instead of apologizing for mistaking the target for a concentration of troops, the Pentagon tried to justify the action. The heavy American presence was evident to everyone as more than twenty war ships were visible from the shore and, we were told, many more were anchored beyond the horizon. The fear was that Saddam Hussein was not a dictator with whom one could negotiate and had we not forced him out of Kuwait, he might, indeed, have continued on to Saudi Arabia.

For the first time, we sensed that we were living in a society that was not completely hospitable to us. The war was over in a matter of weeks but the effects lasted much longer. We no longer felt comfortable discussing Middle East affairs with our Omani friends. While they continued to be friendly, a wall of caution separated us. Additionally, international passenger flights were canceled so we had no visitors or mail service. We felt safe, because we knew that the sultan would quickly put down any unrest, but we also felt isolated from the rest of the world.

On the surface, life continued its idyllic style. One evening we watched with fascination as a group of fishermen cast their nets in a wide arc onto the sea and hauled in huge batches of sardines, flashing silver in the twilight. The fishermen dumped them onto the sand, where other men shoveled them into pickup trucks. The vehicles aside, they were fishing as their ancestors had for hundreds, if not thousands, of years. The scene reminded us of biblical stories of Jesus's disciples fishing on the Sea of Galilee.

Later that evening Felcy and I drove to the fishermen's market, where we purchased the fresh sardines. We also ate very well from the garden Patrick had planted. Fresh produce was quite expensive in

Muscat as it was flown in from Europe. We harvested turnips, spinach, tomatoes, peppers, radishes, coriander leaves and delicious figs. We also had put in petunias, double hibiscus trees, and bottlebrush trees that the sunbirds and hummingbirds adored. With the year-round growing season, our garden had quickly become lush and beautiful.

In April, regular air service resumed. We flew to Kuala Lumpur, Malaysia, where Gene met with the local Oxy manager. Our friends Bob and Ann Cooper, who had moved from Scotland to Indonesia, joined us. Ann spent a few days with us in Malaysia before we flew to Singapore, where Bob met us for the weekend. We continued from Singapore to Los Angeles and Bakersfield.

Afterward, we traveled to Oklahoma for our annual physicals. We were shocked when Gene tested positive for tuberculosis. Ronny Yates, the excellent Oxy physician, sent him to a pulmonary specialist who confirmed the diagnosis and started Gene on the drug Isoniazid with the caution to have his liver function tested monthly and stop taking the drug immediately should any adverse side effects appear. In late June, back in Muscat, Gene fainted in church so we stopped the drug. Fortunately, Gene did not come down with the disease.

While in Oklahoma, we collected Grandmother Thelma from Greenbrier Nursing Home in Enid to spend a few days visiting relatives and friends. Thelma's back had stabilized and she was no longer in much pain but weak from using a wheelchair. She seemed to be content to stay in the nursing home, having formed a close friendship with her roommate.

During our visit, Dana developed unexplained painful swelling in her wrists. Her doctor recommended a specialist who diagnosed systemic lupus. We were stunned to learn that this autoimmune disease had no cure. Thus, Dana began the long process of learning to live with pain, as she continued to fulfill her roles as Patrick's wife and mother to Michael, who was five, and Clay, then three. Many years later, Dana continues to inspire all who know her with her courage and fortitude as she lives with this chronic disease while helping others in her church and community.

The end of the Gulf War brought a flurry of activity for Gene. Chevron sold its investment in Oxy's oil field to the Finnish National Oil Company, Neste Oy. The new partners, to Gene's relief, were knowledgeable gentlemen with whom he knew he could work harmoniously. Oxy president David Martin sent Gene to Doha, Qatar, to talk to the government about an offshore oil concession that Oxy was interested in leasing. Gene traveled back to Qatar to introduce an Oxy team from California who signed a contract with Qatar that became a very successful venture for both the company and the country. Gene was invited to the home of the patriarch of the Al Fardan family, who had made their first fortune trading in Gulf pearls in the late-nineteenth century. With deep roots in many businesses, they were part of the oil negotiations. Mr. Al Fardan expressed interest in buying Armand Hammer's racehorse Monarch and enlisted Gene's help. Dr. Hammer had died in 1990 at the age of ninety-two, but Gene was able to put the sheik in touch with the right person. He lightheartedly added horse trader to his résumé.

Gene and I had a full and exciting life during this period. We were able to travel extensively in a luxurious style. Gene's work was satisfying and productive. However, for me something was missing.

I felt that I had nothing worthwhile to do. At home, Patrick and Felcy took care of everything. I didn't enter the kitchen, make my own cup of tea or water my houseplants. I went to the health club, swam, had a massage, took part in Bible study and quilting groups, and napped every afternoon. To help fill the days, I spent hours cutting recipes from American magazines that arrived by pouch, assembling them into a large notebook. Halfway around the world from our loved ones, especially concerned about Thelma's and Dana's health, I was not available to help. Michael and Clay were growing up and we only saw them two or three times a year.

The inequities in the world were thrown into sharp relief in Oman. For us, Oman was a paradise, but for others it was not. Thousands of laborers from the Indian subcontinent toiled and lived in abject poverty, providing the cushy lifestyle that we enjoyed. Observing these men working twelve hours a day in temperatures that reached over one hundred degrees caused me distress. Knowing that the remittances they sent home to their families probably were the difference between life and death for their loved ones made their desperation all the more evident. To my knowledge, there were no charitable services for them. Our status was the same as theirs; we were "guest workers" and aware of the tenuousness of our situation should we anger the government. For the first time, I was unable to do volunteer work of any kind. Planning parties and lying around the pool made me feel rather useless.

One exciting distraction was the expedition mounted by the famed explorer Ranulph Fiennes to search for the fabled lost city of Ubar, the hub of the frankincense trade thousands of years ago. Ran and Gene had met several times because Fiennes had been the public relations representative for Dr. Hammer in Britain. He had visited Oman in 1990, then returned when the war ended, in late 1991, with a team that included American filmmakers from California and an archaeologist from Springfield, Missouri. Occidental was a sponsor, supplying vehicles and other equipment.

Stories of this city had circulated from ancient times. "Omanum Emporium" was marked on a map by Claudius Ptolemy around 150 BCE. Explorers who had heard the tales of Ubar from guides included Bertram Thomas in 1930, Wilfred Thesiger in 1946, and Wendell Phillips in 1953. The filmmaker used a new tool to aid in the search: satellite-imagery maps that revealed early camel caravan trails that crossed at the ancient well site of Shisr. Believing this to be Ubar, the team began an excavation, with the archeologist in charge of an enthusiastic group of volunteers. Muscat was all abuzz with parties, fund-raisers and trips to the site in the Dhofar province of southern Oman. Gene's office was deeply involved in logistics. We all enjoyed being close to the action and becoming friends with the team members. Artifacts were found at the excavation site that made them believe they had truly found Ubar. All the same, as in most archeological research, critics and naysayers abounded. When they completed their dig, a great celebration was held claiming success. The team departed and, in time, disputes among them surfaced. Undeterred, Ran Fiennes wrote a rip-roaringly good tale of his search for the lost city that was published in 1992, *Atlantis of the Sands: The Search for the Lost City of Ubar.*

In September, we received a call from Patrick and Dana with the sad news of the sudden death of her father, Bob Atchison, of a heart attack at the age of only sixty-three. This was another occasion when we felt we were too far from home, unable to be there to help comfort Dana and her family over the loss of this kind, gentle man.

From Suzanne we had some good news. Memorex-Telex, her employer, was moving its headquarters to Dallas. Suzanne's group was not slated to move so she feared she would lose her job; however, she was offered a position in another section that was part of the move. Having successfully passed her certified public accountant exam, she was excited about the new job and the opportunity to live in Dallas.

While our children gathered with Grandmother to celebrate Thanksgiving in Garber, Gene and I did our best to fill our Thanksgiving table in Muscat. We invited six expat couples and four U.S. sailors from a ship that was in port. Patrick, our cook, produced a fantastic meal using our family recipes. Gene retold the story of America's first Thanksgiving for the benefit of our non-American friends. A tradition in our family was to ask each person to name something he or she was thankful for. Of course, when our children were small, they usually said, "The food." The homesickness we experienced on this quintessentially American holiday made us especially grateful to offer a bit of home to the sailors. We were relieved that the Gulf War had ended with fewer casualties than expected on the coalition side, but grieved for the thousands of Iraqis who had died.

Life in Oman returned to prewar calm. Many foreign companies, which had evacuated their staff and families before the Gulf War began, returned. Gene was glad that Occidental had continued operations during the war as the Omani government greatly appreciated those who remained.

We looked forward to a visit from Lisa, Jim and Suzanne in February, and planned a camping trip to the Wahiba Sands. I secretly arranged a surprise party for Gene's sixtieth birthday. Located on the Arabian Sea, 150 miles south of Muscat, the Sands was forty-eight hundred square miles of desert noted for its spectacularly high dunes. About thirty friends signed up to join us. A tour company set up a tented camp with the dining tent layered in carpets and cushions. A delicious dinner was served on china and crystal by waiters in full uniform and white gloves. Johnnie and Mary Kay Heck provided champagne to go with the birthday cake. As it was held a month ahead of his birthday, Gene was truly surprised and pleased.

The next morning we went dune driving. With a Bedouin guide in the lead car because it was easy to get lost, we rode in SUVs as fast as possible up hard-packed sand dunes, flew off the tops and rocketed down the other sides. This was like riding a roller coaster with the element of danger much greater as the SUVs could easily flip over. Hitting the bottom was jarring but provided extra speed for the run up the next dune. The SUV drivers, Omani and American, competed to see who could go the fastest and yell the loudest.

Late February turned out to be the wettest month in Oman for forty years. One day two inches of rain fell in two hours. While that might not cause a disaster at home, in Muscat the roads flooded as the dry wadis topped their banks. Several deaths occurred as cars were swept away. In our garden, Felcy found some baby laughing doves whose nest was destroyed and nursed them until they were ready to fly. At the same time, Britain was experiencing the worst drought in a century. Shortly after this wet period, the desert burst into bloom with wild flowers in profusion. We city dwellers poured into the desert to view this wondrous sight.

I traveled with Gene to the United States in May. While there, we moved Grandmother Thelma into a private room at the Greenbrier Nursing Home following the death of her beloved roommate. We decorated the room with new furniture and cheerful pictures from home, and she seemed delighted, but shortly began to withdraw, taking most of her meals in her room. She became isolated from the other residents where, previously, she had played the piano and sang for them.

As the year progressed, our children grew increasingly disturbed following tearful phone calls with her. Helpless to reduce her melancholy, we contemplated the possibility of bringing her to live with us. Although Gene and his sister, Betty, both expressed concern about taking her out of the nursing home, we invited her to Oman for a six-week holiday. We told her that we would take her to Muscat after Christmas and that she could live permanently with us if she so desired. We held on to her room at the Greenbrier in case she wanted to return.

In September, we flew to East Africa for a vacation. We were eager to visit friends we hadn't seen since leaving Nairobi in 1983. We went first to Arusha, Tanzania, to visit Mark and Linda Jacobson and their three delightful young daughters. Mark and Linda had met at Johns Hopkins Hospital in Baltimore, Maryland, where both were enrolled in a course on family health. Mark had earned his MD from the University of Minnesota Medical School. Linda was a medical technologist. Both were planning to become medical missionaries. We met them at the Lutheran Church when they arrived in Nairobi in 1982 as newlyweds. The next year, Mark took over as medical director of a small Lutheran hospital in Arusha that had no electricity. He sterilized his equipment by boiling it on a small cookstove. Nine years later he invited us to see the expanding hospital as he met with his staff early in the morning for a worship service, followed by a session with the young people he was training. He did not see patients personally, establishing a model that developed Tanzanians to become highly competent doctors and nurses. Each one spoke with Mark about patients they were treating and asked him for advice about their care. The charge for delivering a baby was $2.50 provided the family had the means to pay; otherwise, it was free. In 2013, Mark received one of the American Medical Association's highest honors for his thirty years in Tanzania building a world-class hospital. Under his inspired leadership, the hospital and its associated facilities continued to grow, adding sophisticated equipment to treat ever more complex medical conditions. In Nairobi, we were able to visit several American missionary couples we had known when we lived there plus our Kenyan friends Jim and Mary Nesbitt.

In December we flew home to Oklahoma, collected Thelma from the nursing home in Enid, had Christmas with Patrick and Dana in Tulsa, and spent New Year's in Washington with Lisa and Jim. Then we flew with Thelma to Oman. We prayed that she would adapt to her new surroundings and be content with us.

Sixteen

MOVE WHERE?

Bakersfield
April 1993 / August 1996

THELMA, EIGHTY-EIGHT, arrived in Muscat in high spirits and was welcomed with hugs and kisses by Felcy and Patrick. We hoped she would not suffer from culture shock hearing the call to prayer five times a day from the mosque just below our house, and seeing men dressed with their long, flowing white *dishdashas*, turbans and khanjars (curved daggers), plus attending church on Fridays. In true form, she welcomed each new experience and within weeks told us that she wanted to stay permanently. I had bought sewing projects for her and she was pleased when Felcy showed an interest in learning to do handwork. They spent happy times together laughing and sewing. Each evening Gene and I took her down to the beach before dinner, where we walked her on the surfaced path. Afterward, settled into a beach chair, she watched us exercise, breathed the sea air and exclaimed over the beautiful sunsets. She took an active part in Bible studies, the American Women's Group, quilters group, grocery shopping and basking poolside at the Intercontinental Hotel while we swam. I took her weekly to an English hairdresser who knew just what she wanted, including the type of permanent she preferred. Everyone she met loved her. She rarely went out with us in the evenings as she wanted to eat her supper and go to bed early, but she felt safe with Patrick and Felcy. She slept in the downstairs bedroom where we had installed a buzzer beside her bed to summon them if necessary. She wrote letters to family and friends at home and looked forward to replies when the company pouch arrived on Thursdays. With her arrival, my sense of uselessness evaporated. Suddenly, I had a purpose—to care for her as she had always cared for us. Gene was glad to greet two cheerful, smiling women when he walked through the door each evening.

Our friend June Evans came from England for a month's visit. We took her and Thelma to Sur, the city famous for making the spectacular Omani dhows. These large vessels were handmade by craftsmen who learned their trade from their fathers and worked without taking measurements using the design that originated in the eighth century. A week after June left, our Kenyan friends Jim and Mary Nesbitt arrived. Thelma was pleased to renew her friendship with them after almost eleven years. In March we took her to Dubai. Everything was going so well. We enjoyed having her with us as she embraced life in Oman.

In late March, the phone rang and Gene began a conversation with someone in Bakersfield. It was not unusual for him to receive calls at night because of the time difference, but I could tell that he was discussing a transfer for an Oxy employee. When he hung up, I asked who was being transferred. His response was "I am." What a shock! That was not what we wanted to hear. We both expected to have six years in Oman and then retire. But Oxy had other plans. Gene's position was a promotion to vice-president of oil and gas in charge of development projects and movements of domestic engineers. We were to be based at Occidental's headquarters in Bakersfield. While Gene traveled the world, Thelma and I would be stuck in Bakersfield. Perhaps due to the stress of that news, I came down with Tietze syndrome, a virus that caused painful cartilage inflammation in the chest.

News of our coming move was met with jubilation by our family at home. Gene's cousin, Anne Stoner, and her husband, Jim, lived in Clovis, California, only 120 miles north of Bakersfield. They offered to host Thelma while we shopped for a house. Thelma seemed quite happy to return. She hadn't lived in Oman long enough to become homesick but I'm sure she had thought of the great distance she was from daughter Betty and others.

Gene and I tried to accept the transfer graciously. We had only a few days to contemplate our fate, as packers arrived and began putting things in boxes. We held a mini-sale of foodstuffs and 220-volt appliances. Gene's replacement, Tony Holt, arrived with his wife, Susanna. We were wined and dined by many friends, and the parties culminated in an Oxy company farewell/welcome party for the four of us around the pool of the Gulf Hotel on a hill with a commanding view of the seacoast.

We encouraged the Holts to retain our staff because they were excellent, the envy of our friends. The only concern was that Felcy's ambition to get ahead sometimes caused friction. Hired on a provisional basis, they didn't follow my advice not to make demands and they were soon put on a plane back to India. For several years,

Patrick worked as a cook with a cruise line while Felcy lived in Mumbai with her mother. She adopted a baby boy and opened a hairdressing salon. Eventually, Patrick was able to get a U.S. visa, move to the States and cook in restaurants owned by a man from his home village. Felcy and their son joined him and they settled in a Boston suburb, where Patrick continued to cook and Felcy, the entrepreneur, started her own business. We were so pleased for them. Felcy's ambition for her family finally paid off.

In April Gene, Thelma and I boarded a plane for Hong Kong on the first leg of our flight home. We hired a car and driver to take us around to show Thelma the sights of that wonderful island, including the bay filled with the large seagoing junks that were home to many Chinese families. From Hong Kong we flew to San Francisco, and from there drove south to Bakersfield. We left Thelma in Clovis with Anne and Jim, recently retired from their jobs as managers of the bookstore for California State University in Fresno.

Settled in a Bakersfield hotel, Gene went to the office and I began the search for a house. Occidental recommended an experienced real estate agent with a sparkling personality and wit who made the job of house hunting pleasurable. After twenty-one consecutive years living outside the United States, I was shocked by the prices of everything, especially houses. When I told Gene the asking prices, he was appalled.

After a couple of days, I took him to see the best choices. We bought an older home on a corner lot surrounded by beautiful olive and birch trees. Like many California houses, it had a swimming pool and hot tub set in a lush garden with a high privacy wall. Although we had visited Bakersfield several times, the idea of living there brought home the desolation of the San Joaquin Valley. Without irrigation, nothing grew. We were effectively moving from one desert to another.

Located at the end of a valley, Bakersfield had mountains on three sides, although thanks to the smog they could rarely be seen. But our sheltered and watered backyard felt like the Garden of Eden.

Pre-Columbian peoples had lived in the region for thousands of years. In 1776, the Spanish missionary Father Francisco Garcia was the first European to visit the area. In 1848, gold was discovered along the Kern River and the town became known as Bakersfield when a lawyer from Ohio, Thomas Baker, settled there in 1860. In 1865 oil was discovered and fueled the region's first prosperity. With irrigation, agriculture became a major economic driver and the region became a national breadbasket, the source of nuts, cotton, citrus, vegetables and a quarter of America's carrots.

During the Dust Bowl years of the 1930s, many emigrants came from Oklahoma. Gene and I always read the obituaries in the local paper and frequently found native Oklahomans listed.

Bakersfield was known as a redneck town, home to country-and-western stars Buck Owens and Merle Haggard. With Los Angeles a two-hour drive away, it had few good restaurants and those that attempted gourmet cuisine usually failed. Politically, Bakersfield was considered the most conservative city in California. I was advised by a neighbor that I should only listen to talk radio's Rush Limbaugh; I did not even know who he was.

On the first Sunday in our home on Avenida Valedor, with boxes stacked everywhere and the kitchen barely usable, we ventured out to church. The rector was out of town, but the welcome we received from the congregation at All Saints Episcopal was overwhelming. Gene and I returned from the communion rail in tears, deeply touched by their warmth as well as feeling homesick for our friends in Muscat. Ed Little, the rector, and his wife, Sylvia, proved to be equally welcoming. After all the years we had been active in Anglican/ Episcopal churches, Ed encouraged us to take instruction and officially join the Episcopal Church, which we did. We joined two Bible study groups. Thelma and I attended the women's weekly daytime study. The women said we reminded them of the Old Testament figures Naomi and Ruth, a mother-in-law and daughter-in-law. Gene and I joined a couples group that met in the evening, and there we became friends with Lane and Phyllis Schumacher. They drove in from a mining town in the desert that was over two hours away. Occasionally, they spent Sunday nights with us and also stayed with Thelma a few times so I could take short trips with Gene. Phyllis was an expert quilter as was Thelma, who loved her and was comfortable staying with them. The first time we went out at night, I hired a teenager to stay with Thelma, but she was indignant, assuring us that she could take herself off to bed perfectly well without us or a babysitter, so we began to leave her alone when we went out in the evenings.

Our first months in Bakersfield were occupied with the business of settling in, learning our way around, and dealing with three tragedies. In July, my first cousin, well-respected portrait painter Ethlyn "Cookie" Crouch, had a stroke in the garden of her home in Carmel, California. Her son, Stephen, who lived in Alaska, called and asked if we could check on her. When it was determined that she would not recover, she was moved into a hospice home. Although she was in a deep coma, the staff had surrounded her with beauty, placing her in a bed with flower-patterned sheets facing the lovely garden outside her window and playing meditative music provided by friends. We returned a week later just an hour before she died. The second tragedy occurred in August when my cousin Marilyn Stephens Bailey's son, Robbie, took his life after struggling for years with bipolar disorder. And in September our friend and matchmaker Sally Caldwell Bauer died at home of a heart attack. I had spoken with her only days before her death; she was on the waiting list for a heart transplant but was dreading the ordeal. These sorrows added to what I ultimately recognized as reentry shock.

Our family had experienced culture shock many times over the years as we moved from place to place, especially in foreign countries. We went through the four recognized phases. The first phase, the honeymoon, produces excitement and fascination when the new culture appears to be charming and intriguing. In phase two, the negotiation phase, which often overlaps the first phase, one figures out where to shop, how to navigate in strange territory, the currency and a host of other differences. This causes homesickness for the previous location and a fair amount of anxiety. Within a few months, by phase three, the adjustment phase, one feels more at home in the new culture. Finally, in the mastery or bicultural stage, one may have learned the local language, made friends and begun to feel truly settled and accepted.

I was not prepared for reentry or reverse culture shock. Having returned to America once or twice a year during the almost twenty-two years we lived abroad, I believed that I would have no trouble returning to my native country. Our two most recent assignments in Scotland and Oman, which had very little crime, were a dramatic contrast with the nightly murders reported on the local news. I was warned to avoid certain parts of the city. Less dramatic but nonetheless disconcerting was the abundance of material goods and the emphasis on possessing them. It took ages to negotiate the cereal aisle in the supermarket or buy an article of clothing in the department store. I humiliated myself in a gift shop when a clerk, upon hearing that I had just moved from Oman, exclaimed, "Welcome to civilization." Without thinking, I replied, "Well, hardly," and then struggled to apologize and explain. Politically, I found myself looking at America with the eyes of an outsider. Disagreeing with the prevailing attitude that everything, such as our medical system and way of life, was superior to the rest of the world, I often had to keep my opinions to myself for fear of alienating friends and family.

Another disconcerting experience was trying to sign up with a doctor. Occidental Petroleum used an internist as their company doctor and recommended him to us. To our dismay, we were told that he would accept us as patients but not Thelma because she was on Medicare. Gene replied that we would not use him if he did not take her, so he relented. We never did feel comfortable having him as our physician, but choices of doctors in Bakersfield were limited.

Because Gene traveled so frequently during our thirty-three months there, I was alone with Thelma most of the time. She and I went everywhere together. Although we were great companions, I needed some time on my own as well. I hired a housekeeper who worked on Fridays, giving me an opportunity to get out alone. I started volunteering in the maternity department of Mercy Hospital while Thelma was content to stay at home.

When Gene was in town on weekends we took drives into the countryside, but were often at a loss for something interesting to see. There was an old oil field, still productive, but with miles of ugly equipment scattered about. The closest agriculture was mostly cotton. Museums and other cultural offerings were scarce. One superb destination 135 miles north, Sequoia National Park, featured the oldest and largest redwoods in the world. In winter, deep snow sparkled beneath these majestic trees silhouetted against a brilliant blue sky. A closer escape from the polluted air was a drive into the Tehachapi Mountains at the end of the San Joaquin Valley.

In the predawn mornings, Gene jogged and I walked around the neighborhood, followed by breakfast with Thelma before he left for the office at 7:15. Many evenings, we swam while Thelma enjoyed sitting poolside in the dry, cool air.

Upon our arrival, we were warmly welcomed by Johnnie and Mary Kay Heck. They had reluctantly moved from Oman to Bakersfield about six months earlier so that Oxy management could evaluate him in order to fulfill his desire to become a country manager. A few months after our arrival, Johnnie was transferred to Russia as manager. Although happy for them, we were very sad to see them leave. John was going into a difficult position but was fully prepared for the challenge, which he handled with the skill and patience it required. Mary Kay got busy learning Russian and became an active member of the expatriate community. They exemplified everything that was good about Americans living abroad, representing our nation proudly while keenly exploring and appreciating the rich Russian history.

We were grateful that other old friends were there: Joe and Mati Snape, Dan and Anne McReynolds, and Marvin and Pat Carter kindly entertained us and helped us get settled. Being able to pick up the phone and talk to the children and friends was grand. We looked forward to family reunions. Son-in-law Jim arrived for a short visit in July when he came to California on business. Suzanne and her boyfriend, Jay Lipscomb, spent a few days with us in August. We were eager to get to know Jay. Suzanne had met him in the church choir and described him and his family in glowing terms. His kindness and easy manner made us instant fans.

In October, Gene and I flew to Tulsa to attend the baptism of our grandson, Michael Grogan, at John Knox Presbyterian Church. Patrick and Dana had chosen dedication rather than baptism for their babies. Eight-year-old Michael now understood the meaning of the sacrament and was eager to be baptized. Being able to be present for this milestone helped us to recognize and accept God's direction in our return to the States. Back in Bakersfield, we eagerly prepared for Thanksgiving and the arrival of Jim, Lisa, Suzanne and Jay.

Suzanne returned for Christmas with exciting news. Jay had proposed and she accepted with a wedding date set for May 1994. With Thelma, we went to San Diego on a trip to enjoy the warm weather and visit SeaWorld but spent every moment with our minds full of wedding fever. This anticipated event made us grateful at last to be back in the United States and closer to our children.

Deciding to bring Thelma to live with us was the right decision. Of that, I had no doubt. My motivation was good. I loved her and could not bear to think of her suffering. No stranger to tragedy, she had held her baby boy Dale in her arms as he died when she was twenty-five years old. By the age of thirty-three she was a widow with two young children. She spent her life caring for others—her family, her parents and everyone who needed her—never complaining and spreading joy and compassion wherever she went. To me she was a living Christian saint.

At the same time, the next two years tested my commitment. I believe that my hubris led me to think that I could care for Thelma, travel with Gene, and respond to our children's needs without cracking under the strain. I learned to my sorrow that was not true.

In January 1994, Gene invited me to travel with him to Yemen and Pakistan. Betty and Bill agreed, somewhat reluctantly, to keep Thelma for a month. I welcomed the respite from caring for her but also realized the burden we were putting on Betty. She had placed her mother safely in the nursing home in Oklahoma until we took her to live with us. Now we were asking her to share in her mother's care. On top of that, Betty was caring for her husband, Bill, who suffered from emphysema, was on oxygen, and spent most of his days and nights in a recliner. Betty flew into Los Angeles, collected her mother, and flew home.

I flew to Washington for a short visit with Lisa and Jim, arriving in London a few hours ahead of Gene. Following a partners meeting the next day, we landed in Dubai with time to shop for gold necklaces for Suzanne's bridal attendants and have lunch with friends before our flight to Sana'a. Gene's new position as vice-president for Eastern Hemisphere operations placed the following countries under his supervision: the Netherlands, Congo, Oman, Yemen, Qatar, Pakistan and the Philippines. Away from home so often, he missed me and also wanted me to have the opportunity to see these countries, so paid for my expenses when I was able to join him.

Located below Oman, on the southern tip of the Arabian continent, Yemen (known as Sheba in the Bible) was home of the famed Sabaeans, who thrived on trade, especially of frankincense, which grew prolifically in the area. Under the control of various peoples such as the Jews, Christians, Muslims, Persians, Romans, Ottomans, British and Portuguese, and with a dizzying number of tribal affiliations, Yemen had always been notoriously difficult to unite and control. During the twentieth century, the densely populated country was ranked as one of the poorest and most corrupt countries of the world. Its major cash crop was khat, whose mildly narcotic leaves were chewed daily by most Yemeni men. For this reason, very little work was accomplished after midday.

The southern part of the country became a British protectorate in 1839, starting as a coal refueling station for ships traveling between Britain and India. The long history of tribal friction and foreign intervention divided the country in 1905 along a north-south border with sporadic civil war continuing throughout the century. In 1963, a communist insurgency forced the British to withdraw. In May 1990, the north and south united as the Unified Republic of Yemen with two tribally and politically incompatible men in power, Ali Abdullah Saleh as president and Ali Salim al-Beidh as vice-president. The vice-president was from the south and in August 1993 he retired to Aden. The two armies, which had never been combined, began massing troops on opposite sides of the border. When Gene and I arrived in January, tension was palpable in the capital. Because of unrest in the city center, we were booked into a hotel on the edge of town. While Gene was at the office, Ali, the Oxy driver, took me on a tour of the city including the ancient souk. We walked through its dark passages where I purchased some souvenirs. He also took me to the roof of one of the highest buildings for a bird's-eye view of the city. I felt a bit uneasy when he urged me to walk to the edge of the roof for a better view. Not knowing his feelings toward Americans, I remember being cautious and standing a safe distance from the several-story drop.

Oxy's manager was keen to show us some of the spectacular scenery outside of Sana'a but there was only one highway that was considered reasonably safe to drive. The twisting road on the edge of the deep escarpment gave us a view that was as breathtaking as our Grand Canyon. For lunch we stopped in a home where the family served meals in a room on the top floor of the house overlooking the beautiful rift valley. We were the only customers. The husband escorted us to our table, his wife cooked and their adult daughter served and flirted with the men. After lunch, the daughter insisted on wrapping me in a scarf, Yemeni style, with only my eyes visible. Once we entered our car and were out of sight, I eagerly removed the hot, claustrophobic wrap, discovering how miserable it was to wear the *nijab*.

We flew from Sana'a to Karachi, which the U.S. State Department identified as one of the most dangerous cities in the world. We did not leave the airport, but flew on to the seat of government, Islamabad, where we were met by the Oxy manager. Islamabad, built during the 1960s, replaced Karachi as the capital of Pakistan. The clean, literate, urbane city was home to several universities, medical facilities, technology and science centers, as well as being the seat of government. However, electricity generation had not been able to keep up with its rapid growth. A schedule of load-sharing meant that for many hours each day homes had no electricity. In spite of that difficulty, the manager's wife prepared a marvelous meal for a party in their home to introduce us to Oxy employees and Pakistani businessmen.

Returning to London, we parted ways. Gene flew directly to California and I went to Dallas to plan the wedding. Jay's mother, Betty Lipscomb, had offered her services as well as the use of their club, Brook Hollow, for the wedding reception. I greatly appreciated the opportunity for us to get to know each other better while we worked. Over three whirlwind days, we made all the arrangements. In the evenings we attended a symphony concert and enjoyed meals with Jay's parents. Betty's relaxed, gracious assistance and Suzanne and Jay's ability to make decisions quickly assured that the mother of the bride flew home relaxed and happy to know that Suzanne was joining such a kind, welcoming family.

We brought Thelma back to Bakersfield. Not long after, Gene left on another business trip to Oman, Pakistan and the Philippines. He had just returned home when Thelma had a small stroke. She had complained of being dizzy and seemed confused. We remembered other occasions when she had complained of dizziness, but had not recognized them as medical events. Thelma also suffered from shortness of breath and back pain and was uncharacteristically cranky. She resisted changing into seasonally appropriate clothes and became picky about food. When Nicole Brown, celebrity football star O. J. Simpson's wife, was found murdered in June 1994, we watched on TV while Simpson's SUV eluded police in a low-speed chase. Thelma did not understand that the film clip of the chase was played over and over for days. This was the first indication to us that she was beginning to suffer with dementia.

She had been home with us for less than two months when I loaded the car and we two started east. I left her in Albuquerque and met the rest of the family in Dallas. Shortly before the wedding, Betty and Thelma flew in. The parties began with a Texas barbecue and a Mexican-themed rehearsal dinner. The wedding at St. Michael and All Angels Episcopal Church on May 5 was led by the revered associate rector Bill Power, assisted by Father Roch, Jay's favorite teacher from Cistercian Monastery School. The full choir, who took credit for being the matchmakers that had put these two together, sang rapturously. The next day the newlyweds flew to Europe, Betty and Thelma departed for Albuquerque, and Gene and I flew to Scotland for a short holiday.

Back in Bakersfield, after taking an antibiotic for a throat infection, I experienced a severe allergic reaction. Prescribed heavy doses of cortisone, I was unable to leave the house for three weeks. Gene canceled his travel schedule to care for Thelma and me. Thelma's back became so painful that she began to use a wheelchair again, and she developed stomach problems. Gene often had to be away while medical issues plagued both Thelma and me. He had declined the retirement package that was annually offered to executives over sixty. Now I encouraged him to consider retiring, though he had wanted to work until he was sixty-five. At the same time, he was concerned about the pressure I was under and planned to take me away on more trips and thus we attempted to ignore the deteriorating situation at home.

In September, Betty came to our house to stay with Thelma while I went with Gene to Helsinki, Finland, for Neste Oy and Oxy's partners meeting, after which we visited the Hecks in Moscow. I traveled home via Washington for a quick visit with Jim and Lisa, who announced that a baby was due in April. I eagerly agreed when she asked me to help care for them following delivery.

Betty and Thelma had fared well in Bakersfield. But Thelma seemed out of sorts. I failed to understand that my absences made her afraid. As her dementia progressed, she needed to be with me to feel safe. And I needed her. I missed her when I was away, worried about her, and felt guilty about asking Betty to care for her mother so often. My health continued to be a concern. The doctor strongly recommended surgery but I put it off.

Our family gathered at Patrick and Dana's house for a Thanksgiving reunion—Gene flying in from abroad and the rest of us from California, New Mexico, Texas and Maryland. We held a belated celebration for Thelma's ninetieth birthday at her home in Garber. She was excited about the party and beamed at the large crowd of family and friends who arrived at the house. At one point in the festivities, she leaned over to me and said, "Jan, who are these people?" I was shocked. Betty took Thelma to Albuquerque because I was, once again, joining Gene on a trip.

In early December, I flew to San Francisco en route to Hong Kong, where Gene met me, then on to Manila. The Oxy manager was waiting for us with a 1947 Packard limousine and liveried driver from the Peninsula Hotel. We rode through the streets of Manila in high style. The rest of the visit was equally elegant and successful for Gene in negotiations with the petroleum ministry for an oil lease. For the grandbaby due in April, I purchased an exquisite hand-embroidered christening gown made of pineapple fiber. Our five youngest grandchildren were christened in that gown.

Knowing we could no longer leave Thelma alone in the house, Gene and I purchased a treadmill as our Christmas gift to each other. Suzanne and Jay arrived to stay with us through New Year's. We spent most of the week along the coast, in Cambria and Carmel, arriving home in time to start the new year with our traditional dinner of ham, barbecued black-eyed peas, rice, ambrosia and corn bread. Aware of the downward spiral we were in, we prayed for a happier, healthier new year.

In January, Gene left for Oman and the Netherlands. At home, Thelma began to resist showering. Unwilling to insist, I hired a nursing service to come three days a week to shower and dress her for bed. When the bell rang and I said, "Your nurse is here," she grimaced; however, she always reappeared smiling. I later learned that dementia sufferers often have a fear of water. She was increasingly grumpy and difficult. One day, she went to her room and stayed there. Peeking around the door, I saw her crying. When she saw me, she threw a tissue at me—astonishing behavior, completely out of character. But, of course, it was not her behavior but my ignorance that was the problem. I took her to the only gerontologist in

Bakersfield. An MRI of her brain revealed damage but he just shook his head when I asked about a prognosis. Thelma and I continued to have our ups and downs, sometimes crying together. Gene brought me flowers when he was in town. I know he was worried about us but felt as helpless as I did. Thinking back, I wonder why we did not seek counseling from either our rector at church or his wife who was a psychologist. I was slowly losing control of myself and our situation, but pressed on day by day. Over the years, being able to handle whatever came our way had become almost a mantra for me. I didn't admit to anyone outside the family that I was in trouble.

Although Thelma now required constant attention, I was determined to be with Lisa for her baby's birth in April. We asked Betty and Bill to take Thelma for two months so that I could have my long-delayed surgery in Bakersfield after being with Lisa. When I arrived in Washington, Betty and Jim Sams welcomed me into their comfortable home, where Lisa and Jim were already staying while an addition to their house was being completed. Gene came to represent Occidental at a black-tie dinner hosted by Prime Minister Benazir Bhutto of Pakistan to celebrate the signing of several oil contracts. With impeccable timing, while Gene was still in town, Claire Najla arrived on April 9 at Georgetown University Hospital. By noon, she had a roomful of admirers: beaming grandparents Betty, Jim, Jan and Gene; new aunt Alicia Sams; and great-grandmother Hajar Hamady. Gene had to fly back to Bakersfield but joyfully held his brand new granddaughter before departing.

Following my surgery, Suzanne arrived to be my nurse at home for the first few days. Then she and Gene went to Washington for

Claire's christening at St. Alban's Episcopal Church on June 4. Our friends the Schumachers came to stay with me, then Gene flew to Albuquerque to bring his mother home.

During this difficult period, I began to write. Discovering a love of writing during my years at the University of Aberdeen, I joined Writers of Kern County, a branch of the California Writers Club, one of the oldest writing clubs in the nation, composed of published writers and amateurs like me. Bakersfield boasted quite a few screenwriters and novelists who found the city quiet and comparatively economical but close enough to Los Angeles to commute with their finished work. Gene was very supportive of my hobby and encouraged me to attend a weekend writers conference held in Pacific Grove, California, that I enjoyed immensely.

In August, I decided that Thelma might perk up if I took her to Garber. She had always been happy to be in her own home. Also, an uncle in Gene's family was having a party to celebrate his ninety-fifth birthday in Pampa, Texas. There would be a large family gathering where Thelma could see lots of relatives.

Being in her Garber home wasn't the tonic I expected. Visits to friends in nearby towns did not help. I could see the sadness and confusion in her eyes and theirs. We closed the house and went to Tulsa to spend some time with Patrick and Dana. She seemed happier there, enchanted by her great-grandchildren. Continuing to Dallas, we checked into a hotel so that I could care for her without disrupting the Lipscombs' routine. The second night, Thelma lost her balance in the bathroom and fell. She wasn't hurt but I had a difficult time getting her up from the floor. After four days in Dallas, we started for home, spending the first night in Amarillo. The next morning I left her alone in the hotel room while I ran next door to McDonald's to buy breakfast. When I got back, she was crying. In the car, she sank into a black mood, refusing to talk to me while my frustration kept me mute as well for the long drive.

After settling her at Betty and Bill's, I drove to the service station to buy gasoline and get a car wash. Driving into the automatic washer, I got outside the rails, realized my mistake, backed up and completed the wash, only to discover that I had crumpled the left front fender. Bill assured me that the fender wasn't rubbing the tire so I could continue to Flagstaff the next day. Fifteen miles west of Gallup, the tire shredded while I was driving on Interstate 40. I was able to get off the very busy highway onto a wide shoulder and called for assistance. The mechanic said it would not be safe to continue without a spare tire so we followed him back to Gallup. One hundred eighty-five miles later, we arrived at our hotel too tired to eat. We fell into bed and started for Bakersfield early the next morning. Completely covered with hives, I called Gene, who was waiting at the house when we arrived and took me directly to the doctor.

We began a tense discussion about moving Thelma into assisted living. Gene was disappointed and I felt that I had failed him and his mother. Again, we should have sought counseling. Knowing we would not stay in Bakersfield when Gene retired, we asked Betty and Bill if they would be willing for us to place her in a facility in Albuquerque. They agreed but seemed distressed at the prospect. We located a small group home only a block from their house. In September, we left for New Mexico. We were too cowardly to tell Thelma that this was a permanent move.

Gene suggested a vacation followed by my accompanying him on another trip to the Middle East. We flew to Washington in time to attend a surprise birthday party for Betty Sams. It was heaven to be with Claire, with her nanny there to help while Lisa was at work. Driving to New England, we stopped the first night for a reunion with Fred and Jean Siefke in New Canaan, Connecticut, and arrived the following day on Cape Cod to attend the wedding of Rita, the daughter of our friends Joe and Mati Snape.

Back in Washington, we flew to Europe and on to Oman in early October, where we attended a church service and renewed many friendships. I sadly recounted Thelma's rapid decline to our friends who remembered her with much affection. They tried to console us and promised to keep us and our family in their prayers.

From Muscat, we flew to Doha, Qatar. Gene had to leave me there when he was summoned to New York to meet with the Congolese foreign minister. We reunited in London, continuing to The Hague for more meetings.

By the end of the month we were back in Bakersfield. We hoped that we had done the right thing for Thelma and for ourselves. Our church family reassured us but we missed her. We comforted ourselves that Thelma had contentedly lived with us for almost three years. Otherwise, she would have remained in the nursing home where she had been so unhappy. Although I know that God forgave me for not listening for His guidance, sorrow weighed heavily because of my failure to keep her with us.

We eagerly accepted Betty and Bill's invitation to Albuquerque for Thanksgiving. Betty had told me that she found it depressing to go see her mother and visited infrequently, so we were especially anxious about Thelma's adjustment to living in the group home. She beamed with joy when she saw us, but we quickly realized that she thought we would be taking her home, heartbreaking for us all. Although it was a cheerful, cozy atmosphere with six other residents under the care of the owner and attentive aides, it wasn't family. During later visits, she seemed more at peace. As her dementia progressed, she became less connected with her surroundings. She died there on February 2, 1997. Following a celebration of her life at the Garber Christian Church, she was buried in the Garber cemetery between her beloved husband, Deane, and their precious baby boy Dale.

The arrival of the family for Christmas helped lift our spirits. We all missed Grandmother but Michael, now ten, Clay, seven, and baby Claire brought the joy that children naturally exude. We were thrilled when Suzanne and Jay shared wonderful news of the expected arrival of their first child in July.

Toward the end of January 1996, Gene called from the office with good news. He had been offered a retirement package that pleased him, containing a two-year consulting contract at full salary, which satisfied his desire to have a forty-year career. March 31 would be his last day at work. After all the years abroad, we were eager to settle near one of our three children, who were located in Tulsa, Washington and Dallas. We chose Washington, a magnificent city with a treasure-trove of museums and other cultural attractions. On two occasions Gene had looked at properties with a real estate agent when he was there on business but we now scheduled a trip together for June.

In the meantime, Gene continued his international traveling. Gradually regaining my health, I joyfully anticipated the arrival of my dear friend Robbie Erwin from Texas for a week's visit. Although separated by time and space, we maintained our deep spiritual connection that began in Tulsa in 1968 when we were in a women's prayer group together. With her, I was able to pour out my deepest feelings about the difficulties of the past two years.

Gene visited all of the countries under his supervision to say good-bye and introduce his replacement. He invited me to join him on one of those trips. Ending his business career was bittersweet for Gene. He had formed lasting friendships and found his work deeply gratifying. Farewell dinners always ended with speeches and toasts in which colleagues praised him for his strong leadership, wisdom and warm personality. It was obvious to me that retirement would be a titanic change for him. There were office parties for Gene and Joe Snape, who was also retiring. The men were asked, "What are you going to do in retirement?" Gene's response was always, "I haven't thought about that yet." Joe and Mati were building a home at Wellfleet on Cape Cod; we were happy that these fine friends were also going to be on the East Coast. Most oil employees tended to retire in Texas and Oklahoma. With our new freedom, we made a quick trip to Reno, Nevada, to visit friends. The Wintours arrived from Scotland for a holiday.

With Thelma settled in Albuquerque, we discussed with Betty and Bill the sale of her home. In late April, we drove to Garber. For the next two weeks, we worked tirelessly going through the house.

We lined the walls in the dining room with cardboard boxes labeled with the names of all the cousins, where we placed items that we thought they would like to have to remember Thelma and her parents, Harl and Jennie Southwick, the original owners of the home. Searching through drawers and closets, we found some of Grandma's gold jewelry in the bottom of a rag bag, so we were extra careful in the cleaning-out process.

We went to Tulsa to attend Clay's baptism at John Knox Presbyterian Church. We met Betty in Garber for Memorial Day, when many families returned to decorate the graves of their loved ones. Grandma Southwick's prolific Paul Scarlet climbing red rose dutifully bloomed at this time of year so we filled the car's trunk with roses for Southwick and Grogan graves. A World War I veteran, Mr. Eby, wore his uniform every Memorial Day and had a starring role in the ceremony at the cemetery on a windy hill outside of town. Both a solemn and joyful occasion, old friends relived happy times growing up in this vibrant small town.

We had hired auctioneers from Enid to handle the sale of the house and remaining contents. We had asked if we needed the Salvation Army to come out to collect the things that didn't sell, but were assured there would be nothing left. The women of the Garber Christian Church offered to sell homemade sandwiches, pie and cold drinks as a fund-raiser for their ministries. The yard filled with people from near and far. A festive air developed as people greeted one another, enjoyed the delicious food, and children chased each other around the house. The sale began at 1:00 p.m. with the auctioning of the brick house, which sold quickly for $21,000, more than we had expected. People interested in the furniture went into the house with the auctioneer. The rest the contents were sold by the boxful on tables outside. By four the sale was over; every single thing had been sold.

When we got home, our agent put a For Sale sign in our front yard in Bakersfield. We were in a state of shock when the house sold the following Tuesday. We drove to Dallas, left our car, and flew to Washington where we spent two days with our real estate agent. At the end of the second day we purchased a new townhouse in Avenel, a suburban community built around a Tournament Players Golf Club. The house had a beautiful long view overlooking a tennis court, meadow and stream, with the golf course on the far side. On the flight back to Dallas, I wondered aloud if we had bought the right home. After all, we were not going to be transferred like we always had been before. Gene's answer put me completely at ease. He said, "Jan, if we've made a mistake, we'll just sell it and buy another."

Suzanne and Jay left for the hospital at 3:00 a.m. on July 13 and William Grogan arrived at 1:50 p.m. An hour later, we went with Jay's folks to greet the bonny boy and his tired but happy parents. Elated grandmas, Betty and I, attempted to buy out the baby super-store and Nordstrom's. Gene spent blissful hours sitting in his Grandfather Southwick's rocking chair with Will cradled in his arms.

Back in Bakersfield, Occidental president David Martin hosted a beautiful farewell party for us at the Seven Oaks Country Club. Two weeks later, we waved good-bye to the van driver as he started for Washington, D.C., then raced east in our car to meet him at our new house in Potomac, Maryland.

Seventeen

JOURNEY'S END

Potomac
August 1996 / November 2013

LIVING OUTSIDE the nation's capital less than ten minutes from Lisa, Jim and Claire and Jim's parents as well provided the small-town feeling that Gene always sought wherever we lived. One of our first outings was to go berry picking with them at a farm a few miles north of us. Claire, a year old, wore one of Jim's old T-shirts and was soon happily covered in purple from juicy mouth down to berry-stained toes. Fortunately, there was no extra charge for what we ate while we picked. If this was what retirement was going to be like, we were ready.

We joined St. Alban's Episcopal Church, located next to the National Cathedral, where Lisa and Jim were members. We immediately felt at home within this lively, diverse group of people under the exceptional leadership of Frank Wade, the rector. Over the years, we have continued to be blessed with inspired priests and dynamic lay people who expressed Christ's love in tangible ways to those in our city and the wider world through feeding and housing ministries for the homeless, volunteering at inner city schools, and supporting the good work of others financially with the proceeds of our outstandingly successful thrift shop. Our faith has been challenged and strengthened through powerful preaching and teaching, small prayer groups, and support groups. Through times of joy and sorrow, we have been surrounded by love.

We began to find our way around the Washington area with the aid of a local map. The new house presented an opportunity for Gene to employ his woodworking skills; an unfinished room on the lower floor was perfect for the large tools he began to purchase: a table saw, drill press, router and planer as well as a vacuum system to prevent dust from circulating throughout the house. Built-in bookcases on two walls of the room adjacent to the kitchen became his first project. A meticulous planner, he told me that drawing the plans would take him as long as building the bookcases and he was right. I could almost hear him singing as he sawed. He only appeared upstairs for meals. Completing this project took almost a year but the result was superb.

In addition to working on the house, we began to contact friends in the area and get acquainted at church. Gene joined the Washington chapter of the Society of Petroleum Engineers. At their monthly lunches, he met other engineers and kept up with developments in the petroleum industry. I joined the Potomac Area Newcomers Club where I made friends who lived nearby. We toured museums and attended concerts and theater productions. Almost without realizing it, we had happily settled into retirement.

Life was filled to the brim. Gene was continually finding more projects to improve our new home. I worked with a landscape designer to turn our tiny back garden into a lush retreat. We enjoyed caring for Claire when Lisa was working and the nanny, Imogene, was unavailable. Lisa and Jim announced that another grandbaby was due in late summer. Gene reveled in his role, making toys in his shop and going to a nearby playground in what became known as Granddad's Park, with a stop to see horses in the field on the way. Gene and I began most mornings with a brisk walk in the neighborhood before breakfast. On these outings, we met other keen Avenel walkers, making friends with people and dogs alike.

When we chose Washington as our retirement home, we thought our location might entice our foreign friends to visit us. It certainly did, but what surprised us was the large number of our American friends who had never been to our nation's capital until they visited us. We were back into our overseas habit of running the Grogan Hotel, and we loved every minute.

Gene developed an intense interest in genealogy. His cousin Gene Southwick provided valuable information on the Southwick clan. He recommended a book that Gene purchased from the Boston Historical Society, written in the middle of the twentieth century, which traced a direct line to Gene's mother, Thelma Southwick Grogan, from Lawrence Southwick, who arrived in Salem, Massachusetts, in 1627. He was granted four acres from the town to set up a glassworks, perhaps the first in the colonies. Gene also researched the Harlan and Grogan families. Over the years, we traveled to many destinations in America and Britain in search of information. Hunting for ancestors found us traipsing through cemeteries, dodging bees in the clover, as we looked for ancient tombstones whose names were barely visible. On one trip in England, we found marriage and christening documents from the 1500s that continued my Rice line, whose ancestor William White was on the voyage of the Mayflower to Plymouth, Massachusetts, in 1620. We visited a church from the Saxon period at Monkwearmouth on the coast northeast of Durham, England, where Harlan descendants continued to have annual reunions into the twenty-first century.

In June 1997, we began what became a tradition. For grandson Michael Grogan's twelfth birthday we invited him to spend a week with us as his birthday gift. Greatly excited, he took his first plane flight alone. We planned a full itinerary that included tours of the Smithsonian museums, the Federal Bureau of Investigation, and the Newseum, a museum on the media, where children could make a video of themselves on TV to take home as a memento. Michael, a keen weather watcher, chose to read the weather. The highlight of his week was a tour of the National Weather Service. He went home more determined than ever to pursue meteorology as a profession. In 2008, he graduated from Valparaiso University with a BS in meteorology and is seen daily on Channel 6 in his hometown of Tulsa.

James Khalil arrived August 5, 1997, at Holy Cross Hospital in Silver Spring. We spent August helping Lisa while we got to know this wee lad. Every afternoon, for weeks, Gene babysat Claire and James while Lisa took a much-needed nap.

Being free to be of assistance to our daughters and their families and to welcome these blessed children into our lives gave us great joy. Suzanne and Jay left fourteen-month-old Will with us while they flew to England for a few days. The first order of business was to buy a rocking chair because Will insisted on being rocked to sleep and Granddad was a champion baby rocker.

Gene and I quietly celebrated our fortieth anniversary on December 7 with dinner at our favorite restaurant in the small, elegant Henley Park Hotel downtown. After Christmas at our house, our family went to Colonial Williamsburg, the restored historical town in Virginia, which was beautifully decorated during holidays with Della Robbia wreaths lighted by thousands of candles.

In early January 1998, my first cousin Marilyn was taken by the rescue squad to Inova Alexandria Hospital's emergency room. Only two years apart in age, we had grown up together in Lawton. The doctor didn't know what was wrong with her but ordered tests. While Marilyn waited for the results, she flew to Oklahoma to visit her mother, my aunt Maudalee. The doctor contacted her there with the tragic news that she was in the final stage of pancreatic cancer with a life expectancy of only a month.

In late February, she entered Walter Reed Medical Center. An intensely private person, divorced from her military husband, she was estranged from her daughter and refused to reconcile with her. One morning when I arrived at the hospital, she presented me with a handwritten will that had been witnessed by a social worker, making me her sole beneficiary. Gene suggested that we hire an attorney to draw up a trust. Marilyn agreed to leave her estate to her four grandchildren and made me executor. She also asked me to take over as guardian of her mother. She died in her sleep on March 21 at age sixty-two. I immediately called her daughter, Elizabeth, with whom I had a loving relationship, and we worked together on final arrangements. By the end of the year, her affairs were settled and we had buried her ashes in Lawton next to her father. When I think of Marilyn, as I often do, I remember a bright, clever girl who played the piano beautifully, made clothes for her dolls on a tiny hand-cranked sewing machine, and sculpted bars of soap into animals. As an adult, she designed dresses that she sold in boutique shops in Alexandria, Virginia. I had looked forward to living near her and was sad when she died so soon after we arrived. For the next eight years, I cared for Aunt Maudalee until she died in 2006, a month short of her ninety-ninth birthday. I administered the trust for the grandchildren until the youngest became twenty-one in 2006 and all the funds were dispersed to them.

Grandchild number six, Elizabeth Agee Lipscomb, was born on September 17, 1998. Named after her paternal grandmother, Betty Lipscomb, and her aunt Lisa Sams, she became known in the family as Little Lisa, a precious, petite girl adored by everyone. Gene and I were there to welcome her and help out.

When driving across the country, our favorite method of traveling, we stopped to visit friends and relatives along the way. We also continued our genealogical research. In Lewistown, Missouri, town records, we recovered the wedding certificate of my grandparents David Crockett Hamilton and Mary Sue Agee. My mother, Lucile, was born on the family farm near LaBelle, Missouri. The rocky, hilly terrain was good evidence for why her father had sold that farm and bought one in Oklahoma sight unseen. They moved to Oklahoma in about 1909 with their five children: Velva, eleven; Lucile, nine; Jack, seven; Roy, five; and Maudalee, the youngest, then two. The farm was near Hulen, Oklahoma, in Cotton County, a few miles southeast of Lawton. The cotton they grew by dryland farming was a precarious existence but by hard work and good fortune the family survived.

Our family gathered at the Lipscombs' in Dallas for Thanksgiving. We were thankful that God had guided us as we helped Marilyn through the last weeks of her life and rejoiced over Little Lisa's birth. Retirement might not be the carefree existence that we had envisioned but we knew how blessed we were. And we were looking ahead to a holiday that we had dreamed of for years.

February 1, 1999, Gene and I flew to Australia. With friends there and in New Zealand, we designed our trip to see the sights and renew friendships. We also planned to visit and photograph rare penguin colonies for daughter-in-law Dana, whose love of these delightful creatures was well known. After stops in London and Bangkok, we were greeted in Sydney with the spectacular sight of half the city glowing in sunlight and the other half in the shadow of black rain clouds overlaid by a brilliant rainbow. We felt it was an auspicious sign.

We picked up a rental car and began the steep, twisting drive into the Blue Mountains. With detailed maps and directions provided by our friend Leo Murphy, we arrived in Katoomba in the early afternoon. For the next month, we drove and flew around the vast country. We visited Leo and Norrie Murphy in Canberra, Australia's capital; saw the amazing fairy penguins on Phillip Island offshore from Melbourne; drove the Great Ocean Road to Adelaide; and flew to

Alice Springs in the Red Center to see Ayers Rock (a holy monolith known as Uluru to the Aborigines). We climbed Kings Canyon and snorkeled on the Great Barrier Reef. After traveling in a gondola suspended by a cable over the rain forest, we flew to Brisbane and drove to Paradise Point on the Gold Coast to visit our friend Susan Bowen (from Oman days) and her daughters.

Australia reminded us of Africa. Although Africa is five times the size, the same great contrasts of topography are compressed onto the island: high, snow-capped mountains; lush rain forests; stark deserts; and unique fauna and flora. The people reminded us of Americans, gregarious and generous, eager to help visitors. On one stop on the Great Ocean Road, we met a couple from Sydney who invited us to their home for a "barbie" and became lasting friends.

Similar to America's native populations, we saw the tragedy of the Aborigines in the Red Center, where they were the majority population. Direct descendants of the people who arrived on the continent about fifty thousand years ago, they were one of the oldest living cultures in the world. These indigenous people had been segregated into reservations and left to suffer unspeakable privations, living in parts of the country that were lightly populated because of the harsh conditions. Man's inhumanity to man seemed to be inescapable on every part of our planet.

Boarding the Sky Princess in March, we began our first cruise, an experience that had been hailed and reviled by our friends. The ship held approximately two thousand passengers and a large staff. Our first impression was of a huge shopping mall that, in addition to the many shops, included a theater, cinema, casino, library, two swimming pools, several bars and about ten places to eat. Food was available around the clock. After an overnight in Melbourne, we were once again at sea on our way to Tasmania, and hearing informative lectures that prepared us well for what we would see and experience. One lecturer, Dr. Bill Romey, a volcanologist from Cape Cod, and his wife, Lucretia, became friends. Lucretia, a renowned quilt designer and artist, sketched scenes that she later used to create fabulous quilts.

Tasmania, a favorite holiday destination for Australians, is a bucolic paradise. Half of the island is made up of reserves, national parks and World Heritage Sites. The other half is agricultural due to the rich soil in the valleys. There were sheep in abundance. And, of course, we visited a sanctuary to see the infamous Tasmanian devils— actually smallish, rather ugly marsupials that smell bad and emit a loud screech. They did keep the island pristine by eating all the carrion.

After two days passage through the notoriously rough Tasman Sea, we neared New Zealand's South Island and began to see albatrosses following our ship. We entered Fiordland National Park on the southwest tip of the South Island. Encased in slicker suits to view this World Heritage Site, which gets over 250 inches of rain a year, we joined the Romeys on the open top deck of the ship as we cruised through the three main fiords, Milford Sound, Doubtful Sound and Dusky Sound. The high bluffs around us were covered with cascading waterfalls. At the north end of the park, mountain peaks of over sixty-five hundred feet rose in the background.

Our ship made stops along the east coast of both islands at Dunedin, Christchurch, Wellington and Auckland. We saw friends in two of those locations. Near Dunedin we were fortunate to visit the albatross colony and the rare yellow-eyed penguin habitat, as both restricted the daily number of visitors.

We arrived home in time to see the cherry trees in bloom in Washington, then drove cross country again to visit our children and grandchildren in Tulsa and Dallas and on to California to see my cousin Gaird Hamilton and his wife, Pat, plus his brothers Jerry and Leon. We cousins had not seen each other in almost fifty years. In September, we visited friends on Cape Cod and Nantucket, followed by three weeks in England and Scotland. In December, we drove back to Oklahoma to check on Aunt Maudalee and attend a surprise party for Patrick on his fortieth birthday.

Gene became active in a group called Companions in World Mission. Nondenominational but composed mostly of Anglicans and Episcopalians, it raised funds for indigenous Christian groups worldwide and hosted visiting clerics. Gene, deeply committed to this group, served as its president for a term. We were both active in several groups at St. Alban's Church. I served on the board of the Crossroads Shelter for men living in the basement of our administrative building. We seemed to have fallen into the retirees' dilemma of having more things that we wanted to do than time to do them. But we were healthy and happy. Life was good.

Angst and exuberance swept the nation as we approached the twenty-first century. Dire predictions of the collapse of the worldwide computer system when the clock struck midnight on New Year's Eve, mixed with the giddy belief that our country's economic prosperity would continue its steep upward trajectory forever, reflected the wide range of emotions across the country. Our family gathered at our house for Christmas and remained to greet the new millennium. Our children were all gainfully employed and content while our grandchildren were beautiful and healthy. As the radio humorist Garrison Keillor described his fictional town, Lake Wobegon, where "the women are strong, the men are good looking, and the children are all above average," we counted our blessings too.

For the next five years, we spent almost every minute together, traveling, involved in good works, delighting in our family and friends, and pursuing our hobbies. We looked toward the future with confidence.

In addition to visiting family and friends, we made two pilgrimages with people from our church led by our rector Frank Wade and his wife, Mary, to Spain in 2002 and to Ireland, Wales and England in 2004. These were times of spiritual renewal as we followed in the footsteps of saints, inspired by their lives of sacrifice and service to others. Relaxing after dinner in small groups, we shared stories of past experiences when we had felt God's loving presence and grown to trust His guidance. Frank led us in morning prayer and evensong daily. St. Albanites, whom we didn't know well before the trips, became trusted confidants. After we returned to Washington, we met periodically with them to strengthen our bonds of friendship. Gene and I became deeply rooted in various small groups within the church, serving and making friends with people in our congregation.

We were also intent on bonding more closely with our spread-out family. We traveled to Oklahoma and Texas two or three times a year to care for my aunt in Lawton and be with our children and grandchildren. Continuing the tradition we had begun with Michael, his brother, Clay Grogan, came to Washington in 2002 to celebrate his twelfth birthday; we took Claire Sams for a week's holiday to Quebec in 2007; Will Lipscomb to Washington in 2008; and James Sams to Boston in 2009. Lisa and Maggie Lipscomb went as our guests with their mothers to New York City in 2010 because, during that period, Gene and I were unable to travel. We were delighted to be present for important events in their lives, such as grandsons becoming Eagle Scouts with proud Eagle Scout Granddad Gene at their side, high school and university graduations, dance and music recitals, and holidays. Our entire family came together each year on either Thanksgiving or Christmas.

On June 23, 2000, veterans of the Korean War were honored at the fiftieth year commemoration on the Washington Mall with President Clinton, veteran aviator Senator John Glenn Jr. and others speaking. Gene and I were given an honor escort to our seats for the intensely moving service. Gene became interested in attending conventions of the Corps of Engineers Officer Candidate School, which were held annually in different parts of the country. He became active on the organization's board and contacted as many of the men from his class of 1952 as he could find. We visited several of them on driving trips around the country.

In August 2000, Jim Sams was transferred to the San Francisco offices of KPMG, one of America's largest auditing firms. Anticipating this move, Lisa had resigned from the Internal Revenue Service and decided to stay at home with the children—Claire, five, and James, three. While we were sad to see them leave Washington, we were delighted for the opportunities this move afforded Jim in his work. In 2004, they were transferred to London and returned to Washington in 2009.

On January 17, 2001, another precious grandchild, Margaret McVoy Lipscomb, "Maggie," made her appearance. During our stay, Gene replaced the rotting wood deck on the back of their house. He had purchased a tool belt for Will, four, who spent happy hours, in unusually cold weather, helping Granddad work.

In September 2002, the writers group I had formed under the auspices of the Potomac Area Newcomers Club had its first meeting. Shelly Ekhtiar and I were the founding and only members for several years. Fortunately for me, Shelly was a retired university English professor with experience in creative writing. At its zenith, our group grew to six active writers. We constructively critiqued and inspired each other and became close friends. Without the encouragement of the group, I doubt that I would have completed this book.

As we aged, illness became an issue for ourselves and others close to us. At his annual physical in May 2000, Gene was diagnosed with type 2 diabetes, a total surprise as he was not overweight nor was there a family history of it. Thankfully, a change in diet controlled it. I enjoyed learning to cook without the four no-nos: white flour, white sugar, starches and alcohol. Gene happily embraced the new diet and remained healthy. Between 2004 and 2014, I had four successful surgeries for deteriorating joints.

My brother-in-law, Jimmie Wade, died November 7, 2000, due to kidney cancer. When my sister, Beverly, had breast cancer surgery early in 2001, I went to spend a week with her as she recovered. She continued to live independently for several years and then joyfully moved into an extension of her granddaughter's home in Norman, Oklahoma. She died on January 7, 2011, at the age of eighty-six. Jim Sams Sr. and Bill Montgomery died with rare forms of non-Hodgkin's lymphoma and my childhood friend, Maredith, with throat cancer.

Early in 2006, Gene was diagnosed with prostate cancer. Because his maternal grandfather and two uncles had died of this disease, we were aware of a higher risk factor for Gene. With our son's help, we chose to travel to Loma Linda University Medical Center in Southern California for treatment. This facility was the pioneer in proton beam radiation that was virtually painless and had no lasting side effects. Because he would receive radiation five days a week for approximately nine weeks, we rented a small house in nearby Redlands, California, and settled in for what the patients called their "radiation vacation." Loma Linda, owned and operated by the Seventh-Day Adventist Church, provided not only state-of-the-art medical treatment but spiritual counseling and comfort. During our three months there, we made friends, worshipped daily and took day-trips around Southern California. My friend Maredith's family lived in the area and graciously included us in their family gatherings.

On the drive to California that year, we became aware that Gene was having difficulty remembering words for common items. As we dealt with the prostate cancer, I attempted to ignore the concern I felt about his forgetfulness. When we returned home we consulted our doctor, who recommended a neurologist. Following tests, he gave us the shattering news that Gene had Alzheimer's disease. The reality left us stunned and dry-eyed. As we left the doctor's office, Gene said, "Well, it might have been better not to have known." That was the only time he verbalized the distress he felt. The doctor prescribed two medications that he hoped would slow the progression of the disease. For the next two years, we tried to carry on as though nothing was amiss. Of course, we told our children and I shared confidentially with some friends but most people were unaware. Although Gene's mother, Thelma, and his sister, Betty, both developed dementia in their eighties, we had never considered that Gene might be vulnerable.

More than ever, we sought comfort in our Christian faith. We tried to live each day, each moment, loving and supporting each other. I believed that my years with my dear mother-in-law as she slipped into dementia prepared me to be more patient, compassionate and wise in caring for Gene. Helping him to maintain his independence as long as possible was a goal. For the first two years, we continued traveling with Gene driving. He sometimes expressed frustration when he couldn't think of a word, but after fifty years of marriage, to our relief, I usually knew what he wanted to say and was able to provide the language that he was losing.

For as long as Gene was willing, he was included in the activities that were so important to him. He served on a board at church that administered a generous trust and he volunteered in the Opportunity Shop. I helped him dress in suit and tie as was his custom for Sunday services and we attended the weekly Bible study long after he could not read or understand what was said.

He continued to attend a monthly men's Great Decisions group and "Gene's Gang" lunches, groups that he had founded with retiree husbands of the Potomac Area Newcomers Club. These thoughtful men took him to the affairs, kindly including him as much as possible.

In December 2006, we flew to London to be with the Sams family for Christmas. We joined Jim's mother, Betty, and sisters Victoria and Alicia to remember his father, Jim, with love, laughter and tears on the first anniversary of his death. While there, we received a call from home that Bill Hurst, Gene's brother-in-law, had died. Gene and I flew directly to Albuquerque to help Betty prepare for the funeral. There we were joined by Lisa, Suzanne, Patrick and Dana for the service. Gene and I remained afterward for a fortnight with Betty. In May, Betty fell at home, badly breaking her leg. Her doctors told us that she should not be living alone. She readily agreed when we suggested that she sell her home and move into a continuing care community, where she lived quite happily until shortly before her death in 2011. We traveled to Albuquerque frequently to visit her and take care of her affairs.

For our fiftieth anniversary in December 2007, we traveled with our fifteen family members to Costa Rica. For our grandchildren, riding the exhilarating zip line with their parents and Granddad was the highlight on their holiday. For Gene and me, being surrounded by our family with their love and delight in each other was a glorious commemoration of our fifty years together. Lisa produced two wonderful books, one filled with photos and letters from our friends and another of photos from Costa Rica. During his years of illness, we spent many happy hours reliving our celebration through those books.

Gene's illness from 2006 to 2013 taught us that, though watered with tears, the ground beneath our feet was solid and abundant with the fruit of grace. God gave us ample time to express our love for each other and be showered with love from Him through our children, grandchildren, our friends, and the strong St. Alban's community.

October 27, 2012, our family expanded once more with the wedding of Clay Grogan to Courtney Gard at the First Presbyterian Church in Tulsa. Gene was not with us in person but we felt his loving presence at this joyous occasion.

Although we were all terribly sad, for the last year of his life Gene could not live at home because of the level of care he required. A passage from *The Prophet* by Khalil Gibran has given me comfort:

> *When you are sorrowful look again in your heart,*
> *And you shall see that in truth you are weeping*
> *For that which has been your delight.*

Gene peacefully died November 20, 2013. We placed him in God's hands at a memorial service at St. Alban's Episcopal Church in Washington, D.C., on our fifty-sixth wedding anniversary, December 7, 2013.

Epilogue

Since Gene died, I have often been asked, "Are you lonely?" I do spend quite a bit of each day alone. Gene was not only my beloved mate; he was my best friend, my confidant, my strong defender. We could sit together for long periods without speaking: reading, watching television, listening to music, walking, driving across the country, in companionable silence. Of course I miss him every day.

However, loneliness is a state of not only being alone but also longing for someone who is no longer here and, if I am to be honest, feeling sorry for myself. Every time I have felt that way, I am immediately aware that Gene would be disappointed in me. He lived every moment to the full. He would expect me to do no less.

Being alone, I am enjoying a solitude that feeds my soul. Solitude is a luxury and a blessing. I have time to reflect on my past life, appreciate the small wonders of the present, and contemplate the future. Solitude gives me the time to pray. I know how fortunate I am. God has opened doors for me to help others in ways that are deeply gratifying.

Every morning, I thank God for the new day and for my loving family. I ask Him to open my eyes to see His work in our world and anticipate the work He has for me to do. I hope that I will not be distracted by trivialities and miss His quiet whisper.

At bedtime recently, I have been reading a closing paragraph from a service of compline (evening prayers) from A New Zealand Prayer Book. The words give me peace. They are:

Lord, it is night. The night is for stillness.
Let us be still in the presence of God.
It is night after a long day. What has been done, has been done;
What has not been done, has not been done; let it be.
The night is dark. Let our fears of the darkness of the world
and of our own lives rest in you.
The night is quiet. Let the quietness of your peace enfold us,
all dear to us, and all who have no peace.
The night heralds the dawn. Let us look expectantly to a new day,
new joys, new possibilities. In your name we pray. Amen.

Patrick's Eulogy
for Dad

I'D LIKE TO FIRST THANK this church for being the Body of Christ to my mom and dad over the last seventeen years. I would also like to thank my sister Lisa for the formidable and caring support she has given over these most recent years to my mom and dad during my dad's illness.

It is an honor and joy for me to speak for our family in remembrance of my father. Fifty-six years ago today, a beautiful love affair was formalized in marriage in Lawton, Oklahoma. My sisters and I are the direct beneficiaries of this love covenant, and as such, so have been our spouses, and each of our children.

My dad's love for my mom was never a mystery to us. It was deep, faithful and demonstrative. It wasn't uncommon in the evening after Dad returned home from work that my parents would embrace in a genuine hug and kiss, which we would try to squeeze into... mainly to break up this "smoochiness." I remember my dad bringing unexpected flowers for my mom. They cuddled together as we watched TV as a family. My dad opened doors for my mom...an act he refused to relinquish even as his Alzheimer's was causing him frailty. When my mom's name was beyond recall, he substituted the word "Mine."

For us kids, watching from box seats—we were given life lessons of what the covenant of marriage means, and how genuine love expresses itself. As I observe mine and my sisters' own marriages, I see a legacy of love and commitment that was nurtured by our parents. What an inheritance!

This was not all that my dad hoped for us to receive. He was committed also to a faith in God that I'm sure he yearned for us to adopt ourselves, but without any coercion. When dealing with faith, what most of us need is a credible witness, someone whose life represents in action—not just words—the love, grace and self-giving of our creator. My dad was that person for me. I watched from the wings as my dad was involved in the life of the church, in Bible studies and prayer meetings, and in acts of service. And as I started to feel an inner spiritual hunger, I asked him candidly one night when I was twelve years old what it really meant to enter into this life. He simply said that right at that point, I was the captain of my own ship, but if I really wanted to experience the life of spiritual abundance that was possible, that I should ask Jesus to be my captain. That night I did. Dad would continue to be a mentor to me in my growth as a Christian, even into adulthood.

As many of you know, my dad had a very successful and fulfilling career. While growing up, however, there was never a sense that his work was intrusive on our home life. In the early years there were times that he had to be away, but we were very young, and I think

Mom missed him most. If he carried burdens from work, I never remember him projecting them on us at home. Perhaps it was that his service to our country in Korea gave him perspective, and not the least his character that brought him through the door at night with a smile and warm embraces. His character, honesty, competency, and tact led him over the years into the highest levels of management in a corporate world often deficient of these attributes. Again, we kids and our kids have benefitted from his example.

My dad had a number of personality traits. He was first and foremost a "people person." He loved to meet new folks and find out in what way were they even remotely associated with his hometown of Garber, Oklahoma. And if that failed, he would explore other connections with other people and places. He would be the last to leave a party, but as all in our family know he would be the first to leave for the airport! Yes, my dad believed that being two hours early for a flight was barely enough. Oddly enough, my kids have accused me of that same trait.

My dad loved geology and engineering. Ever since I can remember, he carried a geology pick under the front seat of our car, and on many a road trip, he would abruptly pull over to examine a rock formation, which included taking the pick to it to see inside. "Hmmm...quartz or malachite," he might say. We also never missed a historical marker. (Remember those?) My dad's engineering mind caused him to break out the slide rule when I had a math problem, or to pack the dishwasher as tightly and efficiently as possible, and later in life to design and expertly build cabinetry and tables. He became an expert craftsman. We kids also learned that to ask Dad a

ALL OF MY LIFE WITH YOU

question would inevitably lead to more of an answer than we were perhaps looking for. Dad loved the details of life, and he was a constant student of the world we live in.

My dad had a great sense of humor and a playful spirit. He loved a great pun, and delighted himself and us with one he created on a tour of Morocco. "Do you know who the Sultan is Raisin a Date with?" He roughhoused with us kids when we were young, and with our kids when they were little. On occasions of great humor as we were older, his face would convulse, tears roll down his face, and he'd literally go to the ground in laughter. As his Alzheimer's progressed his sense of humor, duty and service didn't leave him. As my sister Suzanne observed, this disease robbed him of language and memory, but his personality was intact.

Author Eugene Peterson titled a book *Perseverance: A Long Obedience in the Same Direction*. I believe this title epitomizes my father. His steady and solid temperament, his commitment to his faith, his steadfast love of our family caused him to live a life well lived and to leave an eternal legacy.

December 7, 2013
St. Alban's Episcopal Church
Washington, D.C.

ACKNOWLEDGEMENTS

WHILE ATTEMPTING to be as factual as possible in writing this book, I must frankly admit to inevitable biases—whether by accident or intent—when relating motives and emotions. Nevertheless, I have been able to write in great detail because of a marvelous gift from my sister-in-law Betty Grogan Hurst. She saved many of the weekly letters I wrote home to family members from 1963 onwards and compiled them into albums according to our country location. These, along with my appointment diaries and journals, were my primary sources. That said, all errors are mine alone.

The following stalwart friends and helpful critics deserve recognition and thanks: Shelly Ekhtiar, Ann Skelton, Mary Ann Sestili, and Marilynn Mansfield participated in a monthly critique group over a period of several years. They, in addition to my friend the author Diane Marquart Moore, have read and reread my drafts and made helpful suggestions. I could not have completed my book without their support.

At Posterity Press, my editor and publisher, Philip Kopper, has been an invaluable coach, patient and kind, with a first time author. He has saved me from countless gaffes and made me laugh and relax as we worked. My sincere appreciation also goes to Denise Arnot whose elegant design has produced the beautiful book you are holding. To each and all, I am deeply grateful.

FAMILY TREE

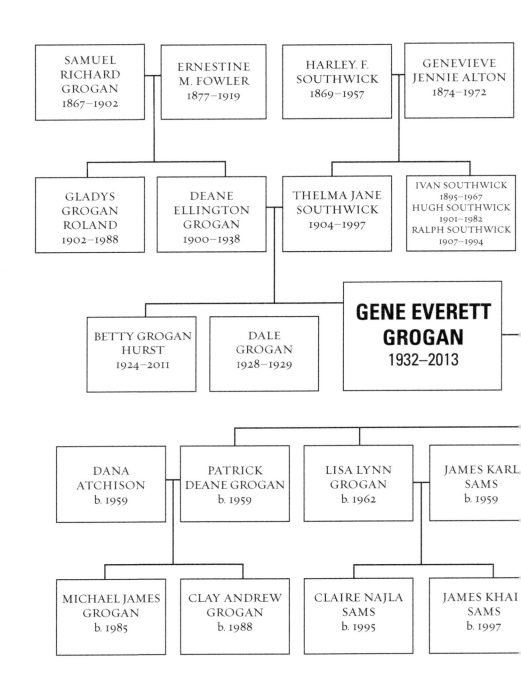

SAMUEL RICHARD GROGAN
1867–1902

ERNESTINE M. FOWLER
1877–1919

HARLEY. F. SOUTHWICK
1869–1957

GENEVIEVE JENNIE ALTON
1874–1972

GLADYS GROGAN ROLAND
1902–1988

DEANE ELLINGTON GROGAN
1900–1938

THELMA JANE SOUTHWICK
1904–1997

IVAN SOUTHWICK
1895–1967
HUGH SOUTHWICK
1901–1982
RALPH SOUTHWICK
1907–1994

GENE EVERETT GROGAN
1932–2013

BETTY GROGAN HURST
1924–2011

DALE GROGAN
1928–1929

DANA ATCHISON
b. 1959

PATRICK DEANE GROGAN
b. 1959

LISA LYNN GROGAN
b. 1962

JAMES KARL SAMS
b. 1959

MICHAEL JAMES GROGAN
b. 1985

CLAY ANDREW GROGAN
b. 1988

CLAIRE NAJLA SAMS
b. 1995

JAMES KHAI SAMS
b. 1997

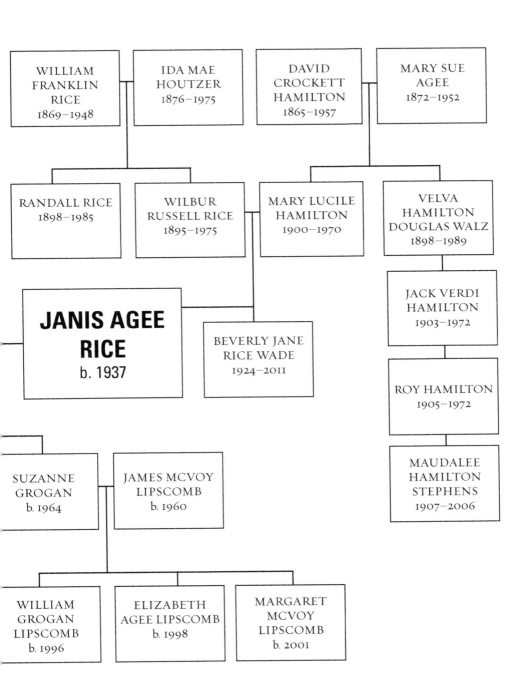

WILLIAM FRANKLIN RICE 1869–1948

IDA MAE HOUTZER 1876–1975

DAVID CROCKETT HAMILTON 1865–1957

MARY SUE AGEE 1872–1952

RANDALL RICE 1898–1985

WILBUR RUSSELL RICE 1895–1975

MARY LUCILE HAMILTON 1900–1970

VELVA HAMILTON DOUGLAS WALZ 1898–1989

JANIS AGEE RICE b. 1937

BEVERLY JANE RICE WADE 1924–2011

JACK VERDI HAMILTON 1903–1972

ROY HAMILTON 1905–1972

SUZANNE GROGAN b. 1964

JAMES MCVOY LIPSCOMB b. 1960

MAUDALEE HAMILTON STEPHENS 1907–2006

WILLIAM GROGAN LIPSCOMB b. 1996

ELIZABETH AGEE LIPSCOMB b. 1998

MARGARET MCVOY LIPSCOMB b. 2001

This book has been set in Requiem, an old-style serif typeface designed by Jonathan Hoefler in 1992. The typeface takes inspiration from a set of inscriptional capitals found in Ludovico Vicentino degli Arrighi's 1523 writing manual, *Il Modo de Temperare le Penne,* and its italics are based on the chancery calligraphy, or cancelleresca corsiva of the period.

CPSIA information can be obtained
at www.ICGtesting.com
Printed in the USA
BVOW06*2000210417
481344BV00005B/5/P